Frank —
I hope you enjoy this
— Dave

Into Light and Shadow

a journey

a novel by Dave Gordon

Comments? Questions? See:
<intolightandshadow.com>

Edited by Brian Doonan

Introduction

This novel deals with a number of themes.

Much has been written on the near-death experience. Many who've lived it talk of meeting a "Light." The effect of such a meeting can cause cataclysmic change, and life can be difficult when an internal shift to a new life pattern obliges deep changes in oneself. One such documented change is a visceral stirring that prompts a search for a spirituality that makes sense. That search often runs counter to ego, shaped by the cultures and traditions we live within.

That raises the question, what does it take to find one's own spiritual path? The Buddha said Buddhism isn't supposed to answer questions but question answers. Certain Buddhists in the United States have come to feel that the Buddha "box" is too small to encompass "true nature." These "nones" are growing in number each year, looking for something more.

But doesn't the infinite plurality of spiritual paths ensure there's a path for everyone, even when we as individuals have to eventually turn a junction to continue on a personal, anarchic "path with heart"?

For the protagonist of this story, that junction was a near-death experience. For me it was the day I helped drag the bodies of two teammates and a Sherpa off Manaslu, the eighth highest mountain in the world. I've been climbing mountains for forty years, but the incident on the "Mountain of the Spirit" and the Buddhist cremation ceremony that followed it changed my spiritual path forever.

I also have a strong philosophical belief in ecumenism. One such interdenominational initiative was a Zen-Christian dialog that started in Japan in the 1960s, eventually manifesting itself into Shinmeikutsu, a Zen-Christian monastery outside Tokyo. This monastery has produced some notable teachers, some of whom reside in the United States today.

This dialog between Zen and Christianity continues, as least in part. To this day, for instance, a Benedictine monk regularly visits a northern California Zen monastery to hold a public conversation with a Zen priest about the similarities and differences between East and West.

But what of the conflict and difficulty that exist in our lives as we pursue our "path with heart"? What is to be done when once more, as we try to deal with our shadow side, it appears that things fall apart and no longer work?

An answer to that question could lie in the Shambhala spiritual warrior tradition, those who turned toward and not away from that which was unwanted. The tradition was promulgated by Trungpa Rinpoche, one of the more charismatic Tibetan Buddhist teachers to immigrate to the United States. Buddhism teaches that difficulty is often a "dharma gate": the entrance into enlightenment.

Of all our difficulties, it seems the most onerous is our clash with others' difficulties, especially those "others" we're in intimate relationships with. In modern conflict resolution, conflict isn't about the other; it's rather nature's way to provide an understanding of those parts of our personalities that we're in conflict with but would rather avoid. This resistance can manifest itself into an inability to connect with teachings that require us to change.

Many of the world's spiritual paths suggest that deep mystical teachings will not resonate with us unless we've already done the hard preparatory work. The problem is we have to be ready to change, and only a visceral connection with those spiritual "tectonic plates" that herald deep change can instigate readiness. By itself, the brain doesn't recognize such shifts, so we have to rely on some other way of working within our interconnected, interdependent reality.

Above all, this is a novel, a story of one man's spiritual journey. It interplays between the mundane and the sacred. Sometimes they appear separate, unrelated; other times they appear as one. I hope you find the story rewarding.

Dave

Acknowledgements

The world has been my teacher, but I feel obligated to acknowledge a few of its inhabitants. Spiritually, I owe a great deal to my former root teacher, Darlene Cohen, who died of ovarian cancer in January 2011. Nine full bows to this greatest of women for helping me plant my butt on a cushion. I also owe a great debt to Tony Patchell, Darlene's widower, for ordaining me as a lay Zen monk in October 2011. Thank you Loren Cruden for the gentle, kind way you put up with me. Without your quiet statement that my original novel required editing, this version wouldn't exist. A full *gasho* bow is owed to all the residents of the three monasteries under the umbrella of the San Francisco Zen Center. You've all been my teachers. On the technical side of things, thanks to my lifetime and best friend Bob Johnson for his help and for serendipitously guiding me to my patient and exacting editor, Brian Doonan, who labored with me for more than two-and-a-half years to get this novel into shape. Going beyond the scope of his job, he came to act as contributing writer to a story he said he strongly believed in.

PART ONE: CHANGES

"Change is inevitable;
(spiritual) growth is optional."

Chapter One

North Ridge, High Camp

There was nothing but the dark and the cold and the doom of the narrative. He was dead, buried under a mound of stone. Such was the power of the dream that it made use of the pasty layers of sunblock and lip balm to add to the effect, but something intervened—perhaps the tent flapping in a gust of wind. All Steve knew was that his eyelids sprang open, setting off his arms and legs, fighting for deliverance.

It was an attempt at self-determination—one of the ten perfections (or virtues) cultivated to help purify karma through which to live a life that leads to the enlightened path, for enlightenment cannot be achieved until awakening is fully realized and the path made clear. That was what the Sherpas believed, but two can stand side by side and a world apart.

For his part, Steve didn't trust them, always smiling, too willing to offer a helping hand—pocketing peoples' hard-earned money, what amounted to the life savings of many. They made more Yuan or Rupee in one season lugging up equipment and cooking for expeditions than their kind typically made in a lifetime. Even so, such grievances were easily overlooked in the Death Zone. It was enough of an effort to gasp for air.

The dream seemed to have been spun from the bleakness of this flipside of Hell, notorious for blurring

1

normal functions of the brain, putting one at risk for mental lapses, leading to uncalculated mishaps and misadventures. Steve's life was being nibbled away as he lay frozen in fear, but as pressurized oxygen pumped through his veins, he slowly became responsive to his material environment: the stygian blackness and freezing cold he'd mistaken for a grave.

Steve had a dream; that was all...except dreams weren't supposed to happen up here. They require REM sleep, and that necessitated an ample supply of oxygen. He felt for the button on his headlamp that was fitted over the balaclava that covered the hair he hadn't been able to wash in weeks. The light stung his eyes, made them water. He forced them open so not to freeze shut while examining the regulator feeding oxygen from the tank tucked in beside his sleeping bag.

What Steve saw shocked him. In all the drama he must have forgotten to turn the regulator down to resting state. He was unwittingly depleting his stored oxygen and in doing so opening himself to dreamland. There being only a limited supply, it was a serious gaffe, but, inexplicably, it was the dream that troubled him more. It seemed more real a threat in his mental torpor. Not since a kid had he had such a fright, and here of all places, perched on top of the world.

Dan's sleeping bag lay empty beside him. Steve knew they'd never team again. Imagine getting into an altercation up here, expending energy on ethics then having to share a tent—what would amount to sleepless hours in accusative silence. All he wanted was a token, a souvenir, some little keepsake that hadn't been bagged and taken away during the 1999 expedition.

Steve could hear the points of crampons crunching on the hardened snow. Someone was approaching the tent. He prepared himself, taking measured breaths, anticipating the cold demeanor of the person he'd need to fulfill a

2

lifetime goal; but when the zipper opened he was confronted by the dark eyes of Nima Sherpa.

"We go, boss?"

Steve pulled down his mask. "Where's Dan?"

The words were raspy, little more than a whisper. All the mucus in his throat had dried. He'd been coughing up chunks for days.

Nima's teeth flashed in the beam of light, a weak attempt at an apologetic smile. "Gone."

Steve paused to gasp into the mask, unable to understand. "Gone?"

"To the top."

"To the top?" Steve said, holding down his mask. "With who?"

"Chiki."

Steve had trouble computing the information. Cognitive response slows at such altitude.

"When?"

"Ten minutes before."

A ghost of a flush stained Steve's cheeks. He crooked his arm up to the beam of light, checking his watch, staring at another serious gaffe. He was supposed to have started preparing over an hour ago. The extent of the fury he could muster in this deepfreeze steamed in his chest. Among mountaineers, a cardinal sin had been committed against him. You never abandon your teammate on summit day.

He grabbed the radio, now livid to the point of shedding tears, risking dehydration.

"It is late, boss."

Steve knew the whole mountain would be listening in, and he wasn't about to make a fool of himself to the international community present, not if his life depended on it. Instead, he allowed himself a single act of weakness, throwing the radio at the fabric of the tent. It bounced back and landed soundlessly on his sleeping bag. For fifteen seconds he did nothing but gasp into the mask, affording himself a moment to think.

"Did you melt the snow?"

Nima blinked crystals from his lashes. "Yes, boss."

"Give me a minute."

Sherpas had long become accustomed to white man's jargon. They knew phrases such as "give me a minute" meant little, for nothing takes a minute at this altitude. Time stretched out as Steve started the process of inserting two chemical warmers inside his gloves, cursing the lost time, the climb of a lifetime and the sacrifice and expense it cost to make it this far.

You need to be on top of your game...

While pulling on his boots, Steve went through the checklist he'd memorized at Base Camp. He had trouble recalling the sequence but eventually was able to confirm all essentials were stored inside his suit, snug against his chest so not to freeze (sunscreen, satellite phone and the all-important camera). In less than half an hour he thumped out of the tent, and clumsily began to strap on his crampons. Even in the dark he could feel the awesome exposure around him, could hear its gaping yawn.

Steve tested his crampons after he tightened them to his boots. The snow was packed firm by the single-minded footprints of those that had set out before him. It glowed diamond-hard under a rising moon—a moon that seemed to radiate cold. Inhospitality may be the pact you make with this mountain, but the dangerous beauty was worth the discomfort. It was a thrill to stand resolute on the edge of nature's boundaries.

Steve felt momentarily heartened, but he couldn't shake what went down earlier that day. It was Dan who'd won him over to the idea. Both felt relatively fit, considering what they were up against. The ascent into the Death Zone had gone better than expected. Their blood oxygen levels remained satisfactory, which likely gave

4

them the stamina to arrive at High Camp an hour earlier than predicted. On the whole, a short pilgrimage wasn't out of the question.

All the same, Steve didn't think it worth the risk. He was finally persuaded by his teammate who argued that his childhood hero was only a couple of hundred yards from camp. A Sherpa on their expedition had already agreed to guide them at the promise of a bonus that Dan agreed to pay in full. In the end, Steve decided to go for the bragging rights it would afford him. It was a decision he'd come to regret.

The route wasn't technically difficult, but anything could go wrong in the Death Zone. Altitude was the objective danger of this mother of all eight-thousanders. Here, even oxygen was outside its element. Added to that was a reduction in barometric pressure, which forces the muscles that draw in air to work that much harder. Heart rates rise at the same time blood oxygen levels drop. From the perspective of the cardiopulmonary system, lying down in a sleeping bag up here is like running on a treadmill at sea level.

Weighted down as they were, they also had to be extra careful with no fixed ropes to clip to for safety. Steve had counted bodies to keep alert; those sprawled out frozen or torn apart by the ever shifting snows. He'd made a game of it, trying to guess the year of death by the gear fixed to the bodies, like those colorful remnants of high altitude suits and the tents that acted as makeshift shrouds that blew in the wind like streamers. Some he knew by name. He was familiar with the story of their demise, having achieved infamy in mountain climbing lore.

But each corpse had been a reminder of the mountain's peril. There were many ways to die in this graveyard in the sky: the ever present threat of avalanche, hypoxia, a fall, a drop into a crevasse, exhaustion and exposure, the mountain sickness all high altitude climbers dread, cerebral thrombosis, high altitude pulmonary and cerebral edema, or simply disappearing, never to be seen again.

Above 26,000 feet, where the body will start to eat itself to combat a progressive loss in mass, few if any have the energy to rescue others. They would only be putting their own lives at risk. If you get in trouble up here, you will likely freeze into an alabaster likeness of your former self unless the mountain chooses otherwise, leaving just your frozen bones. Simply put, you become part of the scenery. It was the pact you made with the mountain.

The exact circumstances of George Mallory's demise were still debated, but information gathering carried out by the 1999 expedition suggested he'd frozen solid while digging his gloves into the loose scree on the slope where he'd been found seventy-five years after the fateful day. It was a standard technique, the only method available to stop sliding after losing your ice axe. What ultimately killed him was believed to be a puncture wound found in the skull. It was speculated his own ice axe caused the injury, as it bounced off a rock and struck his forehead as he slid down the slope after a fall.

The debate of historical significance was whether Mallory made it to the top and died on descent. If he had, that would make him the first to accomplish the feat. Yet like countless others, Steve was skeptical. As far as he was concerned the gear of the time was inadequate to protect against the ruthless elements no matter the skill of the climber. The high-tech shell and lightweight insulation of his suit was a complete contrast to the woolly gabardine jumper and overcoat his predecessor wore. Dan felt otherwise, of course. He hero-worshipped the man.

They had approached the celebrated corpse like astronauts on the moon, muted by masks, encumbered under insulated suits and weighed down by oxygen tanks. As they came upon the mound, Dan slowly bent in reverence, touching the rocks that covered the remains, those the 1999 expedition used to inter the body.

Typical of Steve, he quickly grew impatient. They'd only have a couple of minutes before they'd have to return. Getting caught out here in the dark with no fixed ropes to guide your way was a death sentence, and he knew it. In the end, he callously slumped down beside his teammate and started to pull rocks from the mound, digging a hand into the holes he made; searching for a button, something he could carry that wouldn't add to the burden of weight. Every rock he moved revealed more and more of the mummified remains preserved by the bone-dry cold and parched winds particular to extreme altitude.

"I'll kill you if you move another rock!"

Dan must have had gotten to his feet while Steve had been busy digging his gloves into the holes he made, feeling around. He dropped the stone he had in hand, taken aback. Something crazed had possessed his teammate, staring down at him in hate, an ice axe aimed to strike a deadly blow.

You could lose your mind in the Death Zone...

Steve had scrambled to his feet as fast as he could. He held up his gloved hands and backed away from the mound, at risk of tripping over a rock and sliding to his death. Their Sherpa guide stood observant a little ways away. He whispered a prayer to the mountain as Dan bent down to his knees and restored the rocks to their rightful place. This was a sacred place to Sherpas after all. They call it Chomolungma: Goddess Earth Mother of the World.

Nima handed Steve the bottled water he'd need to keep hydrated for the next 16 or so hours. While he secured them inside the inner pockets of his suit, something dawned on him that made him pause. No one sleeps deep enough in the Death Zone to dream, not before attempting to summit. There simply weren't enough oxygen molecules floating around, and it wasn't only that. He couldn't accept that he

7

(a rope gun if there ever was one) forgot to adjust his regulator. Oxygen was what kept you alive in the Death Zone. You were always mindful of it.

Dan turned up my regulator so I'd fall asleep...

Steve cursed his old friend and then cursed him again for making him expend unnecessary energy. The expedition had been compromised, and for what? Moving a couple of rocks from the sun-bleached weather-beaten body of a dead man? The double standard made him bristle. Dan was probably stepping over bodies that very moment on his way to the summit.

A plan took form that seemed feasible in Steve's present state of mindlessness. He would beat Dan to the summit, regardless of the advantage. It was reasonable to assume the gumbies that swarm the mountain each year were holding up everyone. All he would have to do was get moving and overtake Dan—the slower of the two—not looking back until he stood on the summit, staring down in triumph from the crest. He would win like he always won. He would come out on top.

Nima thumped one of the two Russian supercharged titanium fiberglass-wrapped oxygen tanks into Steve's backpack. He felt the straps of the suspenders bite into his shoulders and remembered he'd intended to adjust them the night before. Carefully, he regulated the flow to his mask, pissed off with himself.

"You've summited before?"

Nima raised two fingers.

"Lead," Steve said, securing his mask.

He waited for the rope to pay out before following Nima's steps, but he started out too fast all the same.

You know the rhythm up here...step, breathe, breathe, breathe, step...

The steepness of the slope and the knife-edge ridge tripped the rhythm he had to spend precious energy recouping. The result was he had to stop to feed on oxygen, panting as he leaned over his ice axe, forcing Nima to stop and wait. As soon as he felt he could, he started out again, rebuffing any sign of weakness in himself. Hadn't he'd spent years training for this day?

The summit ridge that buttressed the mountain on the northeast side seemed endless as it drew Steve into thinner and thinner air. Making matters worse, the confectioners' sugar-like snow wouldn't consolidate, rendering stable footsteps impossible, which cost him more energy as he struggled to find something solid under his crampons. He used his legs to scramble up the slope while he advanced the ascender attached to the fixed rope (a technique known as jumaring).

Up here, if you take a fall and start to slide, you may not be able to stop. Mallory managed, but look what happened to him.

Focus...

Steve used the pinpricks of light he could see of those struggling to summit further up the ridge to map the path ahead. High above he caught sight of a cluster that appeared to be at a standstill. He wondered if it was a bottleneck or an illusion of perspective. He decided on the former, fairly sure he was looking at the First Step—the first of three successive obstructions he'd have to tackle to summit. Being the most technical part of summit day, these steps were a likely place for a bottleneck.

Honey-colored outcroppings appeared in the moonlight. Steve had crossed into the Yellow Band—the sedimentary limestone layer that encircled the mountain between High Camp and the First Step. He'd heard it described as a wedding ring on a colossal finger of stone. Susan had thrown hers at him as he prepared to leave two months earlier. She'd been a distraction since the planning stage, threatening to divorce him and take the kids if he went against her will.

27,500 feet...

9

The surface of the Yellow Band was composed of overlapping slabby yellow-brown rock. To traverse it was straightforward (or would be at lower altitude), but it was slippery as their crampons skipped on the rocks. Steve was grateful for the dark, nonetheless, knowing how many had died here, not wanting the distraction of having to deal with any more corpses.

Jumaring up, he searched for footholds by the beam of his headlamp, glancing up at times in anticipation of the Black Band that marked the beginning of the gray, steeper limestone layer where he'd encounter the first of the three steps; but something was throwing him off, working against what he needed to focus on.

Steve couldn't shake the feeling of whispering around him, so faint it could've been the wind. It was getting to him, making him anxious. Hallucination, as he knew, was an effect of oxygen deficiency. Like all do on summit day, he'd set the regulator to 2.0 liters per minute to compensate for the shortfall, but had he? Did he make a mistake? He considered stopping to have Nima check his regulator but rejected the idea in the end. No mistake had been made. He didn't need to second guess himself.

It took two long hours to cross into the Black Band where they immediately came upon a massive rocky outcropping blocking the way, one which would require proficiency to tackle. The First Step was more of a challenge than most imagined, but it was also an opportunity to really climb, not just scrambling over slabs and snowdrifts. He could see the access point in the step, partially lit by the headlamps of those who waited their turn to climb it, directed at the ones struggling up the ropes.

Steve stepped into the queue behind Nima and took the opportunity to rest among the other climbers. All looked battle-worn, too dogged to do anything but breathe. Most he knew by name, but he hardly recognized them from their time at Base Camp, a place where relationships develop quickly. Up here they had that look of death. It was evident in the gaunt cheeks and the listless sunburned potato peel skin visible around the eyes.

Base Camp was HQ on this mountain, where the preparatory process of acclimatization begins six weeks prior to summit day. There, time is spent adjusting to altitude, progressively climbing higher and higher until the headaches abate and the lungs reconcile (if they ever do). Acclimatization is essentially impossible in the Death Zone, even for Sherpas whose bodies had long ago adapted to altitudes higher than any other people on Earth.

The minutes stretched out at a speed unknown at sea level. It was painful to watch the gumbies, how they exhausted themselves by shoddy techniques they seemed to make up on the spur of the moment. Steve wanted to spray beta at them as it's called in mountain climbing vernacular, bark at them to use the footholds and push themselves up with their legs, but he didn't have the reserves for that.

Instead, Steve made a survey of all present, including those on the ropes. He hadn't expected to meet Dan here, but had his old teammate made it as far as the Second Step? He tried to work it out in his head, calculating the present time by the hour both set out from camp, except he was unable perform even simple arithmetic.

As time went on Steve became more and more impatient, wiggling his toes to fight off frostbite. With growing frustration he looked up at the moon. Staring at it, his mind started to drift. It landed on the dream, how he'd stood at the foot of the mound with his back to the world, staring at the mummified body visible through the holes he'd made.

It was a British voice that addressed him from under the mound—polite with a hint of disdain—a little hard to make out, but that was to be expected. Mallory died face down.

11

Have you followed your ego up the mountain as I followed mine?

Steve hadn't answered, thinking better of it. All the same, he remembered being mesmerized by the voice—posh, elitist and cultured—a voice very much his own. It soon asked another question, not at all put out by not receiving an answer to the first.

Why have you come to climb my mountain?

Steve couldn't help himself. The irony of using Mallory's most famous quote on his corpse seemed too good to pass up.

"Because it's there," he said in the dream, a little smugly.

The callous comment had caused a chorus to sing out from the mountain. It was as if the dead were debating its insolence. By the general tone, they had seemed to think it rude of him to speak in such a manner, that he was in the presence of a celebrated man and should be more respectful.

Steve had paid little heed to the uproar, taking the opportunity to ask a question to the mound himself, the one all mountaineers wanted to know.

Did you summit?

A moment passed before he gotten his answer. It was unsettling. Recalling it, he still felt a chill.

Come closer...I'll whisper it in your ear...

When his turn came, Steve couldn't have been more motivated to move. He clipped in and then clawed a crampon to a foothold, pushing himself up with his legs. It was a straightforward climb, something he could run through at lower altitude, there being no need for any complex technical maneuver. The crux was to stay focused and conserve energy.

Halfway up, Steve found himself blocked. He directed his headlamp at the obstruction. What he saw was a backpack peppered with sewn-on patches from various mountains allegedly conquered, adding unnecessary weight to the overall load. Attached to the backpack was the worst kind of gumby, sitting in his harness like an imbecile, hangdogging, worn-out and used up, a flat-lander if he ever saw one. When the gumby did manage to move, it was excruciating to watch the groveling. There was no technique at all.

The more than 100 foot elevation from bottom to top of the First Step can hit a climber hard. Steve could feel the pressure after topping out. The gumby, hands on knees, expending energy like a fool, wanted to bail; to descend the cliff he'd barely managed to climb, having had enough, it seemed. His Sherpa was using broad gestures to explain they couldn't descend until everyone waiting to climb up the rope made it to the top. The gumby kept slurring swearwords his lips could no longer form. It was a sorry sight to witness.

Gumbies were all the same as far as Steve was concerned, no better than the old ropes, oxygen tanks and tent poles strewn over the mountain from expeditions past. He turned to Nima, standing a little ways off. His guide and porter was regarding the scene in much the same way the other Sherpa had regarded Dan with the ice axe hoisted above his head—ready to dry-tool his teammate's brain to protect the dignity of a corpse. He seemed to be mumbling a prayer under his mask.

Steve released a heartless puff of frosty air. He knew full well the Sherpa would be banging gongs and chanting mantras if he could, wasting everyone's time. Steve signaled to get moving, and without a word they set off into the dark, following the fixed rope, gasping for air each punishing step. Beyond was the second and most demanding of the three steps, approached from below the ridge crest.

28,000 feet...

13

While they clawed their way over rotten, fractured rock, Steve made the most basic slip-ups. He even caught himself holding his breath. Experienced high altitude climbers shouldn't have to think of rudimentary bodily functions or maneuvers and techniques. That was the hallmark of a gumby. He'd specifically trained his body to take over when his mind could no longer be trusted. That's what he told himself as he advanced up the rope.

Sherpas were the ones whose task it was to fix the ropes, sent up each year by the first expedition of the season to lay them out and fasten them together, securing them using hundreds of ice screws and bolting them into cracks in the rocks all the way to the summit. They stretched a staggering three miles to guide the way and act as a safety line. Mallory and Irvine didn't have such luxuries. There was no one to fix the ropes for them.

Steve was ascending back up the ridge when he spotted the silhouette of the summit pyramid, the final destination of a lifetime's preparation. Under it, blocking the way, the Second Step stood resolute. It was lit by a faint glow emanating in the eastern sky. Within minutes he could distinguish the aluminum ladders bolted to the rock face, silver in the soft golden light.

Training for this day meant years of getting up at the break of dawn, but in all those years Steve had never seen a dawn like this. It was a peculiar color, one that couldn't be described as caramel, straw or a muted ocher; it was gold, ingot gold, the color of the wedding band he'd hidden away at Base Camp to lighten his load. It seemed to permeate the gray of the rock face as it intensified and infused it with its precious hue—just strong enough now for him to spot a figure who stepped off the ladder, about to scramble over the headwall and disappear.

Steve reacted in the way he would at sea level. His instinct was to speed up the pace without taking anything else into account; but as he clawed his way up the ridge, he

14

caught sight of the queue clustered at the base. It took what little breath he had away. He was destined for another long wait, one he couldn't afford, not now, not after sighting that backpack—custom-made for the Seattle Expedition.

Hope faded, but as Nima crested the ridge, two aluminum chocks caught the rays of golden light. They were clipped onto a daisy chain on the back of the Sherpa's pack. Steve spied a spare emergency rope looped beside it, all he'd need to lead climb. He would do what Mallory did: climb the mountain like a real mountaineer. It was the perfect solution to the problem at hand, or at least the one that forged in his freeze-dried brain.

Early expeditions had described the Second Step much like a prow of a ship, having frozen solid as it sailed down the ridge, tarnishing over time. If Mallory made it past this point as Noel Odell claimed he had (Odell being a member of the 1924 expedition and the last person to see him alive), he did so without the use of the Chinese ladders first bolted to the rock face fifty-one years after the famed adventurer was lost to the mountain. Whether Steve could do the same was a point of contention outside his control, but anything outside his control was a point of contention.

Steve crested the Northeast Ridge with renewed purpose, but the awesome exposure made him pause. He looked from left to right, from a two mile drop to Nepal to a two mile drop to Tibet, both sides buried under a blanket of cloud, peaks poking out like meringue over lemon pie. The epic exposure had an unexpected, auxiliary effect. It gave him the jitters. Veterans of this mountain could tell you that looking down from the top of the world differed dramatically in the light of day.

The glitch in his nerves was like a switch. Suddenly, the mountain was caught in a whirlwind of vaporous whispers. Somehow, unintentionally, he'd honed into the frequency of the Death Zone. The accents in speech patterns were suggestive of French, Russian and

Italian, East Asian, the Americas, all the civilizations and languages that made up the world—each having offered up a sacrifice to this multiethnic graveyard of mummified mountaineers.

They were riding the bone-dry winds, the dead conversing with the dead, keeping score on the events of the day. While Steve stood knee-deep in terror, Nima was trying to communicate something ten feet away, waving his arms to get his attention. It took a moment for it to register. Being where he was, his eyes were being exposed to extreme levels of UV. He was at immediate risk of snow blindness.

Steve reached up and pulled down his goggles. It cancelled out the golden light and, with it, the voices. He swooned in the deliverance. His nervous system started to slowly depressurize. In its place his brain cranked up to process what he'd just experienced, expounding on a reaction to a reduction of oxygen, that which impedes brain function under stress of a sustained maximum heart rate.

There was a bounty of evidence to that effect. Look at what happened to Dan, raising his ice axe against his teammate. Steve was hallucinating; that was all. It was a known side effect of altitude. That, at least, was what his cerebrum told him, but that talkative more analytical part of his brain was shouted down by his almond-sized hypothalamus.

Take a swig of water…

Steve scanned the rock face before him as he took a series of sips from the bottle, swilling each inside his mouth to warm it up. It was a testament to self-control not to gulp it down, and affirmation that he still had his wits about him. Swallow a gulp of cold water up here and you could fracture a rib, for the coughing fit it could set off was brutal. High altitude cough is triggered by inflammation of the bronchial tubes, flushed with cold, dry air with every breath in, an offering of the body's precious moisture with

16

every breath out. The mountain was insatiable. It would drain every last droplet if allowed.

After tucking the bottle back into his suit, Steve, feeling better for the draught, signaled Nima to advance. Nothing was going to stop him, not even himself. He had worked too hard for this day. They scrambled up the ridge between rocky outcroppings of weather-beaten boulders, climbing to the base of the step. All the while he was surveying the rock face which was festooned with old, unusable ropes, frayed and tattered by the relentless winds, degraded by UV.

Steve had fresh rope. What he needed was to find an alternate route. No one had to tell him he should've been beyond this point by now. He had two oxygen tanks, and that was it. Today would be at least a sixteen-hour climb, eight hours up and eight hours to get as far below the Death Zone as humanly possible. He'd already been inside some fourteen hours and had no intention of spending another night.

The higher-order parts of his brain fired up again, neurons sparking in an oxygen pool in the frozen depths of gray matter. This time it took the form of rationality, an invitation to think things through, such as the fact he'd need more than two chocks for a 100-foot lead climb; but, then again, he wouldn't have to scale the cliff as he first thought. He could see another, safer option, what in mountain climbing terms is called a "project."

The standard route up the Second Step was climbed in three stages, first by a lower ladder that topped at a sloped ledge that climbers scramble up to reach the upper ladder, a thirty-foot vertical climb that terminates at a shelf in the headwall. Scramble over that and the hard work was done, for the Third Step posed little difficulty, even for a gumby, being the least taxing of the three. If he could just make it to that ledge he'd bypass those queued at the base, using the second ladder to top-out, saving an hour or more.

17

Steve moved through the queue of listless bodies, all facing the ladder, sitting on boulders or standing at rest, paying no heed to one another. It was utter silence except for the clank of crampons negotiating the aluminum rungs and the nylon shells of snowsuits rippling in the wind. All were fixed on the task before them: the ladders that would carry them that much closer to the snow-covered pinnacle of their fancy, the finish line of their hard-fought battle to the top of the world.

But the eyes behind the goggles told a different story. They appeared drawn, sunken and ill-defined. On summit day, the body uses up 1,000 calories an hour, having to resort to eating itself.

Focus...

Steve moved through the queue and descended a little way down the right side of the ridge, clutching the rock face, using the sides of his crampons for extra leverage. Until he reached the ledge and scrambled up to the second ladder, he would be out of reach of the safety of the fixed ropes. It was the objective danger of the plan.

Unlike top roping, lead climbing requires the climber to set the anchors during ascent. Various devices serve that purpose, one being a chock. A chock (or nut) is a metal wedge threaded on a looped wire that is inserted into a crack in the rock face and jerked to where it narrows and locks in place. Once secured, a quickdraw is attached and a rope threaded through. Chocks come in different sizes to service different sized cracks. Use the right one in the right crack and they're as good as any bolt.

The technique required a belayer, however, someone at the bottom to pay out or pull in the rope or to put on the brakes if the leader falls. Steve looked up at Nima who stood staring down at him, his mask pulled away from his face.

"No good, boss...wait for ladder."

Sherpas were uniquely adapted to their environment. Studies have shown their bodies inhibit red blood cell overproduction in response to reduced oxygen levels, which in others could lead to a heart attack, blood clots or a stroke. They also had a particularly grating habit of spraying beta in that soft-spoken way of theirs to some of the best climbers in the world.

"Ladder is safer."

"Mallory did it!" Steve barked, having to gasp into his mask from the effort. Nima didn't understand. The words came out wrong, slurred like those of that gumby who obstructed them at the First Step. "Can you belay?"

Nima nodded after catching the meaning.

Steve spoke slowly so he'd be understood. "I give you bonus of 500 American dollars if belay me to ledge," he said, pointing up. He cracked a smile after replacing his mask. He could see the little Sherpa computing the bonus in his head, probably thinking of purchasing a new maggot-infested yak.

"2,000 American dollars," Nima countered, pointing a gloved finger down the mountain.

That was when Steve made his third gaffe of the day. He turned to look at the epic exposure that fanned out below him. It was what in mountain climbing terms was referred to as a "screamer."

"Okay, 2,000 American dollars," Steve quickly agreed, jamming a knee into the rock face for leverage.

The ledge was only about 20 feet above him, give or take, a distance easily scaled with two anchors at lower altitude, but Steve had to step lower down the ridge in search of a place to anchor a chock. It was a source of frustration, for every step down added to the distance he would have to climb up.

While looking up for a route, a yellow snowsuit topped the lower ladder. Steve watched the figure step onto a hidden edge before scrambling up a crack in the rock and

19

onto the ledge above, disappearing from view. His eyes followed the line of the edge as it ran horizontal over his head.

"Give me the chocks."

Nima was beside him, looking up into his eyes even though he was standing higher on the ridge.

"Ladder is safer, boss."

"Chocks!"

Steve grabbed both chocks once Nima released them from the daisy chain. He attached one to his harness and reached up as far as he dared with the other—careful not to raise his heels and compromise his grip on the mountain. He inserted one into a crack and slid it sideways until it wedged. The fit was perfect; nice and secure—a bomb-proof anchor if he ever saw one.

"The rope," he ordered, clipping a quickdraw to the wire loop at the tail of the chock. Once he got hold of the rope he threaded the sharp end through and tied a figure eight knot to his harness, speaking under his mask. "Sure you know how to belay?"

Nima took up the rope as a point of pride and immediately started to tie a figure eight knot to the opposite end, just as Steve had done, allowing enough slack to thread the tail end through the belay loop in his harness, running the remainder back into the figure eight, finishing it off with a duplicate knot.

Steve felt a tug after Nima pulled in the slack. Suddenly, he was reminded of the one piece of equipment he had overlooked, but he needn't have worried. The Sherpa was equipped to the hilt, producing a belay device from a rack on his harness. Considering the weight difference between the two men, the small mechanical device was critical since a belay device (fitted into a bight of rope) added friction, allowing the belayer to control the person on belay with minimal physical effort.

Steve heard a click as Nima connected the belay device to a biner and the biner to his harness in one proficient sweep of the wrist. Once clipped in, the Sherpa took a step away from the rock face, both hands firmly on the rope.

"Wait!" Steve called out, twisting around. "Turn up my regulator to max."

The double flow of oxygen (4.0 liters per minute) was a gift like no other. Steve breathed it in, reveling in it. He could feel his blood take it up, transporting it to his frosted extremities, even with all moisture removed so the components of the regulator wouldn't freeze.

Showtime…

Steve chose a foothold, but before be lifted off, he decided on the next one further up and the one above that. Once having established the beginnings of a route, he turned to Nima and voiced the question.

"On belay?"

Nima responded in a thick accent under his mask, "Belay on."

Steve was free to move up, breathing in deeply, confident, doing what he did best. He could hear the rope slowly pay out as he moved progressively higher. Below, his Sherpa was doing the job required; leaving only minimal slack in case he fell.

So close was Steve to the rock face that he could distinguish the different layers within it, those darker layers interspersed by lighter-colored, crystallized deposits—skeletal fragments of sea organisms crushed by the weight of the ancient oceans. It was mind-blowing to contemplate the irony of it—how ancient coral had settled to the sea floor only to be lifted to the top of the world—or it would've been if he allowed himself the distraction. He didn't. All concentration was centered on the next handhold and foothold. There was no room for error.

Three quarters up, Steve slid the second chock into a crack, turning it sideways to bite the rock. Handholds and footholds got trickier after that. They were barely nubs, some only jibs, just enough of a surface to grip a toehold with the front-points of his crampons, but all he would need to do was make it to the edge and mantel up.

Steve's heart pounded as his goggles crested the edge. What he saw were choices, two means of getting to the ledge. It was possible to either top-out over a flattop block that was directly in front of him or traverse the edge back to the ladder and clip into the fixed rope, climbing up to the ledge in safety. The first route meant he would have to mantel up a second time and the second meant he would have to traverse the narrow edge, stepping over a void to reach the rope.

Steve got his arms up over the edge and pushed down on the rock, leaning forward, clawing his crampons into the fossilized shells and sea creatures. When his strength started to fail he improvised a move more typical of down-climbing, the "sit and spin," except he did it in reverse, spinning his body and plunking his buttocks down on the edge.

Slouched against the rock, wheezing into his mask, Steve gasped for air while blinking at the sun. He could almost see all the way down to Advanced Base Camp (fondly known to all as ABC), tucked away out of sight under the North Ridge. He followed the path he'd taken up the mountain, from the snowcapped North Col where the fixed rope began all the way up the North Ridge to where it intersected with the Northeast Ridge at High Camp, across the Yellow Band to the First Step where he could just make out a bright green snowsuit topping-out, the sweeper of the day.

Steve turned his gaze to the north face of the mountain, to a point a couple of hundred feet from where he could see the bright-colored tents of High Camp. He could just make out a mound, a blemish on the craggy surface. Looking at it, it occurred to him that if he fell from his perch he might come to rest at that very spot. It made him smile. He wasn't sure why.

His eyes then fell on the goggles at the base of the step, all aimed up at him. It made him start. It was a shock to realize he was on display. He was being watched by the gumbies and punters waiting their turn on the ladder, none anywhere near as skilled to do what he'd just accomplished: lead climbing up the Second Step.

Steve filled with pride in the recognition. He felt he was looking out from a throne. Here sat the rope gun of the mountain, the master mountaineer. To play to the crowd, he tapped his boots together, clearing them of excess snow; after which he made a show of retrieving a water bottle from inside his suit, smacking his lips after taking a draught. It would be the fourth major gaffe of the day.

The fit of coughing hit so hard that chunks of hardened mucus sprayed the inside of the mask. Steve had to force it over his mouth to keep it in place. He couldn't draw in air with everything flying out and quickly became light headed, like he was about to topple over the edge. He started to panic, but all he could effectively do was to lift up his legs and dig his crampons into the edge, burying his face between his knees, waiting for the fit to abate.

When it finally did, a sharp pain stabbed at Steve's side, almost as painful as his wounded ego. He pushed himself up against the block, but it didn't do any good. There was no hiding from his folly. He was in full view of all the goggles. Under each mask he could sense a smirk. They were laughing at him, looking up in contempt, tickled that he'd failed. He couldn't bear the humiliation.

Steve held his side as he pushed up against the block. Knowing he didn't have the reserves to mantel a second time, he immediately started off toward the fixed rope, pressed against the rock face, wincing in pain. Slowly he traversed the edge, feeling for nubs and jibs, but just as he stepped over the void, a red snowsuit topped the ladder. For a moment in time the two men stared at each other with a look of surprise, but instinct kicked in, and both reached for the fixed rope.

Survival mode was the protocol in the Death Zone, the modus operandi of the flight or fight response—the brain's most primal overseer, which the fossilized creatures adorned to the rock face could identify. In this mode, no high-order deliberation went into decision-making. The body responded in the most effective way in which to help itself, regardless of courtesy or decorum—those attributes of etiquette that took millions of years for the human brain to work out.

Steve won like he always won, but he had the advantage, not being clipped into the fixed rope. In a state of near euphoria he scrambled up the crack in the rock used to access the ledge, so exhilarated he thought of nothing but forward motion. Upon topping he continued with the fixed rope firmly in hand, scrambling up to the second ladder, blinded by what he'd just achieved—so full of himself he believed the plethora of voices were those waiting at the base of the step, cheering him on.

Poor Nima didn't know what to do. He'd watched the spectacle with growing unease, wishing he hadn't agreed to take part, murmuring a prayer of thanks when his charge topped out and was lost to sight. But he was immediately faced with a new problem. The rope kept paying out, running through the belay device he had firmly in the down position, allowing it to run freely through. Action had to be taken, for the rope was exactly one hundred feet long, a little less than the height of the step. It was sure to run out on the upper ladder.

Nima wasn't told to second—to follow up the lead—but he wouldn't have risked it, not for the world. He had his children to think of and a doting wife he loved with all his heart. His family was the reason he became a porter in the first place. It was a way he could afford to provide for them, to build up his herd of yaks.

There was no call of "belay off," but Nima had to assume his charge had clipped into the fixed rope. He'd seen all there was to see in the two years he'd worked as a porter, watching these foreigners stumble around like ragdolls, having lost all sense of orientation, some even lying down in the snow in the middle of a climb as if to go to sleep; but forgetting something as basic as clipping into the fixed rope was unthinkable. It didn't even enter his mind.

To avert disaster, Nima did what he had to do, hoisting up the rope to lock the belay device in place before his charge made it to the ladder. Looking up, he felt a tug on the rope, but what happened next horrified the Sherpa. The rope went slack and started to slip back over the ledge. All he could do was pray to the mountain, pulling in the rope as fast as he could.

Steve had been halfway up the ledge when he heard a familiar voice. It spoke to him directly, calling him by name; saying something he couldn't quite understand, something about a light.

"Dan?"

As if in answer, Steve was unceremoniously jolted backwards. He fell hard, landing on the oxygen tank, the edge stabbing into the small of his back. There wasn't time to scream. Gone was his grip on the fixed rope. Not having clipped in, he was sliding backwards, head first, picking up momentum on the snow covered slabs. Wedged underneath his backpack, his ice ax was unreachable, and his crampons offered little help as they skipped over rock.

Nima, wheezing from the effort of pulling in the rope, watched helplessly as his charge flew over the ledge, the mask whipping about uselessly in the thin air, having become detached. He shot up his arm to lock the belay

25

device while leaning backward for maximum leverage, digging his crampons in, praying the chocks would hold.

They did. Instead of hitting the base of the step, Steve slammed into the rock face. He was dragged sideways over the rock, coming to rest about five feet from the base, one leg caught in the rope, the other hanging limp, looking out over the world upside-down until his eyes clouded over and his life—an exercise in ego—came to an end.

He quivered like a tear in recognition. How gracefully arms unfurl in death, he thought, as if his body were taking a final bow. He gazed in wonder, but reaching down he rose higher, buoyant as a balloon.

All around, suspended in space, were a million little flames bound to the mountain by a force of their own. It enthralled him—so many hues, no two the same—these votive lights of Buddhist prayers, kindled by heartfelt blessings, invisible to all but him.

The panorama of the mountain opened beneath him as he continued to rise. He called out to Dan, and a body lit up like a beacon. It lay mangled on a shelf—eyes looking skyward, both legs broken in a fall. The head rested as it would on a pillow against the rock that had shattered the skull. Rising still higher, he sent down his love.

A breath, a bubble underwater, he ascended higher, leaving the little flames behind. All was glassy blue, and then it went dark. Summoned, he rushed down a tunnel as if a plug were pulled from a drain, only to emerge into the warm embrace of glorious streaks of gold, streaming from a light.

It would've been the new attraction on the mountain, being so accessible; a gruesome photographic subject for those waiting their turn to climb the ladders. Semi-anonymous in death, a nickname would be afforded, something fitting the particulars of the fatality, such as the "Hang Man" or the "Peter Cross," that first pope of the Catholic Church who had allegedly requested to be crucified upside down out of a sense of humility, claiming unworthiness to being put to death in the same manner as his Savior.

But when the heart and lungs fired up in a burst of inexplicable energy, that grisly fate was put on hold. Steve's chest heaved as air wheezed down his windpipe and into his lungs, filling them with cold streams of air. Bit by bit, oxygen pumped through his body, feeding his vital organs, calling them back to life. His muscles went limp with the disillusionment of it.

It was painful to look upon the world. Steve blinked stiffly at the daylight, bleak in comparison to where he'd come from. It seemed cold, glaring and unloving. He wished with all his heart he hadn't returned, that he could've forever remained in the Light's golden embrace.

On the rungs, the clang of crampons rang out like faraway gongs. Steve looked beyond them, searching for the voices, but he couldn't hear a peep. The dead had gone back to being dead while those yet living were preoccupied with endeavors particular to the living. In resurrection, he'd been abandoned by all.

But something drew his attention, an imprint stamped on the mountain. It was the echo of the little prayer flames, centuries of invocations from a people whom prayer was a daily part of life. Hadn't Sherpas encouraged him since arriving to take a spin each time they came upon a prayer wheel? He was told spinning one would have the same effect as reciting a prayer.

Blood was pooling around his brain. Steve could feel himself slipping away, puzzled as to why he was returned to this broken body. What seemed so clear had faded. Wasn't he supposed to live, to find a better path? It was to be a second chance, but he was no longer certain whether he was shown what could have been or what could be. Perhaps he was sent back to suffer the same indignity he afforded Mallory.

But the Light communicated nothing of that famed adventurer. It was a review of his life that was put before Steve, the whole ugly misadventure; even those little moments he'd failed to notice in life. He was subjected to every quiver of his wife's lips and every frown on his kids' brows—and it wasn't shards of memory passing before his eyes, for he could see himself in the visions, looking the other way, not having witnessed the pain he'd caused; the pain he had to now endure, rerouted for review.

Tears froze in the tangle of his eyebrows, tears for his wife and kids and all those he'd mistreated in life. The Light had set the evidence before him as he, a pinstripe lawyer, had set evidence before the court. It presented those dearest to him, those persons he'd spent a lifetime plundering. It was painful to realize he'd barely given a moment's thought to any of them in two long months since arriving at Tribhuvan International Airport.

The rope would fail. At least there was that. It'd degrade in the winds and fray under the eroding effects of UV, but how long would that take…six months, a year? It was easier to visualize the freefall. Steve was front row center to how it'd play out. All he had to do was roll back his eyes to see how his frozen corpse, once it snapped loose, would crash down the side of the Northeast Ridge, shattering to pieces on the north face. He'd shoot past Mallory's makeshift tomb at a growing velocity, bits of his body disappearing under the clouds, never to be seen again.

Have you followed your ego up the mountain as I followed mine?

It was the question Mallory had posed in the dream. Only now was Steve able to answer with certainty. His life had been an exercise in ego. How callous he'd been, thinking only of himself, his personal triumphs—badges to inflate a hollow heart.

Steve closed his eyes to the world. He wanted to offer a prayer to the mountain, to add his own imprint before he expired; but it was difficult to remember refrains so long unspoken, those he hadn't recited since a fidgety kid in church. His eyelids squeezed tighter as he stumbled on a broken set of words, but they snapped open when he heard a sound.

Steve stared at a pair of black eyes, twinkling behind goggles.

"I made stretcher, boss."

Three Sherpas had been released from expeditions. With Nima, that made four to attempt a rescue. They were whispering to each other as they gathered around him, looking into his eyes. One was middle aged, older than the other three. So intrigued was he that he pressed goggle against goggle, trying to get a closer look. He withdrew only to pull down his mask. Leaning back in, he washed Steve's face with the warmth of his breath.

Already news of the accident had been broadcast over the mountain, and a plan had been hatched. At ABC, the expedition doctor had been notified. The leader of the Seattle Expedition had been informed of the situation while staring out in triumph on the summit. He took charge, radioing one directive: to get his team member as far below the Death Zone as quickly as possible.

Nima had secured the rope before scrambling up the ridge for help, having wound it around Steve's torso, knotting it so it could easily be freed. He'd even replaced the mask before heading up for help, ignoring the whites of

29

the eyes that stared back at him in death. Chomolungma had called to him to act, and that was what he had told the others.

After unraveling the rope, Nima clipped in and stepped away from the rock face. The plan was simple. He'd lower Steve down to the stretcher—a hammock-like contraption tied together with a strand of borrowed rope. Clipped to the stretcher on either side would be two Sherpas waiting for their load. The job of the fourth would be to lay the injured man out and tie him down with rope. He was young, new to being a porter. This would be his first rescue mission, and he was nervous. The injured man looked too far gone to save.

Nima signaled, making sure all were ready before releasing the lock on the belay device; but when he did, the rope slipped through his gloves. Steve dropped before jerking to a stop. The cry that escaped him was dampened under the mask, but still the Sherpas froze, uncertain what to do. They looked to Nima for guidance. It would be his call to make.

All Nima could do was offer a prayer to the mountain before signaling the others to continue as planned. He paid out the rope, gently, inch by delicate inch, as the accident replayed in his head. It was his hope that the insulated suit might've helped cushion the impact as the hood might've helped pad the skull. Holding tight to the rope, he prayed for his prayer to be answered.

Steve fell into a state of delirium before coming into contact with the stretcher, slipping into a semiconscious fog where time seemed to accelerate and lose speed in pace with the sporadic rate of his heart. The pain came in waves. He cried out each time, but the only effect it had was to make the labored breathing of those trying to rescue him halt.

The tears that froze Steve's eyelids shut proved a blessing. He was blind to the callous stares of those he

30

passed at the ladders as he soon would be to the exposure of the side of the ridge—that perilous section separating the first two steps. It would force the rescue party to slow their pace until arriving back up to the relative safety of the ridge's crest.

If the First Step was long in coming, it was miraculously free of traffic. The last of the day's sweepers had long since passed. They had it all to themselves, a window of opportunity that didn't go wasted. A throng would soon be heading down from the summit. If they got caught up in it, their efforts would be for nothing. On this mountain (as it tends to be in life) the slowest loses the race.

Nima and the young Sherpa had taken on the burden at the top of the step, providing the other two a well-earned break. They synchronized their downclimb to keep the stretcher level, each holding a fistful of rope, selecting only those deemed relatively fresh. Expeditions typically fix supplementary ropes at trouble spots for climbers less experienced. The rescue party was quick to take advantage of them. Even so, it was backbreaking work.

In its own way, the Yellow Band proved just as difficult. The slabs were dangerously slippery in places, polished by decades of traffic. Nima insisted on keeping up the pace in anticipation of an unavoidable delay at High Camp. There he'd use the booty (the gear left behind by past expeditions) to stabilize the stretcher, using old tent pole parts to make it more rigid.

As agreed, Nima radioed in once arriving at the cluster of vacant tents—the highest campground in the world. After giving an update, he was informed two spare Sherpas had been sent up to provide assistance. It encouraged the little rescue party, by now feeling the effects of the burden. Steve was zipped into his sleeping bag and placed back on the stretcher with tent pole parts

31

woven into the backing. They rested for ten minutes before setting out again, turning onto the North Ridge.

A muffled cheer rang out after they passed beyond the Death Zone, but exhaustion was taking its toll. Instead of removing their masks, they turned up the flow to compensate. The added weight of the aluminum tent poles and the down filled sleeping bag (infinitesimal at sea level) felt as if they were lugging a sack of stone. It got to the point where they had to swap places every ten minutes.

Benefits of decreasing altitude were slow in coming. In time, however, they slogged into Camp II after descending the fifteen hundred or so feet from High Camp. The middle-aged Sherpa and youngest of the party looked too spent to continue in spite of slurred protests to the contrary. Nima radioed in again and was told the ones making their way up were twenty minutes away at most, having started out from the North Col, the next camp down. He decided to wait.

Dawa and Kamli looked as if they hadn't even broken a sweat. Unlike the rescue party, they hadn't gone through the wasting effects of the Death Zone. Quickly evaluating the situation, they decided that they alone would take the burden the rest of the way down; and they didn't waste time arguing, ordering the other four to lie down in the tents and get some rest, reminding them of their wives and children.

They set out at once, unburdened by the weight of oxygen tanks. They breathed the air freely as they followed the fixed rope down single file with the stretcher clipped between them. They set the pace to keep ahead of the bottleneck behind. The snow was deeper at this lower altitude, giving crampons something to dig into, making it unlikely to slip in spite of the steady pace they set. In the end, they made excellent time.

******

Steve woke bundled inside the same sleeping bag used to carry him down the mountain, pain flaming through a body numbed by heavy doses of codeine. He was wrapped in gauze and set with splints. A makeshift brace was fitted to constrict movement, put together from the available booty, much like the stretcher. Booty was a plentiful commodity at ABC where piles of old castoff equipment littered the camp.

A man lay beside him. It took Steve a moment to recognize the expedition leader even though they'd known each other for years. Like everyone does, Brian had lost weight in the Death Zone. His skin had darkened in the sun.

"Glad to see you're still with us, Steve," he said, a little raspy. "If the weather holds, we should be able to get you out tomorrow."

Silence followed. It couldn't be easy to converse with someone so critically injured, but Brian had always been straight with Steve, even those times when the two had butted heads.

"You know, we'd have never made it this far if the Japanese expedition hadn't released their Sherpas."

Steve tried to speak, to ask if Brian summited, but the task proved too taxing. Recognizing this, the expedition leader made an attempt to lighten the mood, something unusual for him. He was known as a serious type, always busy saving the planet in one way or another.

"You sure picked a helluva place to take a fall."

It was meant to be a joke. Steve tried to grin, that silly, goofy grin that mountaineers were quick to sport in the face of fear, but the best he could do was grit his teeth. Brian grinned for them both before rolling over in his sleeping bag, clearly in need of sleep. If he was concerned the person lying beside him would be dead in the morning, it went unsaid.

******

33

With the help of the cache of codeine provided by Jon, the expedition doctor, who made himself available throughout the night—visiting the tent on the hour to check vitals—Steve managed to live through it. The doctor had already done what he could with the resources available. His recommendation was to get Steve to Base Camp as quickly as possible. There he could be transported by helicopter to hospital in Katmandu.

Tibetan yak herders were sitting in a group, smoking and talking, having had their breakfast. Several times Steve caught them looking his way, nodding knowingly to one another. Yaks stood about, some waiting for their loads as ABC was broken down. Herders were feeding tsampa to others, already loaded with gear.

Steve lay on the ground strapped into a padded aluminum rescue basket called a Stokes litter, a critical piece of equipment on climbing mountains. Nearby, a huge bull yak pulled restlessly at the ropes that secured it to the center of camp. He followed the flight of its red wool tassel, fluttering from a horn.

It wasn't long before a group of Sherpas stepped up to carry Steve to the bull. Its herder stood watch, a cigarette dangling from his lips, holding a rope tied to the bull's bridle. The tassel jerked violently as the bull swung its horns around to examine the burden it was expected to carry. It lunged, deciding against the extra weight, dragging the herder through the rock flakes. The air was immediately full of whistles and yells from other herders as they converged on the bull.

Through a fog of pain and codeine, Steve caught the earthy pungency of the beast as he was lifted onto its back. He never liked barnyard smells, but he found himself breathing it in like incense. One of the stiff wooly hairs brushed his cheek, and for an instant he caught the baleful glare of a dark liquid eye.

Brian's voice called out. "You guys sure this is going to work?"

"No problem, boss," Wongchu Sherpa the sirdar said.

Anyone who'd ever climbed in this part of the world knew how easily that phrase seemed to spill from the tobacco-stained lips of Sherpas, even during times when a most definite problem was afoot. After much lashing, with herders holding the bull front and rear, the basket was tied down. On the count of three (rendered in a Tibetan dialect) all let go with the exception of the bull's herder. The beast immediately swung its massive head around to look at the basket in spite of the herder pulling hard from the front, his heels dug into the rocks.

It lunged, scattering the herders. Bucking violently, its hind legs kicked upward and outward. Steve found himself once again upside down, terrified. The huge horns swung wildly from side to side as the bull bellowed and snorted. The force of movement caused the Stokes litter to shift forcefully onto its side. Steve cried out as stabs of pain shot through his pelvis and lower back.

Herders had to converge on the bull a second time. Once they got it under control, the basket was retied and new ropes were lashed to it under the supervision of a wizened old herder. Things started to go smoother after that, and they were soon able to start out. The first group of loaded yaks followed the bull down the trail for the day-long trek to Base Camp.

"Brian?"

"Right beside you."

Steve rolled his eyes at the expedition leader before returning his gaze back to the jagged rocks that spired up into points in the sky. The short gasps of vapor expelling from his mouth added to the majesty of it all. Rocking back and forth from the movement of the bull, his eyelids slowly closed.

"The Sherpas seem curious about you," Brian said. "Don't know what they're saying, but I noticed how they stare at you." Lowering his voice so he wouldn't be overheard, he whispered "you know how superstitious these people are…"

Steve felt a jerk when the bull's head swung around at a passing herder. The crudely hammered bell tied around its neck struck a sturdy tone. It rang out in complex, earthy harmonies until it was lost to the mountain. He listened to the bell as it continued to clang to the slow steady rhythm of the bull's movement, adding its voice to the bells of the other yaks behind.

For a time, Steve came to believe they were ringing for him, but, unexpectedly, Brian spoke up in denunciation of his worthiness in an awkwardly phrased apology.

"This probably isn't the right time or place," Brian said, "but sometimes, Steve, you've been a sonofabitch," he stated, matter-of-factly. "Getting you down the mountain, I was bracing for this angry, foul-mouthed monster that was going to ream us all out for the pain we were causing him. When I first got the call, I have to tell you, I thought of not even bothering to rescue you at all. Sorry about that."

The codeine, the slow steady rhythm of the bull's stride and the song of the bells lulled Steve into an uneasy sleep. Later he woke to massive blue-white cathedral-sized columns of ice on either side.

"Dan's dead," Steve said, his voice barely a squeak.

Brian grumbled. He hadn't expected to have to deal with that particular issue, at least not yet. "Yes, Steve, Dan's dead," he said, incapable of telling a lie. "He's part of the mountain now."

Steve looked up at the scripture in the clouds. "I saw him from above."

Brian looked down at Steve—questioning eyes shaded under dark sunglasses. "What do you mean?"

"I saw him, before I was sent back."

"Sent back?"

"From the Light."

It was likely the confused rambling of a delusional mind, but, then again, Brian couldn't help but wonder. They'd stood on opposite sides of the aisle too many times in the past. For a moment, he suspected a trick. It wouldn't have been the first time Steve hoodwinked his way into getting what he wanted. The man truly was a sonofabitch.

Chapter Two

"You don't seem to have significant damage to your spinal cord, but there's damage to the sheath," the doctor said, blunt from years on the job. "I have you scheduled for physical therapy in the pool at nine tomorrow morning, but at this point I'd be surprised to see any major changes," he added, heading out of the room.

A mountain sat on Steve's chest. His life was in freefall. For an hour he stared into the sterile room, seeing nothing but the dead-end before him. It was the click of heels that finally roused him. He didn't have time to even run fingers through his hair when his wife stormed through the door, a nurse caught in her undertow. It was her first appearance, and it was going to be a show.

"Please, could you leave me alone with Mr. Forrest?" Susan ordered.

Her composure faltered as she pulled a sheaf of paper from a briefcase. The nurse left as soundlessly as a mouse.

"These are divorce papers. I told you...I said when you left on your fool adventure that I'd had enough. Remember?"

"Yes."

"I'm leaving you, and I'm taking the kids. You're not fit to raise them, not now. Look at you!"

Susan's nostrils flared as she stared down at the hospital bed, her hands balled into fists even as she held the papers. Steve saw in her eyes fractured, broken rock, but he tried to plead his case, regardless.

"I've changed."

"No more!" Susan shouted. "I'm not listening...sign the goddamned papers!"

Susan stepped back and stood against the wall, appearing to rise and fall with each scorching breath.

"Leave them with me," Steve whispered. "I'll look them over."

Susan's eyes bored down into him.

"Can't we…?" Steve blurted out, trying to form a sentence as he followed the path of a tear that wound down his wife's face.

Susan stiffened to stone. "Don't try any lawyer tricks."

"I won't."

"What?"

"I said I won't."

Susan's mouth started to open but then slammed shut. She dropped the stack of papers on the dresser, picked up her briefcase and bolted for the door. It resisted as she tried to slam it, hinges hissing in protest. Giving up, she stormed down the hallway, hammering the tiles with her heels.

Steve had hours to reflect. His eyes only refocused midway through the afternoon when he heard the soft sucking sound of the door. A woman's head peeked into the room, lips quivering.

"Can I come in?"

Steve turned to face the wall in panic, ill-prepared for what was about to happen. Kathy pushed through the door and dashed across the room anyway, throwing herself on him. She began to stroke his hair as she sobbed.

"I know it wasn't your fault," she said, her voice muffled in his hospital gown, "but why did you two have to go? Now Dan is dead and you're a cripple!"

Steve could feel her tears soaking through his gown, anointing him with guilt. In time, Dan's widow released her grip, wiping her face with the back of her hands. She smoothed out her clothes while trying to forge a smile. She couldn't. Finally, she just nodded and left, her lips curled in anguish.

39

A late spring storm darkened the room. Rain splattered against the windowpanes. Steve watched it until he heard the soft sucking sound once more.

"Don't you want the lights on, Mr. Forrest?" a young nurse said.

He shook his head.

"Are you okay?"

Steve stared at her over the bulge in the pillow, knowing the question was beyond the scope of her job. She has yet to be hardened like the doctor, he thought. "Yes, I'm fine…thanks."

Darkness returned. Steve drifted mindless in a whirlwind of thoughts spiraling through his head, craving emptiness. Another hour slipped by in silence. Finally, he pressed on the light switch to distract himself and once again closed his eyes, fading out.

"Hello there!"

An exceedingly tall, heavyset man with a shaven head, hawk-like nose and piercing dark blue eyes stood at the foot of the bed. Steve blinked up at the vision, not having heard the soft sucking sound of the door. Something deep inside his lower belly tingled in warning.

"Are you a doctor?"

"Nope, I'm John Sheehan, S. J., but people call me Jack. I rotate here as chaplain." The man moved to the side of the bed and leaned over Steve, a little too close. "I thought maybe we could chat."

A child's wail erupted. The cry echoed through the hallway. Steve was immediately overwhelmed with emotion. Everything else was forgotten. The room became a blur of tears.

"Do you know the two greatest sins according to Sherpas?" Steve blubbered.

"Why, no, I don't."

"Picking wildflowers and scolding children."

The child's cries jerked violently around him in crimson tassels. Steve pulled them into himself, sending waves of understanding through them and back to the child. The wails dwindled and then stopped altogether.

"Sherpas sound like a compassionate people."

"They were sloppy," Steve said, releasing the strands, not understanding what just happened.

"Sloppy?

"That's what I used to think."

"What changed?"

Steve turned and faced the wall again. "Father—"

"Jack will do fine."

There was no direction to the mayhem of pallid paint strokes. Steve looked at the little insect that got caught in the paint, whitewashed the color of the walls. It had become his only friend. He had cried over its fate, caressing it with a finger.

"Ever heard of near-death experience?"

"Of course...I've researched the emotional aftereffects of the near-death experience."

"What aftereffects?"

"Increased sensitivity to the surrounding world; how relationships change—divorce, things like that."

Steve felt like a kid under the shadow of such a large man. "Did you know my wife was in here with divorce papers today?"

"It's the talk of the floor."

Steve glanced up—way up—into the dark blue eyes only to turn away and swallow hard. "Did you hear that child crying a moment ago?"

"Yes, it stopped."

"I made it stop."

"Did you?" Jack said. "And how did you do that?"

Steve had no answer.

"Field studies have documented claims of paranormal activity associated with the near-death

41

experience, you know. Of course," Jack said with a shrug, "psychologists who study the phenomenon tend to think it's the brain playing tricks on people who've experienced trauma."

"What do you think?"

Jack took his time before answering. "I think most people know very little about the true nature of reality."

Steve looked up at the man. It wasn't the answer he had expected.

"I can see you've got a lot on your plate," Jack said, pulling up a chair. "What's bothering you?"

"To be honest, I'm not sure I want to talk to a priest about what's bothering me."

"Then it's your lucky day."

"How so?"

"I'm also a psychotherapist."

The lawyer in Steve tripped. "You knew about my near-death experience, didn't you?"

"It's in the report."

"You had access to my report?"

"Not exactly."

Steve stared dumb. "What do you mean?"

"Well, I don't exactly have the authorization, being the chaplain and all, but I took a peek at your folder. Hope you don't mind."

Steve pressed the pump, sending a dose of painkiller into his arm. He waited for the meds to kick in. "The reason I wanted to return—"

"Wait," Jack said, holding up a finger. "You had a choice?"

"Ah…yes, after the life review, I—"

"The life review?"

"The Light presented me with my life so I could see for myself what I'd become."

"Fascinating…continue, please."

"I saw what a lousy husband and father I'd been," Steve said, now inexplicably spilling his guts—certainly not something he would've done in the past. "I wanted to make it up to my wife and kids. So I came back...you know...to try to do a better job."

Jack took a moment to think. "So the life review was life-changing?"

"Yes, but I can't see the way forward."

The rain had stopped. Out the window, the clouds hung low in the sky. Nothing moved, not even the air in the room.

"Eastern thought believes the reason change is so difficult to achieve is that plans, agendas and preferences have to be given up to fit a new paradigm. Some people feel like they're losing their identity, and that terrifies them," Jack said, flipping his gaze from one wall to another. "On the other hand, I've heard of a biological law that states that any living thing that doesn't change must be dying."

"So?"

"One wonders if that doesn't apply to spirituality, too." Jack paused, arms now behind his head, leaning back in the chair, looking up at the ceiling before letting his eyes fall back to the bed. "Can you describe the Light to me?"

No one had bothered to ask that question, and because of it, Steve didn't have an answer prepared. He closed his eyes to gather his thoughts, but, strangely, he became distracted. It was as if he could feel the essence of the man beside him more intensely in the dark.

"I'm reluctant to talk about it," Steve finally said. "Words seem inadequate."

"That fits with what others have expressed—those who've claimed to have had a near-death experience."

"Does it?"

"Yes."

"It radiated gold," Steve blurted out. "I didn't so much see it…it seemed to bathe my whole being with…I don't know, love, I guess you'd call it."

"It was the color of love?"

"Yes," Steve said, "the color of love…and, the funny thing is, I've seen that color before, all my life. I just never recognized it until the moment I was confronted by its…pure form."

"Explain?"

Steve tried. "It was the same color I could remember seeing springing from the grass when I was a kid."

"You don't say?"

"I know that color!" Steve insisted, words spilling out like spit. "I've seen its glow on top of clouds."

"And the life review?"

Steve deflated back into the pillow. "A series of random scenes."

"Like what?" Jack said, pressing for information.

"If I concentrated on one scene," Steve said, thinking back, "I'd see it from different angles—how it affected my life—but I'd also feel how my words and actions affected others. I could feel their hurt."

"Really?"

"Yes, but—"

"What?"

Steve stumbled on the words. They sounded odd coming from him. "The review would've been unbearable if it wasn't for the love radiating from the Light."

"Which stands in accord with the New Testament's view that God is complete and unconditional love," Jack said.

"The experience was beyond words," Steve retorted, "even the words of the New Testament."

Jack hooted. Such a statement must have been rather bold to a priest.

"Once my son and I were playing catch," Steve said, now sharing what he'd never shared before, "and I swear I could feel every blade of grass."

A nurse walked into the room. "Visiting hours is over...mind wrapping it up?"

"Certainly," Jack said, lifting off from the chair. "What's on your agenda tomorrow?"

Steve took a moment to think, a little dazed by the encounter. "I'm told I've got physical therapy in the pool, starting at nine."

"What if I drop by about one o'clock?"

"All right," Steve said, watching as the chair was moved back against the wall. "Jack?"

"Yes."

Steve blinked at the brightness of the man's eyes. "Thanks."

Jack stood rocking on the balls of his feet like a little kid. "Think you would've thanked me before the accident?"

It was the first time in ages that Steve smiled.

Jack started for the door, holding onto the doorframe so he wouldn't hit his head. "So you've some inkling of what this change entails, do you?"

"No," Steve said, fanning tears with his eyelashes, tears that hadn't dried since waking up in the hospital a paraplegic. "I don't have a clue."

******

Steve sat hunched in his wheelchair. He stared into his lap, having just related the morning's events to Jack sprawled out beside him on a bench like he didn't have a care in the world.

"So you couldn't look her in the eye," Jack said.

"I couldn't look at her at all."

"Found her sexy, did you?"

"No!"

"You sensed she took offense though…thought you didn't approve of her, maybe?"

"Maybe."

Jack chuckled to himself. "Melody is a topnotch physical therapist. She came to the hospital highly recommended, but she's an attractive girl, a bombshell some might say. Plenty of the boys on staff have a crush on her. I have to admit I've looked her way once or twice myself."

"You're a priest!"

"And you're not," Jack said, debating whether to slip off his shoes. "Would the old Steve ogle over her?"

Steve pushed his legs together and locked them in place with his hands. He couldn't bear the way they flopped to the side. "The old Steve would pinch her butt if he knew he could get away with it."

"What's different?"

It took Steve a moment to find the words to express what he really felt. "I feel like I'm being watched."

Jack sat up a little straighter. "By whom?"

"No idea."

A bee circled Jack's head three times before flying off to the tulips that bordered the flowerbeds by the hospital's back façade.

"Am I right to assume you're not referring to a human being?"

Steve stared blankly at the mottled shadows of the trees—puzzle pieces dumped on the grass, waiting to be reassembled—searching for answers to questions that had never before surfaced inside him.

"This 'watcher' you refer to is known by other names, you know. Some call it the 'silent witness,' and others call it the 'observer.'"

"It's inside me," Steve said. "Maybe it's always been there."

"Do you think it stands in judgment or does it cheer you on, so to speak?"

Steve mulled the question. "Neither."

Jack stretched out on the bench again, resting his head on the fingers he'd cupped behind his head. What he said next was articulated in something that resembled a mumble, as if he were talking to himself. "Ordinarily, it'd take at least ten years of *zazen* to get to the level of observer."

"*Zazen*?"

"Zen meditation."

"What kind of Catholic priest are you anyway?"

"The fact you've reached the point of recognizing your observer is a milestone in itself, although not one which the meditator can celebrate, according to Zen Buddhism."

"What?"

"A person gets it all at once in one horrendous event, like it or not. That's the way it goes. You heard God works in mysterious ways, haven't you?"

"You haven't answered my question."

"What question?"

"What kind of Catholic priest professes Zen meditation?"

Jack smiled up at the sky. "A Zen teacher, of course."

"You're a Zen teacher?"

"Ordained at Shinmeikutsu, outside Tokyo, a Zen-Christian monastery opened back in the mid-70s. I studied there for twelve years before being posted to Seattle twelve months ago, give or take a week or two."

Steve spun the wheelchair to face Jack. "How can that be? Why isn't the Vatican all over you?"

"Well, for one thing, there're only a few of us in existence."

47

"Wouldn't your Jesuit superior in Rome look on this unfavorably?"

Jack lowered his voice to a conspiratorial whisper. "My spies tell me he has a meditation cushion of his own in his office."

Steve was too flabbergasted to move, even if he could. It took a moment for him to recover his train of thought. "Is this why you're interested in my near-death experience?"

Jack pursed his lips. "It's a pet theory of mine that confronting the changes demanded by the near-death experience is exceedingly similar to integrating enlightenment into one's life from a meditation cushion."

Steve scratched at his elbow. That prickling sensation was starting to trouble him again. It had become more pronounced. He didn't have a clue what it meant. Was it a sign his paralysis was improving or getting worse? He suspected the latter. As of yet he hadn't told anyone about it. He couldn't face more bad news.

After a couple of minutes of silence, Steve posed a question. "Do people who pursue enlightenment think they're going crazy?"

"There are Zen tales from the old days concerning people who went stark staring bonkers," Jack replied. "But as a therapist those stories make me wonder how mental illness was perceived back then."

"The last couple of weeks have made me question my sanity," Steve said. "This hypersensitivity and sudden...I don't know...ability to meld my thoughts to others is raising a lot of questions in me."

Jack grunted as he lifted himself none too graciously off the bench. "I suspect you'll want to wheel yourself in as you wheeled yourself out."

"I want to walk again," Steve said with a bite of sarcasm. "Do you think that'll ever happen?"

"*Insha'Allah*," Jack said, strolling away, whistling back at the birds.

******

The next morning's therapy session was as grueling as the night it followed. Steve had awakened in a sweat every couple of hours or so, his heart racing. Melody drove him hard in the pool. She wouldn't accept his wanting to quit. She held him up under his arms, whispering encouragement in his ear. Whatever this woman thought of him, she took her responsibilities as a physical therapist seriously.

After lunch Steve acquiesced and allowed Jack to wheel him out to the grounds. Although he wouldn't admit it, he didn't have the energy to do so himself.

"So, how did the session with Melody go?"

"She's a driver."

"No doubt about it, but so are you."

"What do you mean?"

"Melody is well aware you're a mountaineer. She's driving you hard because she knows you know how to drive yourself hard. Only a driver would attempt Everest."

"Chomolungma."

"Chomolungma?"

"It's the Tibetan word for Everest," Steve said. "It means 'Goddess Earth Mother of the World.' A Tibetan legend says if you approach the mountain with a pure enough heart and you sit quietly at its foot long enough you'll hear the deep bass sound of the Goddess Earth Mother of the World spinning out life on the planet."

"*Qi!*"

"Sorry?"

"*Qi,*" Jack said again. "It's Chinese. It means 'vital energy' or 'life force.' It's said a Qigong master can

49

manifest *qi* with a deep bass sound. It's funny how things seem interconnected. Did you sleep well last night?"

"No."

Jack parked the wheelchair beside the same bench as the day before.

"And why was that?"

"I can't seem to turn my brain off. Too many thoughts are whizzing through my head."

Jack plunked down on the bench. "One writer," he said, "Joseph Chilton Pearce, refers to this as 'roof brain chatter.'"

Unlike the day before, Jack sat with his back straight, legs spread apart and feet flat on the grass. He leaned his body forward ever so slightly on the edge of the bench. He then closed his eyes to slits as he clasped his hands on his lap.

Steve regarded the man for some minutes. "Is this a technique you're showing me that I can use to rid myself of this roof brain chatter?"

A smile as sly as the slits of his eyes curled on Jack's lips. "If you're referring to meditation, the answer is no. Meditation is a skill that takes time to develop. Most novices find it only worsens the problem, mostly because they believe they're not supposed to think, that their mind is to remain blank. That, of course, is wrong since meditation encourages the mind to think."

"Does it?"

Jack cracked open an eyeball and peeked over at Steve. "With that said, already your sense of your observer is strong. You recognize its presence. Perhaps meditation may help, but at this point I can't say for certain."

Jack's eyelids returned to slits. Steve noted how the man's ample chest rose and fell with each breath.

"What does *Insha'Allah* mean?"

Jack sat as still as stone. "*Insha'Allah* is Arabic shorthand for 'if God is willing' or 'God willing.' There are a number of equivalents from other cultures. In t'ai chi/Qigong it's referred to as '*sung*,' which translates both to 'relax' and to 'give up and let go.' The Christian equivalent is 'Thy will be done, Lord, not mine.'"

"Give up and let go?" Steve said, perplexed. "It sounds like a formula for suicide."

Jack's eyelids shot open. "Quite the opposite! It's the most natural thing in the world to at once witness the divine plan and surrender oneself to it."

"I don't understand."

"Two monks, centuries ago, one young and the other old, were travelling together from one monastery to another. They came upon a rushing stream where a young geisha stood frightened. Bound as she was in traditional garment, she could not cross on her own. The older monk stepped up, bowed deeply, picked her up and carried her across the stream. He put her down on the other side, bowing once more. Onward the monks continued on their way to the monastery. At one point the young monk could stay his objection no longer. 'How dare you pick up and carry a woman!' he said, trembling in fury, adding 'it is not allowed even to talk to them!' The older monk stopped, turned to the young monk and said, 'are you still carrying that woman, young one? I put her down long ago.'"

******

"What's wrong?" Jack said, strolling into the room. He leaned his weight on the metal frame at the foot of the bed, staring down at the tearstained face.

"It's raining," Steve blubbered, wanting to crawl away on his elbows, away from this overpowering presence bearing down on him. "It's raining for that poor woman."

"Has someone died?" Jack's eyes were fixed on Steve. "Last night by chance?"

"Yes."

51

"Marian?"

"Was that her name?"

The seconds ticked on the alarm clock on the bedside table.

"How do you know Marian died?" Jack said. "Her room is all the way on the other side of the ward."

"I was with her."

"I'm sure she didn't come to visit you. I know for a fact she's been in an induced coma for days," Jack said, leaning in a little closer. "How did you two manage to get together?"

Steve stared blankly at the valley in the bedding that sloped down from his two dead feet. "I felt her searching, and I reached out."

"Like the way you reached out and comforted that child?"

Steve looked up at Jack, the big bald head eclipsing the light from the fluorescent fixture on the ceiling. "She wanted to show me things."

"What?"

"Her children and grandchildren, her husband who died years earlier, her mother and father, brothers and sisters and all the friends she had in life. She was so happy."

"And this is why you're crying?"

Steve turned his head to the wall, to the little insect incased in paint. "She had so many happy memories to share with me, so many more than I," he said, trying to keep his composure. "She was a good person, Jack."

"Yes, she was, and so were you for comforting her during her time of need."

Steve turned back to face Jack. "She didn't need my comfort. It was her that comforted me."

Jack smiled. "Did she die in peace?"

Steve's eyelids fell like a curtain. "I guess so...the images started to fade and then finally snuffed out. That's all I know. She went away, and what did I have but a pitiful handful of happy memories of my own—and there aren't too many of those if you add them all up."

Jack straightened up and folded his arms. "Have you heard from Susan?"

"She wants the divorce papers back."

"Have you signed them yet?"

"No," Steve said. "I can't."

"*Quid pro quo.*"

"What?"

"*Quid pro quo*," Jack reiterated. "You're the lawyer. Tell her you'll sign the goods for an exchange of services."

"What do you mean?"

"Tell her you'll sign the papers after your demands are met."

"What demands?"

"Ask her first to undergo divorce counseling with you. It may offer an opportunity for her to see you in a new light. As a therapist, I recommend it. It would minimize the emotional stress on both of you."

Steve stared up at Jack, now leaning against the dresser opposite the bed. "She won't do it."

"Doesn't hurt to ask, does it?"

Steve shook his head, unconvinced, until an idea struck him. "Are you licensed for divorce counseling?"

"Being your therapist, Steve, I doubt I'm the right person for the job whether I'm licensed or not. One could argue a conflict of interest."

"Couldn't you act as mediator?"

"I could, in theory."

"Let's do it," Steve said, suddenly determined, rising from his tears. "Maybe if we get to talking, she'll see I really have changed. Maybe she'll withdraw the divorce."

Jack moved off the dresser and strolled to the window. "I hate to burst your bubble, Steve, but if you go into divorce therapy with that idea in mind, Susan will suspect you're trying to manipulate her. You need to stop hanging on to things outside your control."

"All right…I'll stop trying to hang on to things outside my control, but will you do it?"

"It's not my usual practice," Jack muttered, "but I'll make an exception in this case, that is, if Susan agrees."

"I'll let her lawyer know," Steve said, feeling a lot better all of a sudden.

Jack continued to stare out the window as Steve blinked at the light from the ceiling fixture.

"Hey, Jack?"

"Yes?"

"This hypersensitivity…what is it?"

"You tell me."

"I don't know," Steve said. "It's like I've been opened up like a can of peas. I feel…exposed."

"Exposed?" Jack said. "Exposed to what?"

Steve considered the question a moment. "To the world."

"Does it feel threatening?"

"It feels like my chest has been ripped open."

"Like your defenses have dissolved?"

"I don't know how to explain it," Steve said, wiping the crusty residue of tears from his face. "It's like the air is full of flaming arrows directed at my heart, and I don't like it. I don't want to be hurt in this way…it's too painful."

Jack moved from the window and pulled the chair to the bed. "In his preface to Dag Hammarskjöld's book, *Markings*, W. H. Auden describes humans as possessing rings of defenses, all pointing outward. The strongest are the outer rings, the ones others see first. People always appear stronger, more threatening, in relation to how one sees oneself. Do you understand the point I'm trying to make?"

"No."

"We see our perceived faults and foibles when we look at others while at the same time we stand witness to their strongest outer defenses."

"People still react to the old me because they only see my outer defenses. Is that what you're trying to say?"

"It's a theory."

Steve shook his head. "How could they not notice?"

"Our personal experiences always seem like the center of the universe to us, but that's simply not the case. People are going to need time to recognize the changes that have taken place inside you. Just let go," Jack said. "Let go and be at peace."

"How do I let go?" Steve replied. "I can't walk. How do I let go of that?"

The chair creaked as Jack leaned back into it. "*Wu wei.*"

"What?"

"*Wu wei*," Jack reiterated. "Understand that Zen is the end result of a synergistic collision between Taoism and Buddhism, after the latter arrived in China. '*Wu*' is Taoist and '*wei*' is Buddhist."

"*Wu wei?*"

"Yes, *wu wei*," Jack said for the third time, letting the words slip from his lips. "It refers to a state that arises from a sense of being connected to others as well as to one's environment."

"*Wu wei?*"

"Yes," Jack said, smiling, "*wu wei.*" Think of it as meaning 'going with the flow,' which may sound simplistic, but don't be fooled. It's not an easy thing to be conscious both to one's inner self and to the reality of one's environment in a non-interfering, receptive way. One would have to put aside one's ego with all its plans, agendas, preferences and prejudices. One would also have to learn to perceive processes that occur inside and around them in their earliest stages, just as they arise. 'Deal with the small before it becomes large,' Lao Tzu the Taoist sage said."

"How does one achieve this state?"

Jack's face contorted into a big question mark. "How indeed?"

"Meditation?"

"Perhaps," Jack said, not too convincingly. "But knowing yourself, Steve, do you think you'll be able to maintain personal, daily practice?"

"I don't have anything pressing at the moment to distract me from thinking about my life."

Jack smiled down at him. "All right…first of all, you'll need to monitor your progress. Don't push yourself too hard too fast. This must be a natural process or it won't work. I recommend starting out with five minutes per day. Increase the time to no more than fifteen minutes per day in the first week or so and then get back to me as you become more familiar with it. Gradually, we'll increase your practice time."

"Practice?" Steve said. "That's the name for it?"

"Yes, and don't wage a war with your ego while meditating. You'll lose."

"Sorry?"

"Your ego will do all this crazy stuff to try to get you to stop meditating."

"Why?"

Jack's eyes flashed blue in the fluorescent light as he looked up at the ceiling. "It's only a theory, but I believe the ego is aware that meditation is a force destructive to it or at the very least meditation acts to swap loyalties over time, eventually coming to battle against it. At any rate, can you get into a chair by yourself?"

"Yes…if I use the bed frame to lift myself up. Melody has been pushing me to do this."

"Would it help if I leave the chair beside the bed?" Jack said.

"I should practice meditation while sitting in a chair?"

"If not a cushion then a chair," Jack said, standing up and gesturing for Steve to move into it. He looked at his watch. "I've got others to visit before the end of the day. See you tomorrow."

"Okay."

"And don't forget to sit up straight and count your breaths."

******

Jack had to smile when he walked into the room the following day. A look of upheaval had replaced the dejection he'd witnessed the day before. He could see the questions twitching in Steve's eyebrows, and he knew he was about to be flooded by inquiries.

Steve assaulted him at once. "You didn't say how difficult it is to sit still and count breaths. The moment I tried to relax my thoughts, my brain started to jump all over the place!"

Jack leaned against the dresser, staring down at a man who he knew had just taken his first step toward enlightenment. "Buddhists have a name for when thoughts jump all over the place, from branch to branch and from tree to tree, looking for just the right food or friendly female, never settling on anything."

"What?"

"Monkey mind."

"Monkey warfare is more like it," Steve countered.

"You must learn how to expand. Your thoughts explode like popcorn in a lidded pot because they're confined within a restricted space. They need to be freed and allowed to spread out. For this to happen, you must learn to expand the space within your mind."

57

Steve blinked repeatedly at Jack, unable to control the tics.

"Through practice," Jack said, "as you improve your skill at meditation, you'll find you'll be able to be more present within the monkey mind, more reflective of what is happening; but don't beat yourself up, my friend. The mood and flow must be light and easy."

"Zen mediation is not what I thought it would be."

Jack snorted. "Zen appears somber from the outside, doesn't it? All those grave people dressed in black with grim faces and downcast eyes, looking like they're going to a funeral."

"I have a long way to go, don't I?"

"Think of yourself as a newborn."

The comment pricked Steve's pride. "I'm an adult, Jack, a father of three."

"No, you're a child," Jack countered, looking down at him in seriousness; "a newborn baby like the child you heard wailing, the one you said you comforted and helped to stop crying. You're only now starting to take your first steps in learning the nature of yourself and your surroundings."

"My first steps, Jack? I'm a paraplegic. I can't walk. Remember?"

"Just like a newborn baby." Jack raised a hand in a gesture of peace. "*Wu wei.*"

"Oh, stuff your *wu wei* up your yin-yang!"

Jack bent over his knees in a fit of laughter. When he finally lifted himself up he fell back onto the dresser with a thud, his face as pink as the setting sun. "I hope you're not going to debase thousand-year-old eastern concepts in divorce counseling if Susan finally agrees to it."

"As a matter of fact she has."

"Oh, excellent…I can't wait to meet the woman who had to put up with you."

"What exactly is yin-yang anyway?"

"Two tadpoles joined in sexual intercourse."

Jack exited the room in snorts and howls, holding onto the walls for support. Steve listened while the peals of laughter rolled up and down the hallway. Patients in other rooms started to laugh out in response. It was infectious. When Jack finally returned he was holding his abdomen.

"Sorry, Steve, but laughter can be a powerful medicine even for humble Zen practitioners like me."

"I suppose."

"All right, where were we…oh yes, yin-yang. The symbol itself originated from nature, from how light and shadow interplay on a mountain as the sun moves through the sky. The sunny side of the mountain is slowly replaced by shade while the shady side is slowly replaced by sunlight. It's a metaphor related to the harmonious interplay of complementary opposites."

Steve saw Chomolungma, and the sunlight he pictured had an unearthly golden hue. He pondered on the mountain that had claimed his legs and his oldest friend.

"Make no mistake, Steve, meditation can be a compressed can of worms. I'm still not convinced you're ready for it, to be perfectly frank."

"What do you mean?"

"I'm still not sure you can handle the 'critical mind' that meditation arouses to action. Tell me…are you prepared to see who you really are?"

"Do I have a choice?"

Jack looked Steve straight in the eye. "When meditating, let your observer do the work without you making judgments on yourself."

"Okay."

"By the way, how spiritual were you prior to your near-death experience?"

"Not very."

Jack lifted off from the dresser and headed for the door. "Let me know when you and Susan agree on a time."

"Will do," Steve said, his thoughts moving elsewhere.

******

Jack stood motionless with his feet spread apart and his arms folded across his chest while Steve sat tensely, waiting for Susan's arrival. They had scheduled the meeting in one of the hospital's conference rooms. Steve looked up at the clock again. Susan's tardiness had always been a thorn in his side. He suspected she had every intention of being late. It had always been her way to get back at him.

The parts of Steve's body that remained under his authority stiffened when he heard the clicking sound in the hallway. He knew it was her. How many times had he listened to that defiant rhythm as she stamped away from him? He had tried for years to block it out.

Jack greeted Susan after opening the door. She was dressed for business, wearing a fitted blazer and hair tied back into a ponytail. There was no mistaking the body language.

"Thanks for coming, Mrs. Forrest," Jack said, gesturing to a seat across the table from Steve.

"Please, Father Sheehan, call me Susan."

"And you can call me Jack."

"Jack?"

"Call me Jack."

Susan looked up at the towering figure as she took a seat. Steve was well aware of her Catholic upbringing. She had never been on a first name basis with a priest before. It might have thrown her, but she quickly regained her composure, her business face snapping into place.

60

"I appreciate you offering your time, Jack. It's generous of you to do this."

"Not a problem," Jack said. "It's the least I can do."

"Well," Susan said, as she moved her purse from her lap to the table and back again, "how is this going to work?"

"Would you like to tell Jack why you filed for divorce?" Steve hazarded to ask.

Susan glared at him. Steve could see the color rise in her cheeks despite a layer of cosmetics meant to hide any such indiscretion, but she restrained herself and was able to keep her self-control intact.

"Oh, I have my reasons," she said, smiling up at Jack. "He was an absentee husband and father at the best of times. When he wasn't engrossed in work he was out climbing or getting ready for a climb or working out in preparation of a climb…etcetera."

"And how did that affect you?" Jack said.

"In every way imaginable," Susan said, emphasizing each word. Her lips tightened to an incision before she could relax them enough to speak her mind. "I raised the kids, paid the bills and got the cars serviced and fixed. I did everything. I had to. There was no one else around to do it."

"Except what the housekeeper was paid to do twice a week," Steve blurted out before he could stop himself. It was a force of will on his part to remain composed under the malicious glare across from him. Susan continued to stare him down as he started to speak, hoping to repair the damage. "I agree I've been an absentee husband and father, but I've been a good provider. You never lacked for money, and you had plenty to spend on yourself."

"Spend on myself?" Susan's expression hardened to ice. "How much did Everest cost?"

Steve felt the thinness in the air typical of high altitudes.

"Well?"

The chair Jack sat down on shrieked under his weight. "I have an idea. Susan, I want you to tell Steve your chief grievances with regards to your marriage. I want you, Steve, to remain silent until she finishes, then repeat what she said. Susan, it's your job to correct him until you're satisfied he got it right. Then it's his turn to do the same to you. Agreed?"

It took Susan a moment to respond. "You mean he can't interrupt me until I'm finished?"

"That's right," Jack said.

"And he has to repeat it back to me until he says it in a way that satisfies me?"

"Correct."

Susan slowly turned her gaze on Steve. "One doesn't know where to start," she said, a little smirk curling her lips. "All right, even though he wasn't around," she said, clawing her fingers to indicate quotation marks, "when he was available he was bossy, controlling and critical. He wanted everything done his way and was apt to criticize me no matter what, often in front of the kids, when I didn't do things to his specific instructions."

Susan concluded by turning to Jack.

"Please look at Steve," Jack said. "I want you to talk to him, not talk about him like he's not in the room. Steve, can you repeat what Susan just said?"

"Of course," Steve said, twisting his fingers in his lap so no one would see. "I was bossy, controlling and domineering—"

"I didn't say domineering!"

Steve paused a moment to douse the fire he unintentionally ignited. "Sorry, I meant critical," he said, letting out a stream of air. "I wanted things done my way even though I wasn't around much or wasn't…available." Steve flinched at the intake of breath. He immediately regretted replicating the quotation marks with his fingers.

This time he was quick to continue before Susan had a chance to reprimand him for his lack of discretion. "I would even criticize her in front of the kids."

"Susan, is that what you said?" Jack said.

"Yes."

"Okay, Steve, it's your turn," Jack said. "And please address Susan directly."

"Well, I think this is really Susan's show," he said, his eyes wandering around the room in spite of Jack's instructions. "I realize I've been a lousy husband and father, and yes, I've been critical, controlling and bossy, in spite of not being around much." The words trailed off. In a desperate act of spontaneity he decided to take a chance and go for broke. "I know I didn't engage you, honey, nor did I engage the kids. I know that now," he said, pleadingly. "I've seen my errors in the Light!"

Susan stared at Steve without saying a word.

Jack quickly intervened. "Steve believes he had a near-death experience on Everest."

Time stopped. It only started up again when Susan slammed her handbag on the table and shuffled through its contents. She withdrew a tissue paper and shook it out. After dabbing her eyes she blew her nose. She then crushed it in her fist. In an impulsive act of rage she threw it at Steve before clicking her handbag closed and stuffing it under an armpit. She shot out of the chair like a rocket.

"No! I don't trust this! You've played with me too many times in the past, Steve. I know you too well," she added, pointing a reproving finger at him. Her voice rose to a pitch that would've been shrill if she hadn't started to speak in a whisper. "I'm not coming to any more of these sessions. I'm done," she said, turning to Jack in a plea of understanding, practically curtseying in apology.

"Is it because I'm a paraplegic?"

"How dare you!" Susan snapped. Her head moved back and forth in disgust as she glared down at him. In one swift movement she sliced the air with a hand in a patent gesture of finality. "Goodbye and good riddance!"

Mortified, Steve threw out tassels as the quickened steps faded down the hallway. He felt her energy rebuke his force, refusing to connect. A moment later she was gone.

Neither man said a word. It was as if each was waiting for the room to thaw. Finally, Jack moved behind Steve and patted him on the back, pulling him out from under the table.

"Let go of that over which you have no control," Jack said, wheeling him into the hallway.

"Can we go outside?" Steve said, choking on the words. "I need to get some air."

Steve punched the handicap door opener and waited for the two glass panels to slowly open to the sun. "I don't understand," he said, his voice vibrating on the gravel path.

"What don't you understand, Steve?"

"Am I being punished for my past?"

"What do you mean?"

"Why was I shown this magnificent, unconditional love when I'm not allowed to share in it? It doesn't make sense."

Jack parked the wheelchair in front of the bench that faced the beds of tulips. "Research from a number of studies by scholars who've delved into the connection between psychology and spirituality has suggested there seems to be a significant difference between what is termed 'absolute love' and what is termed 'relative love.'"

"Absolute love?"

"It stands to reason that human character is not the source of absolute love. It is a life force beyond our capacity to create. It can only shine through us, and in doing so it lodges itself in our hearts."

"How is relative love defined?"

"Simple," Jack said. "Relative love is absolute love filtered through the imperfect human character, through our fears, deceitfulness, greed and illusions. But there is always a grain that lodges in our hearts. If we don't recognize its presence it's because it's buried under ego and acculturation and other such things that burden our spirit."

Steve regarded the shriveling tulip stems and the petals decaying around them. He knew the flowers had done their job. They had reenergized the bulbs that will sprout anew the following spring.

"The more we're able to rid ourselves of our…stuff, the closer we move toward absolute love," Steve said. "Is that a fair description?"

"Yes, but not if we burden ourselves with what's unnecessary," Jack added. "Learn to love yourself as you are and forget all the rest."

"Tall order!" Steve blurted out with more force than intended.

"Not for a Zen master," Jack countered. "Because they have no wants, they have no burdens. They're up to any challenge that confronts them no matter what."

"I'm not a Zen master."

"Clearly, but think of it this way: Every problem is an opportunity for enlightenment."

The magnitude of the day's events spiked when Steve returned to his room and spied a stack of envelopes on the bed. He picked up a large thick manila envelope and ripped it open with a sinking heart.

"What is it?" Jack said.

"I've been fired and…they're terminating my medical insurance." Steve stared blindly into the room, defeated, but as the seconds ticked by he could feel the lethargy in his limbs being replaced by an overwhelming sense of indignation. "No, this isn't legal," he finally said. "They can't do this. I won't allow it."

Jack regarded the bared teeth and the shoulders flexed for a fight, and he liked what he saw. The animal inside Steve was emerging. He curbed a smile as he headed for the door.

"Go get 'em, tiger."

Steve looked up as Jack disappeared down the hallway. For some reason the tiger reference felt wrong. If anything he was a dog person, and he let out a growl just to make that clear.

Chapter Three

"What did you do for your company anyway?" Jack said from the front seat, strapped in a seatbelt barely long enough to wrap around his expansive chest.

"I was the henchman, defending it against environmental lawsuits."

Not that it was Steve's choice to make, but he knew he could never go back to work there. He had already contacted Brian to see if there was an opening at Justice for the Earth—his long-standing adversary, having squared off with them in court countless times over the years. Brian didn't take him seriously at first. He thought it was a trick.

"I put the house up for sale."

Jack's seatbelt stretched to the point of snapping as he turned to look over his seat. Steve refused to meet his gaze. He continued to stare out the windows at the thrift shops, dollar stores and taverns—a derelict part of town that reminded him of his hardscrabble childhood.

"What about the kids?"

"I did it for the kids."

Downsizing to secure his assets was the only way Steve could ensure his children would have a roof over their heads. He had to be on his game. His initial efforts to sue for breach of rights got sidetracked when the hospital informed him he was being moved to a nursing home. They said they needed his bed, but he knew the truth. They didn't want to get stuck with a liability now that the flow of insurance money was being terminated. At least physical therapy was to continue.

The transport van stopped in front of an inner city monstrosity dating back to the first decades of the last century—a time when red brick was the building material of choice. It might've been a handsome building in its youth, but years of neglect had turned it into an eyesore.

Jack wheeled Steve backwards through the double doors and then spun him around to face his fate. He was met by a blast of urine mingled with institutional odors of discount cleaning products and disinfectants. Also lingering in the stale air was the unpleasant scent of breakfast, reeking of grease and freeze-dried coffee.

"What do you think of your new home?" Jack said, pushing the wheelchair up to the security window that separated the lobby from the front desk.

Steve was too engrossed in an old woman parked in the middle of the lobby to answer. The elastic band used to keep her disheveled gray hair from her face only made her look wilder. She was dressed in a threadbare nightgown showcasing hints of meals past, slumped in a wheelchair with her eyes closed and tongue lolling out. Staff swirled around her like a rock in a river current.

"There's an old saying that the opposite of love is apathy," Jack whispered in Steve's ear.

"I don't like this place."

Jack rocked Steve back and forth in the wheelchair while they waited for the receptionist to get off the phone.

"I'm Mrs. Copeland," a woman said, bending to the hole in the Plexiglas like she was speaking to a child.

She had approached the front desk after entering through a door behind the glass partition. Steve noted how the young woman on the phone shriveled under the shadow of the woman that stood over her.

"But everyone calls me Judy," she added. "Welcome to the Green Lake Retirement and Nursing Home." The woman's introduction concluded with a thin practiced smile.

Steve stared back blankly. "Why has that woman been left in the lobby?"

"Oh, that's Helen," Judy Copeland said, not bothering to look over. "She's sleeping off her medication. Just ignore her."

After signing all the registration forms, they were unceremoniously led to Steve's room by a subordinate in a white smock coat, fraying at the seams.

"What are you feeling?" Jack said, laying out the toiletries.

Steve, huddled in a corner, stared into the room like a trapped mouse. "Nothing."

"Have faith," Jack said. "In its own way this place could work to your advantage, hasten your transformation, so to speak. Use what you learned from the Light. Pay attention to what happens around you. Think of this place as your 'earth school.'"

"I hate it."

"It has a garden in back," Jack said, moving towards the window. "Would you like me to wheel you there before I go?"

"To hang with the inmates?"

Jack chuckled as he stuffed Steve's suitcase into the closet. "You never know, Steve; you may find some of these inmates more interesting than you'd expect them to be. I'll bet one of them could give you the story behind Helen, at any rate."

"The window faces east," Steve said with a sigh, regarding the light spilling in after a cloud passed over the sun. It was one redeeming factor he could appreciate. "Okay, let's head outside."

"I'm going to wheel you out and leave you to explore on your own," Jack said, pushing Steve down a hallway painted baby vomit beige. "The van comes to pick you up for physical therapy in a couple of hours. I'll inform the front desk to look for you in the back as I head out," he added, letting out a little snort of glee. "I expect you'll have some good stories to share with me soon enough."

******

69

The garden had long been left to fend for itself. Walkways were crumbling and inaccessible in places, blocked by roots and overgrown branches. Flies buzzed around rusty old garbage cans that reeked of rot. Steve got as far away from them as possible, fighting his way through the brush, finally dozing off under shreds of plastic bags that got entangled in the trees, fluttering in a breeze.

Steve's peaceful nap was shortened by an old man in a beret, making his way toward the overgrown enclave he'd staked out. The old man was having an easier time getting his walker through. It could be hoisted over roots and used to guard against braches. The old fellow didn't have much trouble in the end. Reaching into a pocket for a pipe, he stuffed it into his mouth.

"I hear you're a lawyer."

"News gets around fast," Steve said, pulling himself up in the wheelchair.

"John's the name," the man said, "but everyone calls me the Professor."

"Why's that?"

"Because that's what I am."

"You're a professor?" Steve said, using the present tense charitably.

"South Seattle Community College, Seattle, Washington."

Steve smiled. "I didn't expect to meet…you know… a person of education here," he said, looking around to make sure no one was in earshot.

"Age and infirmity show no greater respect for the educated," the Professor said as he slowly lowered himself on the remains of a bench, clutching his walker like a floatation device.

The air sweetened with aromatic swirls of smoke. It reminded Steve of church.

"What's your name?"

"Steve."

70

"You won't be here long, I should think. They always put the short-timers in the east wing. I heard that's where they put you. What happened anyway?" the Professor said, waving the pipe at Steve's wheelchair.

"Mountaineering accident."

"Oh, where?"

"Chomolungma," Steve said, knowing he'd have to spend the next hour or so bouncing off questions if he mentioned Everest.

"North or south side?"

Steve stared at the man. "North," he said, "at the Second Step."

The Professor examined his pipe before sticking it back in his mouth. He produced a wooden match from a pocket and drew a flame in a series of short puffs, regarding Steve from the corner of an eye squinting to protect itself from smoke. "No one else here could claim such an exotic misfortune as that."

Steve redirected the conversation as the old man let smoke snake up his nose. "Do you know an older woman here by the name of Helen? She was asleep in a wheelchair near the front desk when I arrived."

The Professor made a face. "She was drugged...did you meet Copeland?"

"Judy? Yes—she said to call her Judy...what do you mean by drugged?"

"None of us can stand the woman. She's a tyrant. We all call her Copeland out of disrespect. It's under her orders that Helen is kept drugged and parked near the front desk each day."

"Why?"

"Copeland pegged her as a first-rate troublemaker, the worst of the bunch."

"I fail to see how an elderly woman in a wheelchair—"

71

"Helen was a schoolteacher, a good one from what I heard," the Professor said, "and good ones like her take no backtalk from anyone. She's been on the staff's case for some of the uncaring ways people get treated around here, you see. Copeland didn't like it, not one bit. She thinks its poor 'public relations,' so she has Helen drugged to keep her quiet. Damn shame, if you ask me—always fancied that one."

"Do the state auditors know about this?" Steve said, trying to decide whether he believed this or not.

"Of course they don't. Copeland makes sure Helen is in the clouds when they come around. She's too afraid someone will blab."

"There's an 800 number she could call," Steve countered. "Has Helen access to a telephone?"

"Yes, but Copeland is smart. She left the telephone and took away Helen's glasses." The Professor shook his head. "In the state she's in, she'd just dribble into the mouthpiece anyway."

Steve kept on trying to find a hole in the story. "Has anyone else tried to intervene on Helen's behalf?"

"We're all afraid of Copeland. You should be too. Helen's only the tip of what goes on around here."

Steve looked from the Professor to the backside of the brick monstrosity looming over the garden. "Has anyone on the staff tried to buck Copeland?"

"A couple awhile back, but it came to nothing."

Steve brushed hair from his eyes. He was probably due for a haircut.

"If this were true—"

"Of course it's true!"

"Then someone should do something about it."

"Copeland has the whole place buffaloed," the Professor said, wrapped in coils of smoke. "If you intervene you'd be going it alone. You may even wind up drugged if you're not careful."

72

"This is—"

"Now, you being a lawyer and all, Copeland would have to tread carefully, but she's gotten cocky lately with nobody but Helen to stand up to her."

A bell sounded from inside the building.

"Lunch," the Professor said, pulling himself up with the help of the walker. "Had the pleasure of dining here yet?"

"Yes," Steve said, listlessly. "I got the evil eye in the cafeteria this morning."

"You probably upset the pecking order. It's silly, of course, but it's a good idea to follow along to keep the peace. I'll show you how to get on without causing waves."

It must have been a question of economy to paint the cafeteria the same vomit beige as the hallways. As Steve and the Professor were finishing off their lunch of canned peas, lumpy mashed potatoes and gristly slivers of thinly sliced ham, a wretched figure was wheeled into the dining room.

"Who's that?"

The Professor, sitting across from Steve, had to turn to look. "Oh, that's Denise…poor thing."

If the Professor was referring to appearance, "poor thing" was a gross understatement. "Filthy thing" would've been a more accurate description of the matted hair and the layers of rumpled clothing stiff from lack of laundering.

"Does she sleep in those clothes?"

"Likely," the Professor said, wrinkling his nose in recollection. "It's lucky we're some distance away. She's often as ripe as a peach if you know what I mean. It's rumored the staff has a tough time getting her to bathe," the old man added, brushing his lips with a napkin. "I've seen some horror stories here, but she's the worst, and just twenty-three years old."

"Twenty-three?" Steve had assumed she was someone on the cusp of old age, but, then again, he hadn't

73

seen the face. The young woman was using her arms as a shield, crossing them over her head, hiding. "Has anyone ever tried to talk to her?"

"A few, myself included, but it's impossible to draw her out of herself," the Professor said, crossing fork and knife on his plate. "You might have better luck though, being that you two share something in common.

"What?"

"You're both WBs."

"What?"

"Wheelchair bound."

"I'll take it into consideration."

"Good luck," the Professor said as he slowly pushed away from the table and lifted himself up with the help of his walker, letting out several grunts in the process. "I better start off towards the toilet or I'll never get there in time."

Steve remembered, early in his career, drilling an old Middle Eastern man in the witness box. Asked why he was allowing squatters to remain in a building he owned, the man replied in broken English, "I wept because I had no shoes, until I met a man who had no feet." The case went to the prosecution. The squatters were forcefully removed and the old man fined.

******

Steve had just hung up the phone when a crash jolted the door. A second crash followed, and this time the steel door slowly gave way to reveal two swollen feet stuffed into a pair of well-worn granny slippers. Helen threw her weight on the wheels until the wheelchair was through, and the door swung shut behind her.

Between Steve and Helen was a golden beam of early morning sunlight. He was about to speak when he got hushed.

74

Helen held a finger to her lips. "They're searching for me. Listen!"

Steve heard the muffled voice of a woman in the hallway. They both sat in silence as it passed the door.

"She must've headed to the dining room to rustle up the others," Judy Copeland said. "Jimmy, check this wing just in case."

"All right," the gruff voice of the attendant said.

Hinges could be heard as doors opened and closed in the hallway.

"Please," Helen whispered, her fingers locked in a plea, "help me."

Steve didn't know what to do about this crazed woman with hair sticking up in clumps. Before he could decide on a course of action the door swung open in a rush of air. A heavyset man in a smock stood in the doorframe, smiling.

"There you are, Mrs. Anderson," he said. "Time for your morning pill."

Steve sat frozen as the attendant pinned Helen from behind and tried to ram a pill into her mouth. She shook her head back and forth to try to escape it, her lips sealed so tight that her face turned deathly white. When she tried to scream, the attendant seized the opportunity. He deftly popped the pill into her mouth and then pulled up her chin to massage her throat.

Helen slumped into the wheelchair, knowing the damage was done. She didn't have the energy to do much else.

"That's right, Mrs. Anderson," the attendant said. "You go to sleep now like a good girl."

Steve was in shock. The burly attendant had burst into his room without even glancing at him. He was a nonentity, just another inmate in this madhouse.

"Better come with me now, Mrs. Anderson," the attendant said in a practiced voice of geniality.

75

He backed the wheelchair out of the door with the crumpled figure in it. Helen's head bounced off her chest, her arms flopping in her lap so they wouldn't get caught in the wheels. She looked like a ragdoll forgotten in the rain. Only the glint of a tear was testimony to the battle she'd waged and lost.

Steve let out the breath he'd been holding all the while. Why hadn't he intervened? It was his inaction that shocked him most.

******

It wasn't until four o'clock that Steve finally heard the long-awaited voice.

"Knock, knock…you asleep?"

Steve gestured for Jack to shut the door, but he was unwilling to talk freely, regardless, even in his room. "Let's head down into the garden."

Jack pushed the wheelchair down the relatively accessible central walkway to a spot by a hedge of old scraggly junipers all the way at the back of the property. It took time for Steve to brief his friend on all that had occurred over the previous days. Jack listened in silence, spread out on a patch of grass, letting ants crawl over him and winged creatures land on his big bald head.

"Well, you and I both sensed something, but I didn't expect this." Jack's eyes followed a fly attempting to land on his nose. "How does it feel to be the new detective on the block?"

Steve sat fidgety in the wheelchair, speaking in whispers. "I wouldn't have dreamt of getting involved in something like this before the…you know…accident, but I feel driven to do something for these poor people."

It was the therapist in Jack that responded. "What do you think makes you feel this way? What changed?"

76

"I'm in the same position as all the others here, aren't I?"

"So you feel connected to them."

"Yes, but before…you know…the Light, I would've just shrugged and let things be. Getting involved in things like this is fraught with difficulties. There are just too many gray areas that'd make most lawyers shrivel."

"Then why bother at all?"

"I'm not looking at this through the eyes of a lawyer, or at least not the lawyer I used to be."

"Why?"

"Peoples' basic rights are being abused!"

"Sounds like lawyer talk to me."

"Can you help?"

"Of course," Jack said, "in any way I can."

Steve took a slip of paper from his pocket and passed it to Jack, peering into the shady parts of the garden to make sure no one was watching.

"This is the number for the state auditors. Tell them to come and remove this person until the effects of the drugs wear off and she's able to fill them in on what's going on around here. I can corroborate her story firsthand from what I witnessed."

"Mrs. Helen Anderson," Jack said, reading the name on the paper.

"I called Brian and let him know what's been going on, and I told Melody everything this morning at therapy. I warned them I'll probably get identified as the whistleblower, and there could be repercussions for me."

"You've got three people on the outside looking out for your interests?" Jack said. "You're still a lawyer at heart, Steve."

"Maybe so, but a lawyer who's not going to sit back and watch defenseless people suffer. I sure hope it's enough backup, though." Steve rubbed his palms on his pant legs. "This is a nasty situation I've landed in."

77

"Apparently," Jack replied, blowing playfully at the fly.

Steve peered around the garden once again, a little jumpy. "We better get back inside," he said. "I think they may be watching me. They seemed suspicious Helen chose my room to hide out in."

Jack climbed to his feet, scattering the winged creatures. They flickered in the light before disappearing into the junipers.

"What about Denise? What do you plan to do about her?"

"I don't know" Steve said, shaking his head. "I tried to talk to her at dinner last night, but all I got were groans."

"*Wu wei*," Jack said, pushing Steve over the rutted walkway.

"*Wu wei*," Steve said in return, his voice oscillating from the knocks the wheels were taking, "go with the flow…trust in the outcome to come."

"If it's meant to be, then something will come of it," Jack said. "Meanwhile, I'll make the call, and I'll try to be here when the authorities arrive."

"I don't know what I'd do without you, Jack."

******

Steve wore a poker face the rest of the day. He wasn't about to give anything up and incriminate himself. He pretended he didn't notice the burly attendant leering at him through dinner—perhaps a pill tucked into a pocket. They knew something was up, and they suspected him. The stress got the better of him in the end.

By morning, Steve was exhausted. He had hardly slept. Every time he'd been on the verge his eyelids would pop open to a sound in the hallway. He hadn't realized how active this place got at night. People kept coming and going, shoes clicking on tiles. Worse was that anyone could enter the room unannounced, there being no lock on the door.

Melody's concern for Steve led her to drive him even harder at therapy that morning. He was mush by the end of it. As the van pulled up to the Green Lake Retirement and Nursing Home, he felt an overwhelming premonition that something went down. It felt like he was being lowered into a grave as the wheelchair descended to the sidewalk, but he couldn't have been more wrong.

Jack stepped out of the double doors, his big bald head as smooth as marble. Steve was dizzy with relief.

"Has it happened?"

"They made a lightning raid in the night, as I advised, and got Helen out before the staff could give her the knockout pill. She spilled the beans on everything. Turns out this place had been under investigation for some time."

"Really?"

"The director of nursing, Judy Copeland, has been relieved of all duties in a storm of tears and accusations."

"Really?"

"Yes, really," Jack said, smiling broadly.

"I can't believe it."

"Ice cream and cake are being served in the dining room in memory of her departure."

"Good grief, Jack. One little puff and the whole house of cards blew over…didn't think it'd be that easy."

"Gautama Buddha's strongest caveat to his followers was 'do no harm.' It would've been wise for this Copeland woman to have taken the advice."

Jack swung Steve through the double doors so enthusiastically that he lost his grip and the wheelchair spun towards a wall. He caught up to it before any harm could come of it, laughing at Steve's almost cartoonlike reaction, the way both arms shot up like it was a stickup.

"The whole atmosphere here has changed," Jack

said, tipping the wheelchair back and wheeling it down the hallway. "It's a happy day for all."

The dining room was strung with makeshift streamers hanging from tabletops and draped around necks and anywhere else in reach of the elderly and infirm. Even wheelchairs were decorated in ribbons. The room rang out in shouts of approval as Steve was wheeled in. They were given a sitting ovation of sorts. An attendant, a little frazzled, handed him a paper cup filled with ice cream and bite-sized squares of cake.

"Christine was always good to us," an old man said from a table by the door. "You can trust her."

Christine the attendant thanked the old man by way of a little curtsey. She then wiped her forehead on a sleeve and ran off to meet the demand for more cups of ice cream and cake.

Steve caught sight of someone staring at him through a pair of vintage cat eye glasses. It took him a moment to recognize the woman clothed in a crisp blouse and tweed suit jacket with a head of hair styled in a sensible bun. They wheeled over to each other, meeting halfway.

Helen laid a hand on his arm, still a little shaky from her ordeal. "Thank you," she said.

"You look really nice, Helen."

Steve saw a blush streak her cheeks that was immediately overruled by a flick of an eyebrow.

"Well now, young man, are we being frisky?" Helen said, smiling mischievously.

Steve would never have guessed that this cheeky old woman with a sly glint was that drugged-out mass of mangled hair flopped in a wheelchair.

Jack bent over and whispered in his ear. "Hate to interrupt, but there's a young woman who's looking over at you."

Steve looked up at Jack, who gestured across the room with a nod of his head. Denise was almost unrecognizable in a change of clothes and clean, brushed hair. Her hands, although fidgety, remained in her lap. Even from a distance, he could detect a hint of cosmetics, a little lip gloss and mascara. The lump in his throat hardened.

"Beg your pardon," Steve said. "I need to freshen up from therapy. I'll come by and talk to you later."

"The key's under the doormat," Helen said, giving him a little wink.

It was Steve's turn to blush as he sailed off, smiling in embarrassment, tears trickling down his cheeks.

******

Steve spotted Denise from his window just as he slid out of bed. She was moving under the canopy of scraggly trees, trying to negotiate her way through a tangle of shrubs. Even three stories up he could see the snow-white hands forcing the wheels, hands too long removed from the sun.

"*Insha'Allah*," Steve said, pumping the wheels down the hallway, still in his pajamas.

Ever the athlete, Steve was becoming deft at operating his wheelchair. He spun himself inside the elevator and waited impatiently for the squeaky old box to descend to the lobby. A throng of residents heading for the cafeteria greeted him when the doors creaked opened. Staff even smiled as he flew past despite being shorthanded and frazzled by the extra work.

She had parked herself in the sun. Steve could see her thick brown hair behind a burned-out rhododendron, the tresses a wonder in the sunlight. Strands of highlights radiated gold. It felt like a sign.

Even so, the young woman stiffened at the sound of his approach. To offset her apprehension, Steve reduced speed and wheeled past her, heading for a water fountain he

81

knew didn't work. He spied a beret in an opening in the shrubs just as he fashioned his face into a look of frustration in the act of trying to operate the fountain.

"It doesn't work?" Steve said, continuing with the ruse.

"Nothing works in this dump," the young woman replied on cue.

Steve buried a smile as he backed up and turned to Denise, raising his hands in resignation, making a show of it. "How long have you been in that thing?"

Compared to the radiant highlights in her hair, her eyes were rather dull. A thick strand had fallen across them that she hadn't bothered moving from her line of vision. It was like she was hiding behind her hair as she had her forearms.

"Six months."

"What happened?"

"Do you care?"

"Just asking."

"Snowboarding accident," she said, curtly. "I was doing tricks, and I fell. Now I'm stuck in this hellhole."

"What do the doctors say?"

"They say the spinal cord is okay but the sheath was damaged. They say I should be able to walk, but they're wrong. I can't."

The golden highlights faded as the sun disappeared behind a cloud. What was left was little better than that wretched creature Steve first saw in the cafeteria. He faltered, not knowing what to say, until the cloud passed and the cheerless figure ignited into golden tones of hope.

"What about you?" Denise said in a feeble attempt at being polite.

"The doctors tell me essentially the same thing. The sheath is damaged, but my spinal cord appears intact. My physical therapist has been driving me hard, but we're not making much progress to be honest."

"How'd it happen?"

"Mountaineering accident...Everest," Steve said, deciding on instinct to use the famous peak to his advantage.

Denise's head snapped to attention. "You climbed Everest?"

"I tried to at any rate," he said, knowing he'd hit on something.

"Liar."

"No, it's true!"

The encouraging spark that appeared in Denise's eyes proved short-lived.

"But now you're in a wheelchair, and your mountaineering days are over," she said. "Just like me."

"I saw a Light!"

"What?"

Steve knew he'd have to follow through on his impulse or lose her. "I had a near-death experience," he said, treading carefully. "Do you know what that is?"

"Nope."

"It's when you die, or are on the verge of death, and you can see yourself—your body—as if you're looking at a different person," he said. "Then all of a sudden, I was brought before a Light."

Denise's expression turned guarded. "What did it look like?"

"The color of your hair."

"Brown?"

"No," Steve said, shaking his head, "like the golden highlights in your hair."

"Are you hitting on me?"

"Of course not!"

Denise grabbed the strand covering her eyes and lifted it to the sun. While she stared up at it, Steve told his story. He told her how the Light revealed his life to him like a picture book is explained to a child, how it changed him, and how he has been struggling to apply the lessons he learned.

The story concluded in silence. Steve couldn't tell if she believed him.

"Okay," Denise finally said, "want to hear my story?"

"Yes."

"I lived year-round in a condo up on Snoqualmie Pass in the Alpental ski area. An ex-boyfriend let me live there rent-free if I took care of the place. I loved it, living in the mountains. I worked part-time as a barmaid at the ski lodge and made pretty good tips. I had everything I ever wanted." As she spoke, she stared skyward like she was looking up at the mountain she longed to return to. "But you know what really turned me on about the place?"

"What?"

"At night, when everyone had gone, I would watch the groomers working on the ski slopes and listen to the deep grumble of the engines. It sounded like the mountain was snoring in sleep." Denise looked down at Steve. "Do you know what's it like to go riding with someone who knows how to drive one of those?"

"What's it like?"

"It's crazy, man," she said, "a million lights flashing all at once…death metal blasting in the cab. We went straight up the mountain like we were blasting off the planet…it was heaven…the best sex I ever had."

Both sat in contemplative silence in their respective wheelchairs until the impatient sound of a cough was heard a little distance off.

"Just out of curiosity, why did you decide to share that with me?" Steve said, glancing over at the bushes.

"You're mountain like me," Denise said, "like the skiers and snowboarders and the Nordic skiers heading off into the backcountry."

Steve knew exactly what she meant.

"By the way, thanks for getting rid of Copeland," Denise said as she pushed off.

Steve watched her go, turning when he heard someone approach from the fountain side.

"We did it," the Professor said, kicking his walker over a hump in the asphalt. His false teeth gleamed yellow in the sun. "She seems like an intelligent girl if a little promiscuous."

"Since you were eavesdropping," Steve said, "what's your opinion?"

"You got her to open up, and that's a feat in itself." The Professor balanced on his two legs to pack his pipe. "So you had a near-death experience? Is that why that priest keeps coming around to see you?"

"I'm not sure."

"Think Catholicism is the way to go?"

"As well as being a Jesuit priest, Jack's also an ordained Zen teacher and a practicing psychotherapist."

"Never heard of such a thing," the Professor said, striking a match.

"There're not many around I'm told, but it's lucky one found me."

"Luck or providence," the Professor muttered between drags from the pipe. "When you get as close to death as I am you begin to wonder if everything we call luck isn't something else entirely."

******

"What's your prognosis?"

Steve took a moment to think it over. "She too easily slips back into herself. I made real progress with her yesterday, but this morning in the cafeteria, she hid behind her hair again…wouldn't even look at me."

Jack turned the wheelchair around to pull Steve over a tree root that had snaked its way across the garden path.

"Denise is certainly capable of opening up," Steve maintained, "but she's equally prone to slipping right back into a deep depression. God knows what would happen if I weren't around. Except for the Professor, everyone has given up on her."

Jack parked the wheelchair near the junipers and plopped himself down on a patch of grass. "She hasn't spoken since yesterday?"

"No."

Jack gave it some thought. "The reasons behind her depression can't be deduced from a single conversation."

"I know the reasons behind her depression,"

"Oh really," Jack said. "Pray tell?"

"It's simple. She's an athlete. She may not know it, but she's an athlete through and through. You can tell by the way she talks. Jack, imagine a pianist without fingers or a ballerina without feet. Her *raison d'être* was taken away from her in a matter of two seconds when she fell and hit her back."

"Did you point out that you're in the same predicament?"

"I didn't have to; she pointed it out to me," Steve said. "To make matters worse," he added, following a train of thought, "it's practically impossible for someone in a wheelchair to live in the mountains, especially in a resort town. Those places aren't built for the physically challenged."

Jack went silent, closing his eyes. Steve needed time to recharge anyway. The whole Denise issue was wearing him out. He closed his eyes and soon became lost in the gin scent of junipers.

"There's something I've been musing over," Jack said, "but I can't decide…it could cause more harm than good."

"What are you talking about?"

"Would you give a paraplegic hope to walk again if there was only the slightest chance of success?"

"Yes!"

"Think, Steve," Jack said, looking serious. "The disappointment could be devastating."

Steve's upper half went as numb as his lower half at the suggestion of being able to walk again. "Please, Jack, speak your mind."

"*Wai Qi Zhi Liao* can't be performed by just anyone. Its success depends on someone who has learned to manifest *qi* to the point where the person can control its flow, even in someone else's body. Only a Qigong master is capable of that degree of control."

"*Wai Qi Zhi Liao?*" Steve said, stumbling on the words.

"External *Qi* Healing."

"Aren't you a Qigong master?"

"I'm only a fledgling in the art," Jack said. "I've only been studying it for ten years."

Steve's hopes started to deflate.

"Understand that a Qigong master would be difficult if not impossible to find outside Asia. It's not like they advertise their services. With that said, before I moved back from Japan, I made inquiries to see if there was someone in the Seattle area with whom I could continue my Qigong training. That's when I heard about a true master who works in Traditional Chinese Medicine."

"There's one here?"

"Yes."

"In Seattle?"

"In Chinatown," Jack confirmed. "I've been talking to him about attempting *Wai Qi Zhi Liao* on you for some time now."

"And?"

"And he's agreed to interview you," Jack said. "Note that the TCM interview process is quite extensive. It could last hours. He will first want to know everything about your life."

Steve couldn't help but feel a little dubious. "It sounds like a lot of talk and not much action."

Jack let out an amused snigger. "Do you know how Chinese medicine worked in the old days?"

"Of course I don't."

"The patient paid the doctor to keep him or her healthy. If he or she fell ill, then the doctor paid the patient until he or she recovered his or her health."

What Steve said next surprised even him. "Do you think Denise could take my place?"

Jack's gaze was steady and unwavering. "And if the Qigong master will only agree to take on a single subject?"

"I'll manage," Steve said after a moment's hesitation.

The shreds of plastic bags caught in the trees fluttered a fanfare in a breeze.

Jack pointed a warning finger at Steve. "Tell no one of this."

"Why?"

"Western doctors aren't partial to alternative medicine."

"I see your point."

"You'll have to prepare Denise," Jack said. "If you get her hopes up and it doesn't work she may fall deeper into depression."

"I'll meditate on it."

And that was what Steve tried to do, then and there. He sat up straight, positioned his legs and closed his eyes, concentrating on his breathing, but doubts and fears flew at him like arrows. Before he could get a handle on it, his improvised meditation session was cut short when the wheelchair jerked forward and Jack started to speak.

"How are your therapy sessions coming along?"

Steve moved a branch out of the way before it could take out an eye. "Melody and I have hit a plateau, and it's hard to get beyond it now that I only go to therapy once a week."

"Once a week?"

"My bills are piling up, Jack, and I've no idea how I'm going to pay them. It seems Justice for the Earth isn't interested in employing paraplegics either."

******

"You lied to her?"

"Yes, Jack, I did. I had to. I told her I knew of a practitioner of Chinese medicine who is an expert at dealing with problems specific to wheelchair users."

"And what problems are those?"

"I improvised," Steve admitted. "I said chronic constipation and bedsores. At least that's what's been plaguing me."

"And she agreed to see him?"

"Reluctantly," Steve said. "I had to corner her in the cafeteria. She's relapsed. She won't even go out into the garden anymore."

Steve knew she hadn't been out in the garden because he'd been looking out for her, staying close to the windows that faced it, hoping to catch a glimpse of the golden highlights in her hair.

"Looks like it's on for next Tuesday," Jack said.

"Sorry?"

89

"The interview with Master Feng will take place next Tuesday if I can get around the staff," Jack said. "It'll be another week or so before he can see you."

"He'll see me too?"

"Yes."

Steve stopped himself from pressing the matter. He wasn't about to put himself in a position of vulnerability. If Denise were at risk of being devastated by disappointment, so was he. He'd come to realize how heavily he'd been leaning on the hope of walking again.

"Jack, I don't know how I'll ever repay you."

"Repay me by doing what you've been doing here. I don't know if you've realized it yet, but you've had an amazingly positive effect on this place."

"You think so?"

Jack reclined back into the pillows and stretched out his legs, letting his feet dangle off Steve's bed.

"See if you can make sense of this story," Jack said. "Centuries ago a fully realized Zen master moved into a large dwelling where many lived—what would pass for an apartment building today. It was not a happy place. The residents were always arguing and fighting and yelling and screaming at each other. The master came and went, smiling cheerfully at everyone without getting involved in any hostilities. In time the residents started to notice a growing calm washing over the dwelling. They couldn't understand how it had happened since no one had made the least effort to lessen tensions. Everything was like it had always been except for the arrival of the Zen master who'd quietly moved into the dwelling without a fuss, bothering no one."

Jack turned to Steve and smiled.

"That's it?" Steve said, staring back from the wheelchair. "That's all there is to the story?"

"Yup."

"So the whole atmosphere of the dwelling changed due to the Zen master's influence, even though he didn't do anything?"

"Grass will grow sooner on undisturbed soil when the sun is shining bright."

******

Steve's window faced the garden, opposite the front entrance. He wouldn't loiter in the lobby like Helen was forced to do before being liberated, so he scoped the hallways instead in spite of all the people wanting to talk to him. Three times he passed Denise's room, listening at the door.

On his fourth pass the door opened just as Steve was about to press an ear against it. He quickly glimpsed a little Asian man stooped beside a teenager with a mop of black hair. They stood above Denise, the old man speaking and the teenager translating the words. She was turning her head from one to the other, looking annoyed.

Steve had to back up his wheelchair to gaze up at the man towering over him.

"How's it going?"

"Slowly," Jack said, "but I believe Master Feng is near to completing the interview process, at least I hope so."

"Why?"

"Denise is puzzled by the questions, the ones related to the accident and life in a wheelchair. They seem to irritate her. She doesn't understand the point of it. I had to intervene to explain to her that TCM is a type of holistic medicine, so everything matters, even questions seemingly unrelated to the problem at hand," Jack said, rolling his eyes heavenward. "I'll be glad when this is over."

"What happens next?" Steve said.

"The procedure."

91

"How does it work?"

"Master Feng will hold a hand two inches above the location of the injury for a period of nine minutes. He will keep the palm of his other hand face down away from Denise. After the specified time, he'll vigorously shake his hands and repeat the process, although this time the palm of the other hand will face up."

"Why nine minutes?"

"The Chinese find multiples of three irresistible," Jack said after a moment's contemplation. "Since he's a Qigong master, however, it could be any amount of time. Who knows how long it'll take? It'll all depend on the flow of *qi*."

"Will Denise feel anything?"

"She may feel a warm sensation at the spot where Master Feng's hand hovers over her back, especially during the second nine minute session. Increased *qi* flow creates heat."

Steve buried his doubts. "Why must it be done twice and with the palms reversed?"

"The first session pulls the bad *qi* out. In *feng shui* this is sometimes referred to as 'cutting' the *qi* out of the affected area. The point of the second session is to replace the bad *qi* with good *qi*. The whole process is based on the Chinese concept of the energy anatomy of the body."

Steve knew nothing about this Chinese concept and was sure most people didn't either. He voiced his immediate concern. "Won't Denise get suspicious when Master Feng places a hand above the spot of the injury? If she thinks we've been lying to her, the whole thing may implode."

"I'm well ahead of you," Jack said with an impish little curl on his lips. "I told Denise that Master Feng will probably have to work around the area of her injury since there's likely *qi* blockage at that particular location, and *qi* blockage is known to exacerbate constipation and bed sores."

"Do you think she bought it?"

"I think so," Jack said, slowly, "but she's a tough one to read."

The teenager with a mop of black hair appeared at the door and motioned them inside.

"I don't want to crowd her," Steve said, pushing off. "I'll come by when she's alone." He spun the wheels and headed for the garden to meditate.

******

Steve woke to a crash at his door. It was Denise.

"My feet are cold!"

"Your feet?" Steve said, propping himself up on an elbow, blinking crust from his eyes.

"It woke me up!"

"Your feet woke you up?"

"My feet woke me up!"

It took a second for it to hit. "You can feel your feet!"

"Yes, stupid!"

Steve pulled himself up against the pillows and held a hand over his mouth, overwhelmed with emotions. He was cut off when he tried to speak.

"You guys lied to me, didn't you?" Denise said in a flash of anger. "That old doctor wasn't who you two said he was!"

Steve was caught off guard, stumbling on words. "We didn't want to get your hopes up."

As quickly as her anger appeared, it blew over. Denise's lips burst into a smile. Emotions were running high.

Steve sighed with relief, but he was cut off again when he tried to speak.

"What I need from you, Mr. Liar," Denise said, pointing a finger, "is the phone number of your physical therapist."

"Want me to make a call on your behalf?"

******

"So there are more signs of improvement?"

Steve was studying the blade of grass Jack had handed him. "This morning she felt a tingling sensation in her legs."

"Did she?"

"Melody is working her hard, I hear, as hard as she's ever worked me."

The day wasn't dampened by the clouds. Somehow the leaden sky made the color of the shrubs and the weedy wildflowers in the neglected beds more lavish than they would otherwise be. Even the back façade of the decrepit building displayed a subdued regal elegance.

"Good," Jack said. "How're you doing?"

"A little antsy to tell the truth."

"Patience, my friend," Jack said. "Master Feng will be here a week from tomorrow."

A week from tomorrow seemed a long way away to Steve. All at once the day became duller, a little less opulent.

"But don't get your hopes up," Jack was quick to add, running his fingers through the grass, looking for a blade for himself.

The comment wasn't appreciated. Steve couldn't help but get his hopes up after what had happened to Denise. "Don't I have almost the exact same injury in the exact same location as Denise? If it worked for her, why wouldn't it work for me?"

Steve had to wait for an answer. Jack was busy trying to make a grass blade whistle.

"There are no guarantees, and remember, what may look like an identical injury to doctors of western medicine may appear entirely different to a Qigong master."

Steve started to fill with doubts.

"There's no Qigong master alive skilled enough to cure a paraplegic whose injuries are beyond repair," Jack added, "nor has there ever been. If there were, a master would spend his life traveling the world, helping all who needed healing."

"Denise calls you 'Father Liar' by the way."

Jack let out an explosive hoot. "I hope she forgives our little fib," he said, blowing a papery note to test a grass blade.

"I think we're still in her good graces," Steve said. "By the way, I noticed she's wearing sports attire since starting therapy with Melody."

Jack stood up and stretched. He seemed as tall as a tree from the perspective of a wheelchair.

"Time to go?"

"I've got some problems to work out." Jack started off before stopping and turning back. "Steve?"

"Yes?"

"I know a week seems a long time, but don't waste it waiting."

"What do you mean?"

"There are three good reasons to use this time productively."

"What reasons?"

"Well, first, interacting with people here may help you in difficult situations you're sure to encounter later, like establishing new relationships with your children." Jack stared down at Steve, hands on hips. "You haven't seen them since the accident if I'm not mistaken."

"I haven't," Steve said. He'd been deeply disappointed they hadn't come to see him, much more than he'd admit.

Jack smiled. "This 'new you' must still be a novelty. Spend time getting to know the person you've become. Everyone in this nursing home only knows this new person, so they'll take you at face value. See yourself through their eyes. I think you'll like what you see."

"All right," Steve said, nodding his head.

"Another reason is that it won't be long before you'll be faced with the world and all its hurry and hubbub and the 'ten thousand things' Taoists say hit us every day we're in the world. This will happen whether *Wai Qi Zhi Liao* works for you or not. Remember, you've been shielded from most of that since the accident. Use this time to meditate on what you'll soon have to face, and how you wish to face it, considering your new ideal."

Steve swallowed hard thinking of the future.

"It's out in the world where lessons take place," Jack continued. "From the perspective of Zen, the world is both *Maya*—illusion—and the source of the most important lessons a person experiences. Use this time to prepare for the impact the world will soon have on you."

"I'll try."

Jack smiled softly. "It's my belief that what you've been doing here is helping to serve your spiritual quest. All the major religions and spiritual paths tell us one of the best ways to experience interconnectedness and negate feelings of separation is through service to others."

When Jack turned and walked away, he greeted everyone he passed with a smile—those bold enough to venture out into the hazards of the overgrown garden. Steve noted how the smile transferred to the faces of the old and infirm like each was a candle lit by a flame.

******

Steve was contemplating the feel of the afternoon sun on his forehead when Helen was wheeled up to join him with the help of an attendant who she thanked for his trouble before sending away. Her hair was pinned in a complex style.

"Going somewhere?"

"No," Helen said, looking pleased. "I like to put a little effort into my appearance. It always gave me a level of authority with my students."

It was Steve's opinion she would have asserted authority with her students dressed in rags.

"Speaking of students," Helen said, "I've heard a rumor you and Father Jack have a special type of teacher-student relationship." The cat eye glasses remained fixed as she spoke. "He's helping you in your struggle to come to terms with what you've experienced from a near-death experience. Is that so?"

Steve smiled, looking around to see if he could spot the Professor eavesdropping behind a shrub. "Yes."

"What happened?"

Steve spilled it out unabashedly. He told her about the man he was compared to the man he's starting to see blossom in himself. She listened without interruption. When he concluded she asked specific questions pertaining to the near-death experience, wanting details. His story seemed to impact her, and she soon admitted why.

"I'm old, and I'm going to die," Helen said, checking to make sure the hem of her skirt was just below the knee as it should be, "but I'm not dead yet. I have a lot of questions about what I'm going to face when my time comes."

"Like what?"

Helen swept a handful of painted fingernails in a circular motion, red to match her lipstick. "I'm surrounded by old people hanging onto life, yet…it's meaningless. Do you know what I mean? What do we have to look forward to besides death…our next meal? Sometimes I feel like a garbage can waiting by the curb." She looked up at the leaves in the trees, sighing. "There must be more to life than this."

"There is."

Helen smiled. "Mind if I waylay Father Jack the next time he comes to visit? I want to ask him his opinion on things. I find it fascinating he's both a Catholic priest and a Zen teacher."

"I'm sure Jack would be happy to talk to you," Steve said, "but Buddhists tend to constrain themselves on the subject of Buddhism when speaking to non-Buddhists."

"Oh?"

"Jack once told me that Buddhists wait until someone asks about Buddhism on three separate occasions before responding."

"Whatever for?"

"Awareness of ego is a big deal in Eastern thought from what I gather from Jack. Owing to this, proselytizing is discouraged since it could be motivated by ego, and a Buddhist should always be aware of ego's machinations."

Helen seemed amused. "The Bible thumpers that keep coming around here to save us old sinners could take note. The way they go on, it's like their primary motivation is to hear their own voice pontificating from memory," she said, rolling her eyes. "Anyway, tell me, after the near-death experience, how would you describe your feelings about religion?"

"Why?"

"Just curious."

"Well," Steve said after a moment's contemplation, "I'd say my focus is on my personal spirituality rather than on institutionalized religion. You know," he added, "I was never truly present when I'd go to Mass on Christmas or Easter Sunday. It was more a sense of Catholic duty than anything else. Since the accident, though, I haven't been to Mass once, but I feel much more spiritually aware."

"Really," Helen said, holding her chin on her knuckles, listening intently.

"Before the accident, it never occurred to me I had a divine purpose, but I've become aware that in order for me to experience any real fulfillment in life I must seek out and find what that purpose is and, I suppose, embrace it."

Helen's cat eye glasses had slipped down her nose. She left them there, forgotten, focusing on the words and not the physical person she faced.

"The reason I chose to live was to try and repair the damage I caused. I'm convinced repairing my earthly relationships is part of my divine purpose."

"You had the choice to come back?"

"I believe so."

Helen sat back in her wheelchair and stared at a Pacific dogwood that must have once been the prize of the garden. Minutes passed before she pushed up her glasses and turned to Steve.

"So it's not just some dogma someone handed you, but something specific to you. Is that the difference you mean between being spiritual and being religious?"

"I guess so...I mean, for me, I'm still trying to figure things out, but I'm not just going through the motions anymore; and I'm certainly not going by what someone else says is right just because they say it is."

"And what if they claim what they say is correct because the Bible says so? They often do, you know, especially these Bible thumpers."

Steve considered the question. "I think there're many ways to interpret the Bible. When I was young I was taught the Roman Catholic Church was the one and only true church. Much like other religions, it believes only one true church can exist in order to provide people with the one true interpretation of the Bible."

Helen nodded, having clearly mused on this before.

"But they got it back to front, I think," Steve said. "Jack told me of a Tibetan Buddhist saying, 'there are many spokes to the wheel, but they all point to the center.' Perhaps the many valid interpretations of the Bible are a reflection of the many, many spiritual paths possible, one to fit everyone's spiritual need."

"What a lovely thought."

"Did you like being a teacher?" Steve said.

"Oh, yes, I loved the children most, of course, and they loved me," Helen said, smiling softly. "Not that I would suffer backtalk or shenanigans. Children need a strong authority figure to teach them right from wrong, and that was my task, day in and day out, a stern but compassionate disciplinarian. I had to look out for their interests. That was my job!"

The cat eye glasses magnified a tear.

"I guess you've lost contact with your students over the years," Steve said, thinking about his own children.

"Not in the least," Helen snapped back. She breathed in through her nose to dry out her tear ducts. "They call from time to time, and a number send Christmas cards. Without their support, I don't know if I could continue. Old age is…oh, never mind, I'm just a sentimental old fool, carrying on like a teenage girl."

"What you're feeling seems to be the core of human existence."

Helen pulled a tissue from a sleeve. "You've no idea how much you've improved our lives here. We're all indebted to you."

"For what?"

Helen blew her nose to end the flow of tears once and for all. "I'm not sure. That's why I want to talk to Father Jack."

******

100

Monday night was a kaleidoscopic rampage of emotions from euphoria to frustration to acceptance of whatever fate was going to deal. It was impossible to sleep. Too much was at stake in the coming hours.

Steve found it difficult to remain composed during breakfast with everyone clip-clopping and gliding over to greet him. He finally had to forge a sneeze and excuse himself, parking in a corner of his room with a biography on George Mallory opened on his lap. He stared at the ink, debating with himself.

Steve questioned whether to go through with the procedure for reasons he couldn't quite understand, but everything changed the moment the door opened and he caught the flash of Master Feng's eyes, led in by his teenage grandson. Jack introduced the Qigong master. The interview process then began.

The hours passed slowly. It was a laborious process to have every question translated and every answer translated back. At one point Steve realized the old man was reading his body language as much as listening to his answers.

"Grandfather will now take your pulse," the teenager said.

The old man started to speak rapidly as he held Steve's wrist.

"Grandfather says you have big *qi* flow. He is puzzled. He asks if you do Qigong?"

"No."

After receiving the answer, the old man asked a quick succession of questions.

"Do you practice t'ai chi or kung fu? Have you studied acupuncture?"

"No."

Master Feng looked at a loss for an explanation. He scratched his head and frowned.

101

"I have an idea," Jack said, viewing the procedure from the vantage point of the bed. "Perhaps this elevated *qi* is a result of Steve's near-death experience. It fits the criterion."

"What criterion?"

"The criterion of *qi*," Jack said, turning to the teenager. "Michael, can you provide Steve with a definition of *qi*?"

"Grandfather calls *qi* 'vital life energy.'"

When Master Feng spoke, all went silent.

"Grandfather would like to know what 'near-death experience' is please."

Steve explained it as best he could one sentence after another in order to provide time for the translation. This went on for several minutes before the Qigong master stamped a foot on the floor and started to speak excitedly.

"Grandfather has heard of such thing, but it is not common in China."

"Why?" Steve said.

"Chinese are more sensible."

"How so?"

"They make bigger effort to avoid death."

"Sociologists have been studying the near-death experience in this country for over 30 years," Jack chimed in. "The after-effects have been well documented."

"What after-effects?" Michael said, translating the words of his grandfather.

"Changes in electromagnetism," Jack said, adding, "an increase in psychic sensitivity and being able to discern energy in the form of auras and *chakras*. This could explain Steve's high *qi* levels."

After receiving the translation, the old man said nothing until all at once his hands clapped together like a gong.

"Grandfather will start now."

Jack got up from the bed to make room for Steve who was positioned face down with his shirt pulled up to expose his back. Michael moved the chair beside the bed for his grandfather to sit. The Qigong master placed his left hand over the exact spot of the injury. He then extended his right palm downward to the floor.

"I feel a warm sensation," Steve said almost immediately.

"Grandfather feels the same."

The warm sensation quickly turned uncomfortably hot. Steve gritted his teeth. He wasn't sure this was a good or bad sign.

"Grandfather will now switch hands."

"It hasn't been nine minutes yet," Steve said, clutching the sheets.

"Try to relax," Jack said from somewhere in the room.

A short grouping of unintelligible words was exchanged. Steve was doing all he could to keep himself composed. The inner fire in his lower back intensified when the Qigong master released his hands and reversed their positions after vigorously shaking them out.

Steve pulled at the bed sheets as if he was trying to crawl away. They came undone from the mattress. Tassels shot out of him in an automatic attempt to latch onto something. They brushed the residents in the nursing home. He felt flashes of vital energy of those he touched. It calmed him, took his mind off his burning back.

"Grandfather says treatment has concluded."

Steve lay panting, sprawled on the mattress in a pool of sweat as three voices casually conversed above him. When they started to move off, he became alarmed that Master Feng would leave before he had a chance to ask him his opinion on the outcome. He quickly rolled over and shot a leg out in the direction of the wheelchair. All conversation stopped when he yelped in pain.

"What did you just do?" Jack said.

It took Steve a moment to realize exactly just what he'd just done, and the wince on his lips curled into a painful smile.

******

"Seen Steve?" Jack shouted, gesturing at the empty bed.

"Out back," an irritable older man barked from its twin across the room, eyes glued to the TV screen.

Jack found Steve on a bench with the Professor, packing his pipe. The bench was a recent purchase by the nursing home. It commemorated the departure of Judy Copeland, replacing the old rotting ones she'd always refused to authorize. A walker was parked at both ends.

"Getting tips on how to use a walker?" Jack said.

The lawn chair Jack borrowed from an attendant buckled like a slingshot when he sank into it.

"Monitoring the pruning," Steve said, "making sure they don't cut too much."

Along with the new benches, a landscaping company was hired to prune the shrubs and trees and make the walkways safe for wheelchair passage. There wasn't money in the coffers to afford anything costly. In the end, a startup was hired. The young men were being bossed around by a growing group of residents who took it upon themselves to make sure the job was done to their satisfaction.

Jack sat squished between plastic armrests with a great big smile on his face. "I just met your new roommate. You could hear the TV from the elevator."

Steve ran his fingers through his hair. "The staff has to come in and turn the damn thing off at night after he falls asleep, if I don't get to it first."

"Always preferred the radio myself," the Professor muttered, lighting his pipe.

"You know what TV reminds me of, Jack?"

"What?"

"The cotton candy you get at fairs," Steve said. "Chomp down on it and all you'll get is sweet air and sticky cheeks."

"Sweet nothingness!" the Professor proclaimed, puffing vigorously on the pipe. "Like my poor departed wife's cooking...bless her soul."

Jack chose to ignore the comment. He turned to Steve. "Looks like your slack time here is coming to an end," he said. "You'll soon be out on your own."

"True enough," Steve replied, giddy with news. "Listen, Jack, I got Jake, my new roommate, to turn down the TV long enough to talk to Brian on the phone. I have a meeting scheduled with several of the bigwigs from Justice for the Earth next Monday. What do you think of that?"

Jack's attention was averted as a starling began whistling in a tree. He whistled a tune of his own, one with an oriental twang. The bird whistled it back, note for note. Soon the two were absorbed in a little duet.

"Jack?"

"What?"

"Never mind."

Jack refocused after the bird turned its attention to the pruning effort below. "How did Melody react to your sudden turn in physical condition?"

"She's pleased if a little taken aback," Steve said, looking suspiciously at the little black bird, eyeing a branch being cut in a tree. "She's started researching alternative medicine on her own."

Jack followed the bird as it flew to another tree. "Have you spoken to Susan lately?"

"I think she's finally coming around to reality," Steve said. "At least she's starting to realize she won't be able to demand big support payments or deny me visitation rights with the kids." His smile faded, thinking about the future. "Somehow, though, I've got to get a place of my own, big enough for the kids. I'll also have to figure out how I'm going to pay the bills."

"Problems, problems," Jack said, winking.

"Father Jack," the Professor said, cutting in, "I believe Steve here thinks you're some sort of hot air balloon."

"How so?"

"He talks about how light you are, always ready for anything that's carried on the wind."

Pipe smoke sat around Steve's head like a helmet. "I meant lightness of being."

"Well," Jack said, "lightness of being is something to strive for when traveling down Zen's path."

The Professor took several contemplative drags from his pipe. He looked like a man with a question on his mind.

"Anything up?" Jack said, offering his services with a smile.

"Problems, problems," the Professor finally said, looking very French all of a sudden with his pipe and beret.

"Oh?"

The Professor sighed. "I peed on my walker this morning."

Jack drummed a finger on his chin, taking the confession seriously. "The eighth of the Ten Ox-Herding pictures—"

"The what?"

"The Ten Ox-Herding pictures," Jack said for the Professor. "They're a pictorial representation of the path to enlightenment in the tradition of Zen Buddhism. In the eighth, the ox disappears out a window and into the 'absolute.'"

The Professor held his pipe away from his face, looking at Jack.

"See my point?"

"No."

"Only the ox's tail remains in the mundane."

"Zen stories are a bit hard to follow," Steve confided to the Professor.

"Not at all," Jack countered. "The absolute, or God, or the Tao if you like, is present with us within the mundane, and if it is present with us within the mundane then the mundane is also present within it. Our problems, in one sense, are our salvation, or would be if we could come to understand them for what they are and learn to let go of our attachments to how we should or shouldn't manage them."

Steve chewed on his lips. Thinking back on the Light, he could see how perfect it seemed in comparison to the world, or the mundane, as Jack dubbed it. He didn't see how the two could possibly coexist, and he decided to express his opinion as best he could. "I don't see the...interconnection," he finally said.

"An Eastern paradox, no doubt," the Professor interjected, using the pipe's mouthpiece as a pointer.

"Unquestionably," Jack agreed. "On the topic of enlightenment, the Zenrin-Kushu states, 'you cannot get it by taking thought; you cannot get it by not taking thought.'"

"Who's Zenrin-Kushu?"

"It's a text," Jack explained, "an anthology of Zen passages written by Zen masters over the centuries."

"What's this about a paradox?" Steve said, steering the conversation back.

Jack sat reflective. "This paradox is sometimes referred to as 'the molten iron ball.'"

"The molten iron ball?"

"The point is to swallow it."

"You have to swallow the molten iron ball?"

"Yes, you have to swallow the molten iron ball even though it makes no sense," Jack said. "It has to become part of you."

"Can't be worse than my daily pill regime," the Professor mumbled, distracted by something moving behind the shrubs.

Steve shook his head. "Why does it have to become part of you?"

"It's said once you've swallowed the molten iron ball, it slowly, inexorably, changes you from the inside out, and it won't matter if you drop away from the path of enlightenment after that. You'll be changed forever, regardless."

"All the same, Jack," Steve said, "My problems are real. I'm not making them up."

"They get worse as you age," the Professor added, having lost interest in what he was spying on. "You start peeing on your walker for one."

The lawn chair threatened to buckle as Jack started laughing. Steve noted how all the birds in the scraggly trees responded as if they were laughing too.

"Let me remind you," Jack said, patting his stomach, "it wasn't long ago that your biggest problem was getting out of your wheelchair. You solved that and replaced it with a whole new set of problems. See my point?"

"Problems, problems," the Professor said, knocking the pipe on the side of the bench.

Steve was about to argue the point when Jack interrupted his train of thought.

"Your problems are smaller than you think."

"You think so?"

"You're not the center of the universe as your ego likes to suggest."

Steve's retort got lodged in his throat. He ended up breathing it out as vapor, dispersing the little demons. He breathed the garden air instead, garbage cans and all, straightening his back, his feet planted firmly on the overgrown weeds.

"I see you've been continuing your practice," Jack said, approvingly.

"Yes."

"Busy yourself with the problems of others," Jack advised, trying to squeeze himself out of the chair. "That should get your mind off yourself."

******

Steve thought he'd appear more put together with the borrowed walker than his dented loaner provided free of charge by the nursing home. The Professor generously complied, agreeing to swap for the day, his being a fancier model paid for by his insurance company. Yet, moving slowly down Justice for the Earth's ill-lit hallway, Steve's nerves started to get the better of him. He thought he caught a whiff of urine emanating from the walker.

It had long been a running joke in town that the office floors of Justice for the Earth were carpeted in granola. If anything, the law firm was renowned in Seattle's legal community for losing cases. Once Steve asked Brian why he took such cases, those he couldn't win, and he was forced to listen to a drawn-out lecture on mass extinction and the poisoning of the planet.

Brian was a good mountaineer, respected in the local climbing community. Nevertheless, Steve had always enjoyed going up against him in court. He'd sport his best attire when he did: his alligator shoes and a gold tie clip with an environmental footprint that was meant to throw Brian off his game. If anything, the tactic had an even greater effect on the other partners of the law firm, notably Katherine.

No matter how much she tried, Katherine always looked out of place, and it wasn't for lack of trying. The problem was she'd only wear outfits made from recycled or natural fibers like jute and hemp, colored using natural dyes. What that usually meant was she would show up at court sporting a cacophony of juice-stained pant suits and skirts that clashed with her eco-couture shoe collection and fabric briefcases.

Katherine had never disguised her dislike for Steve. During the times they had gone up against each other in court, he'd catch her staring at him, waiting for one of his famous bombshells. In an offhanded way, he respected her for it. She was a good lawyer, or she would've been if she took on winnable cases and wore something fitting for the courtroom.

Steve brought his attention to his breathing in a mini-meditation session in front of the door to the conference room that the meek little receptionist had directed him to. After releasing three deep breaths from the diaphragm, he knocked and entered.

Brian, Ryan and Katherine sat at a table behind three water bottles, one for each of the interviewers. They weren't those disposable ones clogging up the oceans; these were reusable, meant to last years.

Steve rode in with a manufactured smile.

"Morning Steve," Brian said, taking him in.

Ryan murmured a greeting while Katherine sat silent.

"Morning," Steve said, pulling out a chair. He sat down the way he rehearsed it, careful not to stumble.

Three sets of eyes watched every move he made. Steve caught Katherine looking down at his tie, and he instinctively patted it to feel for the tie clip that Susan probably had pawned by now. The silence in the room was as palpable as the courtroom after he dropped a tactical bombshell on the very people who'd today decide his fate.

"You'll see a list of questions," Brian said, handing him a paper. "We'll take turns as we go down it."

"All right," Steve said, pushing the walker as far from Katherine's upturned nose as possible.

Brian cleared his throat. "Can you explain your personal feelings in relation to the environment?"

It was a question formulated to undermine him. All three were well versed on Steve Forrest's feelings toward the environment. Hadn't he made a career using the ever-increasing environmental degradation taking place in the world to increase his prestige as a lawyer? The more problems that surfaced, the more lawsuits were filed and the more he was called upon to champion continued corporate irresponsibility. It was what made him a star.

"Well, you know perfectly well how I used to feel," Steve said, speaking plainly, "but my outlook has changed…irrevocably," he added, making a point to look each partner in the eye. "I feel deep concern for the planet now, a deepening appreciation for the natural world, and I'm increasingly concerned with environmental problems facing this country and elsewhere."

Brian stared at him with his arms folded across his chest while Ryan pursed his lips. It was Katherine who spoke up.

"That's nice," she said, too much the professional to roll her eyes. She popped the lid off her water bottle and took a draught of tap water. Watching her, Steve recalled what Jack had said about people who knew him prior to the accident. They would see him for the person he once was and not the person he'd become. If Susan couldn't see a change in him, how could he expect Katherine to?

"Why were you fired?" Ryan said.

"They said I'd taken too much time off going on climbing expeditions."

"But you have a different perspective on the matter," Brian added.

"Yes," Steve said, breathing slowly to calm his nerves. "I became a liability. Once disabled, I was no longer their star lawyer, not to mention it'd cost them out-of-pocket to comply with the Americans with Disabilities Act."

"So?"

"They're in the business of making money," Steve said, "not paying out."

Brian placed his hands behind his head and leaned back in his chair. The other two waited for him to speak. He was a man who commanded respect.

"We all know you professionally, Steve. You can't blame us for being skeptical."

"I don't."

"Then what made you do a total about-face in your attitude toward the environment, and why should we believe it?"

It was an improvised question not on the list. Steve could feel a warm sensation flooding his cheeks. He knew the three weren't going to buy a word he said. They were decided, looking at the old Steve.

"You know about my near-death experience?"

Katherine's eyes ballooned in astonishment but immediately reverted back to slits. Steve could only assume she was thinking the courtroom bombshell master had detonated another stink bomb.

"All I can say is the experience changed me," Steve said. "I'm not the same person you used to despise."

The final statement seemed to breach a barrier. The three lawyers shifted in their chairs, eyes drifting. When they looked back at Steve, the hardened lines had softened somewhat, even Katherine's.

Brian handed down the verdict.

"I think I can speak for all three of us when I say we wish you the very best," he said, sitting up in his chair and knotting his fingers together on the table. "Frankly, Steve, we could use a lawyer of your caliber, but we simply don't have the budget to hire you at this time. Let's wait and see if there's an opening in the future, at which time we'll certainly consider you as an applicant."

Steve's heart deflated. It was clear what was happening. There was never an intention to hire him. They were only doing him a kindness.

"I could—"

"Thanks, Steve, perhaps in the future," Katherine said, embarrassed for him.

An uncomfortable silence filled the room. A crow cawing through a screened window finally broke it.

"Thanks," he said, using the table to get to his feet.

Steve made a point of shaking hands with each before grabbing for the walker. He clip-clopped his way to the van parked out front with the nursing home's name stenciled on its side, thinking of a spot by a garbage can out in the garden where he could be alone with the dry rot he felt inside.

Chapter Four

Jack made his way under a wrought iron and glass pergola tall enough for even him to pass through safely. Surrounding him was a hodgepodge of styles of stone and brick masonry. He knew this neighborhood was once the heart of the city, but it had been repossessed by nighttime revelers over the years. Although dotted with small businesses, art galleries and cafes, it all the same gave the impression of being a late riser.

The door to the apartment building off Pioneer Square had been painted so many times it could neither be fully opened nor fully closed. With a little effort Jack managed it and started up the stairwell, trying to make out the graffiti in the light leaching from the landings. The garish pictograms commanded attention, even in the dim light. To Jack, they spoke of journeys past.

Steve cracked a smile when he opened the door. He'd been so busy he hadn't realized how much he missed Jack. He propped the crutches behind him and swung backward to provide space enough for entrance into his attic domain where spider webs long absorbed gave the walls a crackle effect.

"And I once thought the nursing home dingy, if you could believe it," Steve said, apologetically. "Guess I've moved down the ladder renting this dump."

"But you're moving up, nevertheless," Jack countered.

"In what way?"

"You're a whole two floors higher than you were at the nursing home."

Steve smiled. "Yes, Jack, I'm climbing the proverbial mountain."

"Does the roof leak?"

"No."

"Then it can't be that bad."

Steve gestured from right to left, showcasing the entire apartment. "Basically, I sleep and shower and get out as fast as I can. If I hadn't needed a change of clothes, you wouldn't have caught me."

"So you've found a job?"

"Well, as an unpaid intern for Justice for the Earth. It was the Professor's idea. He said they couldn't refuse me if I offered to work for free."

"Indeed," Jack said, contemplating whether the furniture would take his weight. "But how do you pay the rent?"

"I lit a fire under my former employer and the insurance company," Steve said, leaning into the crutches, nearly as proficient with them as he'd first been with the wheelchair and then the walker. "I told them I'd sue unless I saw a settlement."

"Did you?"

"Yup," Steve said, smiling mischievously. "I put on the old Steve voice, and that did the trick."

"They agreed to a settlement?"

"It's not much," Steve admitted, "but it'll allow me to volunteer my time for a while at least."

"Well done," Jack said, bumping his head on the ceiling.

Steve didn't want to spend another minute indoors. "Let's head to the park."

It was debatable who was in greater peril as they descended the cramped, dimly lit century-old staircase carpeted in a thin, badly worn covering that curled up at crusty corners: Steve on crutches or Jack having to bend over double to avoid splitting his skull. They made it down without incident, merging into the eclectic diffusion of urbanites moving on the sidewalk.

"Aren't they going to miss you at work?" Jack said.

Steve noticed how expressions softened as people looked up at Jack, even those sporting studs in lips and tattoos on shaved heads.

"I'll stop at a payphone and let them know."

"They won't mind?"

"Not at all," Steve said. "At the rate I'm going, I'll be averaging sixty to eighty hours a week."

"Where's the walker?"

"Swapped it for these crutches."

"Melody must be thrilled."

"Yes," Steve said, hesitantly, "but she's worried about my state of mind."

They settled onto a bench under the gaze of big city buildings. In the midst of it, a totem pole looked out from the treetops, the seriousness of its many faces a contrast to the frivolity of its surroundings.

"Want to discuss it?"

"What?"

"Your state of mind," Jack said, glancing at an older woman feeding squirrels. "Now that you've moved on and gathered some perspective, for instance, how did helping those people at the nursing home make you feel?"

"Glad to be of service," Steve said, playing along without much enthusiasm.

"Let's look at it from another angle," Jack suggested, sensing Steve's disinterest. "Why do you think you weren't more concerned with your own problems during your stay there?"

Steve shrugged. "I was busy, but I'm busy now."

Jack took a moment to plan out his next question. "How did being part of a community make you feel in comparison to being on your own?"

This time Jack hit upon something that had been bothering Steve.

"I wish I felt that sense of connection now, but it's been all business at work. Can't say I blame them; they've got enough to do," Steve said, fiddling with the crutches. "I guess I feel isolated...that's how I feel."

"You can always go back to the nursing home for a chat."

A squirrel approached the bench, sat up on its hind legs and started sniffing the air for peanuts. Jack lowered his voice so not to scare it off.

"Every spiritual tradition I'm aware of from Buddhism to Christianity to Judaism to Islam all point to how spiritual fulfillment can be attained through service to others."

The squirrel moved in a little closer.

"It is all well and good serving others," Steve whispered back, "but a bandage would do equally well." He ran his fingers through his hair, almost long enough now to tie in a ponytail. "Look Jack, I'm changing, and I'm not sure who I am anymore."

"Be the change you want to see."

The squirrel finally decided it wasn't going to profit from these two benchwarmers and hopped off to where the others were circling the old woman with the bag of peanuts.

"Be the change you want to see," Steve repeated, embracing the words. "That's beautiful, Jack."

"Mahatma Gandhi said it, not me."

Steve meditated on the words a little longer. "I could modify it to 'become the change I've seen,' you know, to fit my particular situation."

"The person you saw in the Light?"

Steve started to feel a sense of serenity hovering nearby, just out of reach. The proximity, however, was reassuring. Since leaving the nursing home, he'd felt a deep sense of insufficiency in himself. He had come to realize as Jack had forewarned that the residents of the nursing home were as vital to him as he had been to them. The way they perceived him provided him with a sense of the person he felt he was becoming. That all changed the day he moved out. Melody was right to worry about his state of mind. He was starting to worry too.

"How's Denise?" Jack said.

"Last I heard she's working to get back to the mountains."

The bench bowed as Jack crossed one leg over the other.

"What're you doing at Justice for the Earth sixty to eighty hours a week?"

"Two things, mainly," Steve said, "acquainting myself with current cases and preparing cases to go to court."

"Show them how invaluable you could be to them."

"That's the plan," Steve said, "but the research and prep work drives me nuts. I haven't done that in years."

"No?"

"I didn't realize how spoiled I'd become having assistants do the tedious work. No matter, though," Steve said. "I know what I'm doing, and I think I can put things together in a way they'll appreciate."

"Good for you."

Steve took in the noise of the traffic. "The Professor's pushing me to set up a practice of my own to advance his cause to have the smoking ban lifted in the nursing home."

Jack laughed, and the most extraordinary thing happened. A squirrel hopped over with a peanut in its mouth and laid it down by his feet. What was more extraordinary was how Jack bent over, grabbed it and popped it in his mouth.

"Keep your ears open for news on Denise."

"Worried about her?" Steve said, marveling over Jack's way with the world.

"It's just a hunch, but I feel she may need further assistance."

"All right, I'll keep my ears open," Steve said. "I would've anyway, you know."

"What's next?" Jack said.

"A cane by autumn if everything goes to plan."

******

Ryan had instructed Steve to look for a big navy gray house with a covered porch. He wasn't sure what navy gray was, but he recognized it at once. It was the color of Chomolungma the first time he spied it on his approach in Tibet. He hoped it was a sign despite the other houses that lined the street. They were all in need of a fresh coat of paint. Around them, trees and shrubs were left to grow where they seeded, compromising foundations and threatening to punch holes through windowpanes.

"How many bedrooms?"

"Four bedrooms and a bath and a half," Steve reported as the taxi pulled up to the curb.

"What have they done to remodel it?" Jack said, stretching out his limbs after unfolding himself from the back seat.

"Practically everything as I understand it."

"And all this for the same rent you're paying for your little apartment?" Jack said, massaging a kink in his neck.

"That's what I'm told."

Jack mumbled something about karma that Steve didn't quite catch. They both stood on the crumbling sidewalk, Jack taking in the house and Steve, beside him on crutches, turning this way and that, anxious about the state of the adjoining homes.

"They don't build houses like this anymore," Jack said, approvingly.

That was what likely attracted Ryan and his wife Ellie to the property in the first place. A big old house in

119

the city located in a different neighborhood would cost a fortune. They probably picked this one up for a steal, jumping on rumors of a neighborhood buyout. On the other hand, if this section of the city was slated for gentrification, it was still early in the process. Ryan's house seemed to be the only one on the street that had any attention paid to it.

Steve unlocked the door and breathed in the house, stepping across the threshold before releasing the air from his lungs. There was an overpowering scent of disinfectant, but underneath he sensed something else. It smelled good for the most part, but one particular scent seemed at odds with the others. It gave the house a vile undertone.

"There's something about this place that bothers me," Steve said, all of a sudden unsure about the house.

"That's the business Ryan an' Ellie scrubbed up on their hands and knees."

A big black woman in slippers and a flower-printed dress stood in the doorframe behind them, wiping her hands on a dishrag.

"It smelled something terrible."

"Good morning," Jack said, bowing his head.

"I'm Lila…live next door," the woman said, using the dishrag to clean her hands of whatever she was preparing for lunch. "I keep an eye on things over here best I can. Even so, a bunch got in last week—came squatting with no respect to all the time and money put into the house, making a mess, squalor all over the floors."

"Do you mean the squatters didn't use the bathroom to do their business?" Jack said.

"They did until the toilet plugged up," Lila said, stepping inside. "Ryan an' Ellie had the water turned off, see, so real fast the toilet jammed, and then they just did it on the floors like dogs."

Steve had a hand clasped to his mouth.

"It almost killed Ellie to do it," Lila added. "You just can't leave no place 'round here empty or they'll move right in and trash it."

It suddenly became all too apparent why Ryan was willing to rent the house so cheap.

"Pretty soon they'd have been cooking in here if I didn't blow the whistle on them."

"Cooking?" Jack said, confused.

"Making crank."

"Crank?"

"Methamphetamine," Steve said, turning back to Lila. "Has your house ever gotten broken into?"

Lila stood counting fingers. "Five, six times, I think, in the last couple years."

"What'd they take?"

"Last couple of times just food and some beer I keep 'round for my boys," Lila said. "If you smart, you lock up anything valuable 'round here and pray to the Lord it'll all be there when you get back."

"Did Ryan and Ellie call the police?"

Lila stared at Steve as if he were from another planet. "The cops don't hang 'round here, honey."

"No?"

"We too poor for the police."

Jack, always the optimist, chimed in. "Other than that, would you say the neighborhood is quiet?"

Lila smiled broadly. "Before all the drugs this was as quiet and peaceful a street as you'll ever find."

"This man moving in here," Jack said, patting Steve on the shoulder, "will turn it around in no time."

Lila took a clump of tissue from her cleavage and wiped her nose. "I work nights, honey, so it'd be good to have somebody watching over my place too."

"What do you do, Lila?"

"I'm a checker and stocker at the Safeway over on Rainier Avenue," she said. "Best they got."

121

Jack moved into the living room. "Looks like they refinished the hardwood floors."

"They put lots of time and work in this old house," Lila said, rolling her eyes around their sockets, "and money...Lord! More money than I ever saw in my life. They ripped out the wiring and plumbing and started from the bare boards."

Steve started to move into the house, looking at the state of repairs.

"If you boys need anything, I'll be right next door. Use both locks now," Lila added, heading out and down the steps, waving a backwards goodbye with the dishrag.

"Come look at this."

Jack followed Steve into the adjoining room.

"A big family kitchen," Jack said, nodding approvingly, "and look at the appliances."

"They're all new!"

They poked around the first floor before climbing the stairs to see the bedrooms. Later, as Steve carefully locked the door, he said "I know a certain young man who'd love that bedroom up under the eaves."

They decided to walk to get a perspective of this neighborhood on the south end of Capitol Hill. Garbage cans were everywhere. One was jammed upside down under a porch, keeping it from collapse.

Jack's size was so striking that he could easily be mistaken for something other than the Jesuit priest he was despite his conservative attire and pleasant demeanor. Steve felt confident they wouldn't get mugged. In fact, everyone they passed on the street just stared. Some even smiled.

"I like it's on a hill," Steve said, "but where will I get the stuff to fill it?"

"Didn't you tell me Susan bought six of everything?"

"Yes," Steve said, rolling his eyes in Lila fashion.

"Well, then, couldn't she give you some stuff? Is she so angry that she'd rather give the stuff away to a thrift shop?"

"Why would she have to give it away?"

"Because she's not in your huge house in Bellevue anymore," Jack reminded him. "Didn't you say you sold it and split the difference?"

Jack had a point. A lot of that extra stuff must be in storage, which would mean an extra expense for Susan.

Steve was suddenly struck by an idea. "How much do you think our relationship would change if Susan was the one helping me?"

A little band of teenagers in hoodies and ragged jeans crossed the street when they spotted Jack, steering clear of his size.

"Considering you were always the dominant one in the relationship, it certainly could bring about a change; but with relationships, there're no guarantees about anything when introducing change. On the other hand, could it be any worse?"

Steve started to swing the crutches forward one at a time like two independent legs instead of both at once, testing whether he could increase speed and keep up with Jack's long strides. As they moved south, Steve noticed several other houses in the midst of refurbishment. He started to see what Ryan must have seen.

They hailed a taxi at the bottom of the hill. Almost immediately their surroundings reverted to what Steve was starting to despise, the surplus of shops selling the same thing: the latest hairstyles, tasteless burgers from a plethora of fast food restaurants that all smelled like catsup and cafes where the ambience was the true selling point and not the coffee they sold in their stylish cups and saucers.

"Look at all this," Steve said, shaking his head.

"The culture around us is certainly not geared to face the big questions of human existence, but how much grief are you causing yourself by railing against it?"

Steve remained defiant as he stared out the window, an ear pointed towards Jack.

"When you perceive things as opposite poles, thinking dualistically, then you invariably get hung up on one side," Jack said. "The culture we live in isn't evil, it simply is."

"You think?"

"Part of the reason you're rebelling against it is that a portion of the ten thousand things that vex you every day derive from it. Keep in mind these vexations are lessons that can lead to a breakthrough in how you perceive the world around you."

Steve was slow to acknowledge the point, but Jack didn't press him. He just continued talking.

"Are you familiar with the 'love frame' concept?"

"No."

"It describes how one or both participants in an intimate relationship often maintain a 'love frame' of what the ideal mate is expected to live up to. Instead of dealing with the person they're with, they're attached to the 'love frame' other. They pat, slap or kick their mate to get him or her to behave like their love frame counterpart."

"Why are you telling me this?"

"The mention of Susan brought it to mind."

"I haven't been in her 'love frame' in years."

The joke went down better than expected. The taxi driver had to take back control of the steering wheel after Jack let out a rip-roarious snort from the backseat. He apologized to the man, promising to behave himself for the rest of the journey, hinting at a generous tip that Steve would be obliged to pay, Jack being under obligation of the vow of poverty he took.

"This love frame," Steve said, "is it based on physical intimacy?"

"Well, yes, of course, but typically not," Jack was quick to add. "Many avenues exist to coerce our intimates into the love frames we foist on them."

"So if I ever get a chance to reestablish any relationship with Susan, I'll need to check my love frame at the door. Is that what this is all about?"

Jack looked preposterous pressed up against the roof of the taxi, grinning like a fool. "I think that's a good idea, and, by the way, do the same for your kids. Too often the unique personalities of children are overpowered by parental expectation."

Even the mention of his children started to cause Steve pangs of guilt. At least before the accident he had provided them with a good home. Now, he could only offer the most basic financial support.

"I hope to get Susan to agree to let me have the kids for a visit as soon as I get the house in order, but I'm worried they won't want to come."

Jack remained silent for a time, thinking. "One of the most difficult goals to live up to in Buddhism is to retain no expectations and no attachments to the outcome of our actions and, at the same time, to put our heart and soul into the effort."

Steve wasn't in the mood for esoteric Buddhist philosophy. Instead, he stared out at all the moms and dads in their suits and ties and blouses and skirts doing what they could to feed and clothe their kids.

"It must seem an impossible task," Jack said, never one to be stifled by silence. "But it's a worthwhile goal nonetheless."

"To sever attachments to my expectations of my kids?"

"To sever attachments to the outcomes of your actions towards your kids," Jack clarified. "When you're

125

dealing with people, especially children, imagine how much more they'd feel accepted and loved if you have no attachments to what your ego demands of you."

"All right, I see your point, but you're proposing a Herculean task. How can I even begin to do this?"

"By being present," Jack said. "Be with your kids at the same time as you're with your old self, your old habits, your ego, seeing everything for what it truly is. Tell your kids when those old habits intrude on your relationships with them. It won't hurt to include them in your redevelopment. You may even establish more intimate relationships with them by letting them see you struggle."

"Easier said than done, Jack."

"Yes, but I firmly believe God provides us what is needed when we need it, especially when we're handed a colossal task to perform."

"You think?"

"God loves to see us grow," Jack said. "He won't abandon us in our hour of need."

"I guess."

"Remember the unconditional love you experienced in the Light?"

"Yes."

"You were shown that for a reason."

******

"Life is full of *dukkha*," Steve mumbled, curled up on the springy mattress, unable to sleep.

The toilet hissed like a whistle. He had earlier tried to fiddle with the handle, even shaking it to the point where it threatened to detach, but it only exacerbated the problem. In the end it didn't matter. There was no way to achieve the desired effect. The shouts and cries outside the apartment building only intensified as midnight approached.

Steve's attempt to achieve a state of total silence was prompted by the words Jack had quoted from a Benedictine monk earlier that day.

"Silence has become frightening because it will reveal the truth about them."

The "them" that the quote referred to was all the people with the "hole in the soul," as Jack put it, those holes we try to plug up with drugs, sex, work or the constant desire to purchase needless items—invariably those that make lots of noise. Jack borrowed the term from the New Age movement but was quick to point out that the Buddha talked of this very issue twenty-five hundred years ago.

"Silence exposes this hole in the soul, so people fear it."

Steve wasn't certain he wanted to expose his hole in the soul anyway, but he quickly realized that even a state of moderate silence was unattainable. The racket surrounding him couldn't be shut out even when he stuck his fingers in his ears. It led him to think he'd never known what true silence sounded like. Even the thin air on the highest mountain peaks made the act of breathing deafening.

It was after relating the concept of the hole in the soul that Jack had told Steve about the first of the Buddha's Four Noble Truths.

"Life is full of *dukkha*," Steve said into the pillow, repeating Jack's words, words first uttered by the Buddha shortly after achieving enlightenment.

Steve went over what he'd learned that day under the elusive lights moving across the walls and ceiling, lights the flimsy curtains couldn't shut out. Jack had explained that *dukkha* was traditionally translated as "pain and suffering" but had since been amended to "pervasive unsatisfactoriness."

The room suddenly turned red, shards fragmenting and passing over the bed, moving from the ceiling to the

127

walls and then out the exposed parts of the windows from which they came. Steve, sprawled out on the bed, realized the second of the Four Noble Truths was staring him in the face.

"The second of the Four Noble Truths," Jack had said, "is that *dukkha* is caused by man's attachments and desires, seeking and attaching himself to pleasure and avoiding pain or painful situations."

To be honest, Steve was relieved that he couldn't recreate a condition of total silence. He actually feared seeing the extent of the size of his hole in the soul. A shadowy part in him didn't even want to deal with the issue at all, but Jack's words from earlier that day resurfaced, refusing to let the issue go, even in absentia.

"We interact with our interpretation of reality, not with reality itself."

Steve had climbed many mountains in his life, but he was starting to realize that no mountain was higher than the one Jack was presenting him. He felt overwhelmed; it was too much for one person to cope with. That's what he'd said to Jack that afternoon as the two sat side by side on a bench.

"There's an old Zen saying, 'when you are ready, a teacher will appear.'"

Steve remembered how all of a sudden he'd felt he was in the presence of a divine being. He looked up at Jack in awe, but the look returned had been anything but divine.

"*Qi* doesn't flow from me," Jack said, his eyes piercing Steve's. "It only flows through me. Don't confuse me with a guru or a saint or anything of the sort. All I did when I first met you was respond to the needs of the environment around me because I believe that that is God's will."

Steve asked Jack how he managed it; how was it that he was able to maneuver through the maze of life toward a more enlightened state of being? Steve felt if Jack revealed the route he took then perhaps he would be able to see his own journey clearer, but the answer he got was evasive.

"My way was to find my own personal spiritual path. The result might seem an eclectic mix to others, but it suits me. Your spiritual path will be as personal to you as mine is to me."

"Am I at least going in the right direction?"

"You're moving forward, aren't you?"

"Isn't a teacher supposed to teach?"

"The Buddha said that Buddhism is not supposed to answer your questions, but question your answers."

Steve remembered almost getting up and walking away after hearing that.

"If you follow a direction that feels right in your heart then you're on the right path, a path particular to you. If you follow a direction that your heart is suspicious of, turn away."

A little ball of fluff had passed in front of the bench, a seed encased in a glove of fine white down. Jack had held his breath, enthralled, careful not to sway the direction the seed had chosen to take.

"It's a dandelion seed," he whispered, excitedly, covering his mouth. "It's heading for the rose bushes."

Steve responded by way of his mood. "It's going to get caught in the thorns."

Jack kept his gaze fixed on the seedling as he chastised Steve. "Karen Armstrong said we fall easily into despair, you know."

"Who's Karen Armstrong?"

"She's a Roman Catholic nun who left her order to become a religious historian and commentator on comparative religion."

"A mere mortal?"

"A mere mortal who writes about good and bad religion," Jack pointed out. "Bad religion, she purports, is the stifling of the individual's anarchistic search for transcendent meaning and absolute truth beyond ego, and good religion is the embrace of compassion and confrontation with the 'other,' which are the matrix teachings of all the great spiritual movements."

Steve hadn't been impressed. "What does this have to do with me?"

"Your anarchistic search for transcendence has begun; therefore, in Karen Armstrong's view, you're on the path of good religion."

Steve tossed away the pillow that came complementary with the apartment and rolled over on his side. The lights continued their waltz on the ceiling as he fell into a tangled sleep.

******

The lawyer in Steve decided to inform his landlord he was moving out of the apartment. He would've likely gotten away with it if he'd just quietly left the premises. All his stuff would've fit into one standard-sized taxi. No one would be the wiser, at least until rent was due; but the landlord could technically come after him for breaking the lease, even if it was on a month-by-month basis.

In the end the landlord was surprised a tenant would bother to inform him at all, being accustomed to the constant flow of people moving in and out. He responded to Steve's honesty by wishing him luck, telling him not to worry, that he'd have the place rented in no time.

Steve hired two young men that worked at a thrift shop near his new premises. Even though he could only offer a paltry sum, they were more than willing to take on the job. They said they wanted the experience more than the money. Both were keen to get out of the thrift shop business and get jobs with a real moving company since a mover made far more than a thrift shop employee could hope for.

Lila came sliding in on her slippers unannounced soon after the delivery truck arrived. The two young men, Dean and Peter, took her to be the commander and chief and followed her every directive.

"That must be the glasses and cups."

"You psychic, Lila?"

"I can hear 'em rattling 'bout in the box, honey," Lila said to Dean, the younger of the two, a boy about seventeen.

Dean was carrying two boxes at once. Steve feared that would mean Peter would next attempt three. Although thrift shop boxes have as many lives as cats, they had to be handled with care. The good news was the move would be over in an hour at the rate they were going.

"Put it on the counter in the kitchen, honey, by the toaster."

Sure enough, Peter came lumbering through the door with three boxes loaded one on top of the other. He had to squat as he moved to keep his jeans from falling around his ankles. It was a disaster in the making and everyone knew it, including Peter.

"Put those on the floor!" Lila commanded.

And on the floor they went. A look of doom came over Peter's face as the bottom came out of the bottommost box. Everything spilled out in a deafening clatter. Gravity took care of the rest.

"Look at this mess!" Lila said as Peter nervously pulled up his pants. She tapped a slipper on the floor as she inspected the damage. "It's just utensils and kitchen stuff…ain't nuthin' got broken."

Nuthin' matched either. Almost every item that came in was purchased at the thrift shop. Steve walked in there with five hundred dollars to spend and not a penny more, determined to furnish the entire house as best he

131

could. He thought the most expensive item would to be the four mattresses he needed—three singles and a double—but he got them for a steal. The most expensive items turned out to be the bedding he had to buy to cover the stains. He had to go to a dollar store for that.

Steve could only imagine what Susan would say if she saw the orange plastic colander he bought for the bargain price of thirty-five cents. It was a shame to fill this beautifully restored kitchen with thrift shop purchases, but he decided not to ask Susan for anything even though, technically, he was the one who paid for it. If she wanted to sit on her hoard of possessions like a dragon on a mound of gold then who was he to judge? He had his own problems to work out.

"How many kids you got?" Lila said as Dean and Peter cleared the mess.

"Two girls and a boy."

"I got myself three girls, two boys and…let me see, nine grandkids. What're your kids' names?"

"KariLyn is the oldest," Steve said. "She turned fifteen this year."

"Fifteen," Lila said, shaking her head. "There'll be trouble there soon."

"Maybe not," Steve interjected. "She's always been the serious and responsible one. Talitha, my youngest, is another story."

"Oh?"

"She knows how to wrap her father around her little finger."

"And the middle child?" Lila said.

"Josh," Steve said, with a father's pride. "He's only twelve years old and the girls are already trying to win him over. The boy's a natural at sports and good in school, too…a parent's dream."

"You miss 'em?"

132

"Like you can't imagine," Steve said. "I'm hoping they'll be allowed to stay with me now that I got a place for them to sleep."

Dean and Peter next brought in the lounger Steve bought for the bargain price of nineteen-ninety-nine. They unloaded it in the living room, opposite the couch. Steve could have gotten a faded but matching vinyl suite in black for not much more, but he decided against it. Instead, he bought a mismatched couch to go with the corduroy lounger.

Somehow Steve felt proud he was filling up the house with the rejected items of people of differing tastes and backgrounds, cultures and religions. It might be true the corduroy lounger clashed with the festive pattern on the couch—sunbursts of ochre over a guacamole base—but what did it matter?

"You'll need curtains."

"Curtains?"

"Yes, curtains," Lila said, pointing to the bare windows. "Teenagers like privacy, honey."

"I didn't think of that."

"I can make 'em for you if you get me fabric."

Steve had already spent the five hundred dollars, and he knew how expensive fabric can be. Susan practically bled him dry with the silk curtains she insisted on in every room of their former house. He could still hear her trying to explain to him that curtains are the first thing that neighbors see, "and we want the neighbors to see silk!"

"I don't think I can afford it, Lila."

"Sure you can, honey. Measure your windows and head to the thrift shop. They sell fabric there, too, you know. How much could you spend?"

"Thirty dollars at most," he said, cringing at the thought of how poor that sounded.

"That's plenty," Lila said, "more than enough."

"It is?"

133

"Here's what we'll do. Measure the windows and I'll pass by the thrift shop myself, pick up the fabric and have 'em all sewn and ready in a couple days. Should be able to get curtain rods too for that price," she added.

"All right," Steve said," if it's not too much trouble."

"With all that new gray paint, this house needs a feminine touch."

"Can't thank you enough, Lila."

"'round here, before the druggies took over, we neighbors helped each other out. I'll make you curtains and you watch my house when I'm at work."

As predicted, the move was over within the hour. Steve paid Dean and Peter each five dollars extra as he had planned, the amount already tabulated from the original five hundred. Lila had gone by then. She followed her expansive bosom out the door, down the steps and off to the thrift shop after Steve measured the windows with a tape measure he got for a buck fifty.

Steve could feel the indentation of its former owner as he sunk into the thrift shop lounger. It made it cozier than it would have been new. He closed his eyes and wondered if Lila went to work in slippers too. Being so seemingly comfortable in her own skin, he wouldn't put it past her.

******

With the methodology of a lawyer, Steve went through all that had happened that day, from the move out of his dingy apartment off Pioneer Square to the move into this restoration on the south end of Capitol Hill. It had been a busy day, and a lot had happened; but there was something else: a certain something that had taken place somewhere in the midst of it that he couldn't quite put a finger on.

Steve soaked in the claw-foot bathtub, impressed by the sensitivity of Ryan and Ellie's restoration. The vanity and toilet and the hardware that served them had a vintage appeal despite providing all modern convenience. It was a pristine example of a combination turn of the century aesthetics and contemporary design with the exception of the thrift shop towel hanging from the towel rack—looking like a frayed banner of privation in such a sparkling room.

The answer came after pulling the plug as Steve meditated on the vortex that formed above the drain. It was a revelation. He started to move through the house, flicking on lights, naked as the day he was born—too absorbed to notice he was exposing his nakedness through the windows yet to be fitted with curtains.

For half the night Steve tossed on the mattress, contemplating his life. The next morning when the doorbell rang, he was fast asleep, exhausted.

"Is it a bad time?"

The thrift shop towel unraveled and fell to the floor before Steve could answer. Jack used his massive frame to shield him from view of the street, unable to stop laughing. Steve didn't bother with the towel. He kicked it out of the way with his good leg and made his way back up the stairs unapologetically, inviting Jack to make himself at home while he changed.

Steve was anxious to discuss his discovery, but Jack wasn't in the living room when he returned downstairs, and he wasn't in the kitchen either. He was about to call out when he spotted Jack through a window.

Steve was warned about the backyard. The owner— the one Ryan had purchased the house from—had planted a single bamboo he had gotten on clearance at some garden center in the city. The man readily admitted to not having known about bamboo's special properties: that it's one of the fastest growing plants in the world and, more troublesome, one of the most invasive. By the time Ryan got the keys to the house, the backyard was a tangle of fifteen foot spears, greening in the rain.

Jack disappeared into the bamboo as Steve moved out onto the deck. He reappeared looking like a giant panda bear with his black blazer and white shirt.

"Listen," Jack said with a hand cupped to an ear. "I love the sound the leaves make in the breeze."

"I told Ryan I'd take care of it."

"Chop them down!" Jack said, horrified. "Try taming them instead."

It wasn't a bad idea. Dean and Peter could be hired to help dig out the rhizomes and install metal edging to keep a set number of allotted bamboo beds from spreading out. It wouldn't cost much and would be easier than chopping it all down and digging it up.

"I need to talk to you about something," Steve said.

Jack stepped up onto the deck without another word and sat down, testing his weight on one of the lawn chairs Ryan and Ellie had left at the house. Steve took the other.

"I'm going to take a short trip."

"Oh, where?" Jack said, looking lovingly at the bamboo.

"Inchelium."

"Where might that be?"

"It's on the Colville Indian Reservation."

"And why would you go to the Colville Indian Reservation?"

"To see my mother."

A smile curled on Jack's lips. "Your mother's Native American?"

Steve swallowed the lump in his throat. "Yes…and so am I."

Steve had spent his adult life playing the quintessential white man. He had gotten away with it because few ever guessed he was Indian despite the olive tone to his skin and his straight black hair. But in the mirror he could always see what no one else seemed to: an Indian that escaped the trials of reservation life by pretending to be someone else.

"Did Lila have anything to do with this revelation?" Jack said, pulling the lever on the side of his chair.

"Yes," Steve admitted. "It was the way she felt so comfortable in her skin. You know, Jack, Susan wouldn't leave the house if she wasn't completely satisfied with her outward appearance...a pimple was the end of the world."

The lawn chair was of such quality that it didn't even squeak while Jack held his stomach, shaking with laugher.

"And then there's Lila going out in public in her slippers and thrift shop dresses two sizes too small, shamelessly exposing herself to the world."

"She's an inspiration," Jack said.

"All night long I tossed and turned, my heritage staring me in the face," Steve said. "Then, all of a sudden, it hit me. Why couldn't I face being Indian? Why was I so intent in hiding it from the world? I suddenly couldn't grasp the reasoning behind denying myself my birthright. It confused me like you wouldn't believe."

"Do you know what Zen says about confusion?"

"What?"

"That it's the beginning of wisdom."

Both sat staring at the wall of bamboo, Jack in complete and total peace with himself and Steve in internal upheaval.

"Tell me about your past," Jack said, closing his eyes, "if you're ready."

"Both my parents were Indian. Dad was part Salish and mom Sin Aikst, known as 'The Lakes' to some."

"Where do The Lakes come from?"

"Traditionally up and down the Columbia River," Steve said, remembering what he'd been told as a kid. "They'd journey to Kettle Falls for the salmon runs then

137

head back up into the Arrow Lakes region in what is now British Columbia. Later some got absorbed into the Colville Confederated Tribes, if I remember."

"What was your life like on the reservation?"

"I don't remember much about it," Steve admitted. "We moved when I was seven."

"Is your father deceased?"

"Yes," Steve said, a little dryly. "I was told he died of cirrhosis a few years back."

"What was your relationship with him like?"

The question brought up a swarm of memories that stung Steve in the heart. "He was a falling-down drunk that sometimes half-heartedly beat up my mom, but most of the time he wasn't violent, just drunk."

"How did that affect you?"

"I came to equate being Indian with being a drunk, I guess. Many were," Steve was quick to add, "those who couldn't hold down jobs. For them, life was a series of failures."

"Why do you think that is?"

"If you'd asked me that a year ago, I would've given you a different answer."

"What's your answer now?"

Steve let out half a lungful of air. "This culture we live in is hard on Indians, especially the men. It runs counter to their traditional ways of life."

Jack absorbed the words with the sunrays. "What's your relationship with your mother like?"

Steve thought about it a moment. "Mom was the anchor of the family, the breadwinner."

"I asked about your current relationship with your mother."

Steve would've preferred to pass on the question. "I have no relationship with my mother. I haven't for years, since she moved back to the res."

"But things have changed since the near-death experience, haven't they?"

"Yes," Steve admitted. "I feel a need to see her."

"I should think you do," Jack said, as if he'd known Steve's history all the while. "I'm curious about something, though. How did you escape alcoholism when so many didn't?"

"I came close," Steve confessed. "As a freshman in college I can remember getting up some mornings not able to remember anything about the night before. I vowed that wasn't going to happen to me. I quit drinking cold turkey, and that was that."

"Like bamboo," Jack said, blinking at the spears. "How so?"

Jack smiled. "It's a grass of steely resolve, if you haven't noticed," he said, closing his eyes and locking his fingers over his chest. "Did you ever attempt a spirit quest?"

"No," Steve said, surprised by the question.

Jack didn't press him. He seemed satisfied with the answer he got. "How would you characterize your feelings toward your Indian heritage before Chomolungma?"

"I rejected it completely."

"Let's review," Jack said, crossing one leg over the other. "Lila's ease in her own skin led you to realize you needed to visit your mother in Inchelium. How are the two related?"

Steve didn't have an answer until he realized the question provided it, and all the confusion inside him drained away. "There's a sense of quietude in her nature that reminds me of the people I knew as a child, the elders who still held the traditional ways close to their hearts, living in harmony with the land."

"Perhaps this state of quietude comes from their close association with their surroundings," Jack mused, "as Lila has with hers."

A memory of Steve's long dead grandmother surfaced out of nowhere. At one time he had been in awe of her. She knew every name of every plant on the res, which ones could be used as herbs and which could make medicine. To a seven-year-old, she seemed like the wisest person on the planet.

"Someday you might consider going back and attempting the spirit quest you missed," Jack said, matter-of-factly. "You never know…it could be a part of your unique spiritual path."

******

A horn sounded as the Gifford-Inchelium Ferry pulled away from the quay on the Inchelium side of Lake Roosevelt.

Steve leaned against his car. It was lined up with the others, waiting on the Gifford side. The secondhand Honda he had splurged for and all the other jalopies waiting to be ferried over the lake were a colorful bunch of rust and body work. Still they paled under the colors of the surrounding landscape—those Steve's ancestors extracted from the land to dye their cloth and paint their faces.

Yesterday had been the first time Steve had spoken to his mother since his father died. The slow way in which she articulated her words brought back memories of the pace of his youth where only the watercourses rushed and the salmon within them, laboring to arrive back to their spawning grounds. Reservation life was a speed unto itself. It retained a certain quietude he was hoping to rediscover.

Steve had been taken aback by the beauty of it all as he drove across the bridge at Fort Spokane, his body resonating to the panorama of the landscape. He became more absorbed the further north he got, gawking longingly at the mountains and swooning in the vanilla scent of the sun-warmed ponderosas. It was as if he were being welcomed home by the land in its Sunday best.

After docking, a burly man in pigtails directed traffic off. When cleared of cars, those heading to Inchelium were signaled onto the ferry with a finger, one at a time. Even though Steve had no idea how reservations worked, it struck him that in a country where everything had a price tag attached to it, this ferry service was mysteriously free.

Four Cummins diesels growled to life, blowing dense black smoke into the clear blue sky as the ferry pulled away from the quay, heading back into Steve's past. A steady, gentle breeze blew from the south as it made its way across the lake, dispersing noxious fumes. Steve took in the sights as people sat talking, vehicle to vehicle, shouting leisurely over the engines.

Steve was last off the ferry. There didn't seem to be a pecking order; people just drove off when signaled by the authoritative finger. Last was fine with him. He wanted to drive into town at his leisure without a line of cars stuck behind him. Turning on the main drive, he was confronted by the dusty little town of his earliest memories. Nothing had changed but all seemed different.

Steve drove around a corner past Inchelium School, turned left onto the cutoff road and then onto the road to Twin Lakes, driving slowly, savoring the sights and smells. The deception of the landscape didn't escape him, knowing firsthand the underlying poverty of his youth. The money generated by the Two Rivers Casino he passed on his way didn't seem to flow back to the reservation. The lawyer in him wondered where the money went.

Sally was watering flowers in front of the double-wide when Steve turned into the driveway. The mobile home was a little worse for wear, and by the look of her, so was his mother. Her long black hair was peppered with gray, and she stood a little stooped. It seemed that life was a struggle for an Indian woman as much as for an Indian man.

Steve wondered whether he should've exchanged the crutches for a cane that morning. He might've allowed himself time to get used to it, but he wanted to give a certain impression: be seen the way his mother had known her athletic, successful son. As it happened, he lost his balance trying to retrieve his bag. It was his mother that saved him from a fall.

"Here, I'll take that," she said, grabbing the bag from him.

The voice was raspier—simple and sweet like the rustle of bamboo. It brought a sudden rush of tears to Steve's eyes. He turned away so his mother wouldn't see, but she'd have none of it, dropping the bag and clasping him around the shoulders.

"Tears, son?" Sally said, hooking one with a finger. "Yes, I see big changes in you. As a boy, you never cried."

Steve could feel how his mother's cheeks had softened through the years and how the wear of the world had chiseled itself around her eyes.

"You were always my hero, you know," Sally said, letting go only to look up at him. "Let's go in and talk."

Steve hobbled inside over the shag carpet to a chair in the kitchen. He sat down slowly, hooking the cane on the backrest. Sally watched his every move.

"It's hard to see you hurting," she said, shaking her head. "Was it worth it?"

It took Steve a moment to grasp the meaning of the question. "If you mean the pain of recovery and the divorce and all the other things that climbing that mountain caused, the answer is no, definitely not; but as I said over the phone, something else happened, something meaningful."

"What, son?"

"Do you know what a near-death experience is?"

142

Sally remained standing, massaging her hands. "You die and come back," she said, softly. "That what you mean?"

"Yes, I died and came back."

Sally moved around the kitchen, opening windows, letting in air. A sprinkler could be heard on the back lawn and, further away, conversations rippling across the lake. Steve kept his eyes on his mother. He saw something graceful in her he never had before. He wondered whether it was her or his perception of her that had changed.

"Tell me, son," Sally said, sitting. "Don't leave nuttin' out."

Steve told her everything from the moment of the accident. He told her about the Light, the divorce, meeting Jack, the nursing home, the Qigong master, his new job and all the people he had met. When he finished, she sat quietly, blinking like a butterfly.

"Want lemonade?"

"That'd be nice," Steve said, following her with his eyes as she got up from her chair and moved to the fridge, wondering if she'd remark on what he told her.

"You're here 'til tomorrow?"

"Maybe Tuesday, depending on how things go."

"Good," she said, pouring out two glasses of lemonade. "Is it okay if we go to Steemus for Indian tacos with the Simmons?"

"Sure, if you want," Steve said. "Friends of yours?"

"Old friends," Sally said, moving towards the table, a glass in each hand. "They're why I moved back out here, so far from town."

Their eyes met as Sally put the glasses down.

"I know you're ashamed of your ancestry."

"Yes," Steve said, caught off guard, "but things have changed. I want to know more about it now. Other than seeing you, it's the reason I made the trip."

"Really, son?"

"It felt as if I were coming home when I drove up today."

Sally's smile was as warm as sunset. "Then there're things here you still treasure?"

"Yes."

"Do you treasure the memory of your father?"

Steve felt beads of lemony condensation trickle down his fingers. "I don't know," he finally said. "I'm not sure I understood him like you did. Maybe I was too hard on him…I don't know."

"He did the best he could for us."

"Do you miss him?" Steve said, reflecting the topic to something less toxic.

"Yes," Sally said, softly, "terribly sometimes. He didn't have your iron will, you know. If he did, he'd been a successful man like you or, at least, a happier one." She shook her head back and forth, staring down at her lemonade. "I know you think he treated me bad, but because I stuck it out with him, we came close in the end. He got to telling me how much he loved me."

"Glad to hear it," Steve said, noncommittal.

"Tell me more about this teacher," Sally said. "He's a Jesuit priest?"

"Yes, and an ordained Zen teacher as well as a psychotherapist."

"How can that be?"

Steve told her about the Shinmeikutsu monastery on the outskirts of Tokyo as Jack had related it to him. Whether she approved or not, she didn't let on. When he finished, she got up and came around the table, giving him a warm hug, her lips close to his ear.

"Welcome home, son. I missed you something terrible."

******

144

"What exactly are Indian tacos?" Jack said.

"Same as regular tacos, except on frybread."

Steve had heartburn for days after his visit to Steemus with his mother and her friends even though he liked the restaurant—owned and operated by the reservation. It was a no-frills greasy spoon in every sense of the word, but it had its own special charm. More than anything, it was a gathering place for locals.

"And it was there you were approached to act as their representative?"

"Yup," Steve said, letting go a little burp of nostalgia, "by John Little Bear and the others. After mom let them know I work for Justice for the Earth, they circled me like a bonfire."

"So there're real environmental problems at the reservation."

"Heavy metals and dioxin have been measured in the lake for years."

"Good Lord!"

"Gets worse," Steve said. "Any decline in the lake's water level causes toxic dust to blow through the reservation."

"Toxic dust!"

"Yup, and the cancer rates on the reservation are concerning."

"Are you going to help?" Jack said, holding a hand to his heart.

"It depends on Justice for the Earth."

"Have you approached them about it?"

"Yup."

"Good!"

"They're also considering putting me on the case."

"A paid job?"

"That's my understanding," Steve said. "It'd mean becoming a full-fledged member of the team," he added with a tinge of optimism.

"I couldn't be happier for you."

"It's not that surprising," Steve was quick to point out. "Being Indian, I'm a natural fit. It'll all depend whether Joseph, one of the lawyers in the office, gets transferred to the Missoula office. If he does, my name will be added to a list of potential replacement lawyers."

"Added to a list?"

Steve sipped the lemonade he prepared according to the recipe his mother gave him, with modifications. He couldn't bring himself to add the amount of sugar it called for. He reduced it by half, and it came out tart.

"Yup, added to the list," Steve affirmed, smacking his lips. "They still see me as a down-and-out corporate lawyer, grabbing at straws. They don't fully trust me, and they don't believe I possess the environmental knowledge required for the job."

Jack was silent a moment. "Do you?"

"Nope," Steve admitted. "You know, I thought I was helping the environment by buying a second-hand Honda, but according to my coworkers, I should've bought a bicycle."

"Who at the office is the most knowledgeable on environmental issues?" Jack said.

"Why?"

"You can approach that person and ask if he or she would agree to be your coach."

Steve scoffed.

"There's nothing unusual about a seasoned member of a team helping out a novice."

"I guess," Steve said, knowing that the person in question was likely Katherine, the most hostile to his presence.

Jack changed the subject to brighten the mood. "So Susan has finally agreed to let you see the kids?"

"Yes."

"What?" Jack said, looking at Steve. "Are you nervous about seeing them?"

"I'm ecstatic."

"Then why the gloomy face?"

"Mom's insisting I bring them up to see her before the summer's out."

"What a lovely idea."

"It won't be for Susan," Steve said. "She'll object in a heartbeat."

"Why?"

"Once mom called her a woodrat to her face."

"Woodrat?"

"Yup, a woodrat," Steve said, adding "better known as a packrat on account of its habit of hoarding shiny objects. Susan never forgave her for it."

Jack broke out into peals of laughter. The deck shivered at every stomp of his foot. He had to finally take a sip of lemonade to recoup his composure.

"On a more practical note," Steve said, "I'm not even sure my little Honda can fit the four of us."

"You're just making excuses," Jack said, mollified by the acute power of citric acid.

"True, but Labor Day's coming up, and mom made it clear she wants to see the kids by then."

"Problems, problems," Jack said, getting up from the lawn chair and stepping off the deck. "Ask the kids their opinion on the matter. Maybe the four of you can convince Susan."

Steve scoffed a second time.

"How old is KariLyn again?" Jack said, disappearing into the bamboo.

"Fifteen."

"And Talitha?"

Steve spoke up to be heard through the shoots. "Seven."

"And Josh is twelve, correct?"

147

"Yup," Steve said, trying to spy Jack through the bamboo.

"And each possesses a unique character particular to themselves?"

"That would be an understatement."

"A Garden of Eden!" Jack said, stepping out of the shoots and throwing out his arms.

"Sorry?"

"You and your kids can turn this backyard into your own personal Garden of Eden."

Jack continued to hold out his arms like a ringmaster.

"Isn't the Garden of Eden the origin of sin?"

"It's also synonymous with paradise," Jack countered. "It could be an excellent way for you to reestablish unique relationships with each of your children," he added, clearing this throat.

"You're about to tell me another Zen story, aren't you?"

Jack brought his hands together. "A student approaches his master and says he'd like to achieve enlightenment. The master asks whether he's yet eaten. The student answers he has. The master tells him to go and wash his bowl and spoon, and instantly the student achieves enlightenment."

"That makes no sense whatsoever."

"If it makes sense, it probably isn't Zen."

Even with Jack standing in front of it, the bamboo seemed taller and denser than the last time Steve was out in the backyard. New shoots had sprouted, advancing towards the house. If something wasn't done soon, Ryan and Ellie's expensive cedar sundeck would soon be overrun.

"According to Buddhism, every single person on the planet is enlightened," Jack said, stepping back onto the deck. "It's not the achievement of enlightenment but the

148

realization of one's own enlightenment that takes place in those that achieve it."

"My kids are enlightened?" Steve said in disbelief.

"Yes," Jack said, "according to Buddhism; but more importantly, the narrative I just shared illustrates the nature of the relationship between teacher and student."

"How?"

"Let's say you're a Zen master, and being a Zen master, you're fully aware of the nature of enlightenment. You know it can't be expressed by words even though words are one of the few ways to transmit knowledge to a student. How can you then proceed to teach?"

Steve shrugged. "No idea."

Jack's eyes flashed as he turned them on Steve, having sat back down in the lawn chair and made himself comfortable. "A Zen teacher proceeds by being aware of the nature of the student. The teacher must lay aside his or her ego long enough to do what Thich Nhat Han calls 'deep looking' into the 'true nature' of the student."

"Are we still discussing my kids?"

"Most definitely," Jack said. "This is an opportunity for you to reestablish new and infinitely better relationships with them."

"How?"

"By communicating directly to the true nature of your children," Jack proclaimed. "They may be puzzled at first, but sooner or later their true natures will respond to your appeal."

The bamboo seemed to be waiting for a breeze.

"Do you now see the point of my little narrative?"

"Nope."

"The Zen master took the opportunity that arose at that moment to communicate with the student's true nature, and it worked—enlightenment was realized."

"How?"

"How indeed?"

"What?"

"It may not make sense to us, but it obviously did to the master and student, and that's the point."

The folds on Steve's forehead deepened.

"Don't take life too seriously," Jack said with a smile. "It's not permanent."

"Is that another Zen proverb?"

"Saw it on a t-shirt."

Part Two: Toward Maturity

Opening to Possibility

Chapter Five

KariLyn lowered the window as the car pulled up to the curb. "Hi dad," she said.

Steve was on pins and needles, barely able to keep his composure, but his smile froze when he spied the lip-gloss painted on the beaming smile. It was his daughter's liquid brown eyes that obliterated any hard feelings he might have had, despite being framed in mascara—something he and Susan had discussed at length in the past (she for it and he against).

"Hi," he gushed. "It's great to see you all…you too, Susan," he added, looking at the stony profile.

"Make sure you get all your things," Susan snapped, staring straight through the windshield, her knuckles popping white on the steering wheel.

Soon a pile of duffel bags, sleeping bags and other stuff was piled on the sidewalk.

"Bye Mom," Talitha and Josh called out.

Susan gunned the engine and sped down the street.

"C'mon in," Steve said, bending over the cane to pick up the largest bag. "Let's get settled in your rooms."

"Look what we got here!"

Lila was wiping her hands on a dishrag as she cut through her front yard.

"Hi Lila," Steve said, dropping the bag to regain his balance. He moved between his son and daughter. Talitha, small for her age, wrapped herself around Steve's leg, not sure what to make of the approaching figure.

"Let me introduce you to my kids," Steve said. "This is KariLyn and Josh and hiding between my legs is Talitha."

Lila did her best to bend down far enough to press Talitha's nose.

"Fine looking bunch of kids you got."

Steve felt Talitha's hold relax after Lila straightened. His neighbor stood looking at KariLyn, fists pressed into her expansive hips.

"Aren't you a pretty young thing?"

KariLyn, loaded down in gear, thanked her graciously, flipping her long brown hair from her face. Lila next stepped back to inspect Josh.

"Could this be the handsomest white boy I ever saw?"

"Yes," Talitha said, looking up from Steve's leg.

Talitha's hair was no longer flaxen. It had turned dishwater blond. It wouldn't be long before she'd be a brunette like her brother and sister.

"Nice to meet you," Josh said with an easy smile.

"And I just took out a tray of fresh-baked, straight-out-of-the-oven cookies. It'd be a shame to let 'em go cold."

Talitha released her grip on Steve's leg and started to jump up and down. "Can we, dad, can we have a fresh-baked, straight-out-of-the-oven cookie?"

Josh grabbed his sister out of the air. She clung to him and turned to her father with those dimples that always could charm him. He was about to make excuses, but then decided to go with the flow on impulse.

"If Lila doesn't mind," Steve said.

"Don't mind one bit."

Steve scuffed up Talitha's hair. "All right, I'll take the stuff into the house and be right over."

"I'll help you, dad," KariLyn said, giving him a little look.

Josh slid his little sister onto his back. She clung to his shoulders as he jogged after Lila.

When the last of the gear was piled in the living room, KariLyn stood looking at her father, a question on her lips.

"What's up, honey?"

"Are you okay?" KariLyn blurted out, looking anxiously at the cane.

"I'm fine."

"Dad?"

"Yes, honey."

"Has something changed?"

Steve blinked at his daughter. There was something of Sally in her. She wasn't just the brunette clone of her blond mother that he used to think she was.

"Could daddy have a hug?"

Steve knew he'd failed. He had asked for the hug so his daughter wouldn't see the tears welling in his eyes. He was holding himself back like he had always done with his kids, exactly what he was determined not to do this time around.

"Is something wrong, dad?"

"No, honey, I'm just very happy to see you," he said, failing again. His voice cracked as he spoke. "We'd better get over to Lila's before your brother and sister eat all the cookies."

They made their way out the door and down the steps.

"Dad?"

"Yes."

"You never called me 'honey' before, but it's okay if you do."

Before Steve could answer, Talitha bounced out of Lila's front door with a cookie in each hand, her eyes dancing. "All gone!"

153

"Don't you believe it," Lila said, holding open the screen door. "C'mon in and help yourselves."

The bright and brassy curtains hanging from Steve's windows courtesy of this most generous of neighbors were nothing compared to Lila's. He had stepped through the screen door into a thrift shop wonderland of clashing furniture, revival textiles and bric-a-brac.

"That Talitha," Lila said, leading the way to the kitchen. "Never in all my days seen a girl so full of tomfoolery."

As if to prove Lila's point, Talitha brushed passed their legs to make it to the kitchen first. There, Josh was sprawled out in a chair, looking content.

"Comfortable, son?"

Josh grinned up at his father, savoring the cookie in his mouth.

"That boy of yours is a golden child if I ever saw one."

Steve had often heard such comments about Josh. Lila picked up on what everyone did. Josh had an ease about him rare for someone his age, even when around adults.

"But all three so different," Lila was quick to add. "It sure is funny how things work out."

"Sure is," Steve agreed.

"Hey dad, what're we doing this weekend?" Josh said, swallowing.

"I think we should have a family meeting to figure that out," KariLyn interjected, nibbling on a cookie.

"That's not a bad idea," Steve said, turning to his other two. "Think you can handle that?"

Talitha answered by crawling under the kitchen table.

"Sure, dad," Josh said, taking no mind of his youngest sibling.

No one knew how she did it, but Talitha sprang up on the other side of the table with a third cookie in her mouth.

"You've got chocolate smeared all over your face," Steve said, shaking a finger at her.

KariLyn took control of the situation, something Steve hadn't seen before.

"Can we use your bathroom?"

"Sure thing, honey" Lila said. "First door on the left."

Talitha sighed, biting down on the magically appearing cookie. "I suppose I got to wash my face now," she said, chewing glumly.

"Don't talk with your mouth full," KariLyn said, grabbing her sister's free hand and leading her down the hallway.

Through the kitchen window Steve could see the sprawl of bamboo over the fence. By some miracle it hadn't yet infiltrated Lila's backyard.

"If it helps any, they're going to be a bunch of kids 'round here tomorrow," Lila said, using the dishrag to wipe crumbs from the table. "My grandkids are coming, and they might even be able to wear out your little one long enough for her to sit."

A squeal rang out from the bathroom.

"Okay, gang," Steve called out, "time to go."

Talitha burst from the screen door and sprinted across the lawn to be the first one home.

******

"Check my harness, dad," KariLyn said.

"Mine too," Josh chimed in, standing by the wall with his younger sister, already reaching for handholds.

"Wait until daddy checks your harness, pumpkin," Steve said, wrapping his own around his waist. It felt odd clipping in, automatic and novel all at the same time. After he wrapped his waist strap back through the buckle he turned his attention to his kids' harnesses, yanking and adjusting them all with care, making sure nothing went wrong.

Talitha, raring to go, was bouncing up and down before he was done.

"Now, daddy?"

"Where's that video game thingy of yours?"

Talitha looked up at her father like she didn't know what he was talking about. "Oh that!" she said. "In the car."

Throughout the family meeting, Talitha had sat between her brother and sister on the guacamole couch consumed in the game she was playing on a hand-held video gaming device she had brought with her, the little thumbs turning the dials and pumping the buttons. She squealed with delight every time a little ditty erupted from it. Steve had to stop himself from grabbing it and throwing it in the trash.

"Do you remember the signals?"

"On belay?"

Talitha said it in that high-pitched squeal only a very excited little girl could manage. Several people stopped to look as she stood facing the wall, trying hard not to fidget, waiting for her father's command.

"Belay on."

"Climbing!" Talitha blurted out, launching herself at the wall.

"Okay, you two know the commands, right?

"Right."

"KariLyn," Steve said, pulling in Talitha's slack, "feeling rusty with the ATC?"

"Let me watch you a bit," she said.

"Spoken like a true climber," her father replied, approvingly, keeping his eye on Talitha's progress. "Josh, mind holding up a minute?"

"No problem, dad," Josh said, looking up at his younger sister. "Go Talitha!"

Talitha giggled, but nothing was going to distract her ascent. She continued up on a down-sloping hold. Steve could sense people gathering behind him to watch the little spitfire go.

"Okay, dad, I think I got it," KariLyn said. "Josh, you can go now."

"Say the command."

"On belay?"

"Belay on!" Josh said, correctly, stepping up onto the wall.

The family meeting had been Steve's first attempt to connect to his kids in a new way, shelving his ego while allowing their individual personalities to fully express themselves. He had used the opportunity to tell them about his near-death experience, and when Josh had asked if he had died, he didn't try to sugarcoat the answer. He told the truth, that he wasn't sure. He then told them about the Light.

"That little girl's almost halfway up already," some woman said from behind.

Steve was monitoring both his kids at once. He was surprised at how smoothly Josh moved up the wall. He was nothing like his fearless sister whose goal seemed to be to make it up as fast as possible. Josh took his time, staying on route, not just grabbing the nearest holds like Talitha.

After the revelation about the Light, all three remained silent, Josh and KariLyn and Talitha between them, oblivious to everything but the game in her hands.

"Say whatever's on your mind," Steve had said, encouraging dialog from the lounger.

"Sure you didn't imagine it, dad?" Josh finally said, hesitantly.

"If he said he saw a light he saw a light," KariLyn said, coming to her father's defense.

"It's only just…you know," Josh said, cautiously, glancing at his older sister. "Remember what mom said?"

KariLyn's lips had tightened as she looked at her father. "Mom said you made the whole thing up."

"Did she?"

"Yes, making excuses for—"

"For what?"

"Ruining the family!" Talitha had squealed as another triumphant ditty rang out on the gaming device.

That was when the family meeting came apart. Josh grabbed the device from his sister's hands and tossed it across the room. The resultant tantrum shook the house. Steve had never seen his youngest react in such a way. He had to finally get up from the lounger, kneel down and brush the hair from her teary eyes, whispering a secret in her ear.

Josh was attempting to tackle a difficult route. It was Steve's opinion that Talitha may have had the enthusiasm, but it was her older brother who was coming to terms with what climbing was really about. A roar of approval rang out from the people gathered when Talitha touched the pipe on top of the wall. She looked down at her audience to acknowledge their adulation before sagging back into the rope, letting herself be lowered down.

"We're Indian?"

"Part Salish and Sin Aikst, on your grandmother's side."

Steve had smiled into Talitha's big brown eyes as he said it, caressing her hair. On either side of her, her brother and sister had remained silent. Steve gave them the gift of time to reflect on their heritage, suggesting they might want to spend the afternoon at that mall with the big climbing wall like they used to do.

As Talitha was being lowered down, Josh was making a difficult transition over a small roof that simulated an outcropping on a cliff face.

"Way to go, Josh!" Steve yelled up in encouragement.

At that moment, Steve heard giggling behind him. He glanced around. A little distance off, three young girls were looking up at his son, whispering among themselves.

******

"Got a lot done since I was last here," Jack said, looking down from the safety of the deck.

The backyard resembled an archaeological site. Dirt was piled in little mounds. What remained of the bamboo was now an informal hedge, loosely following the border of the property in confined clumps, having the space to fan out it hadn't before. The excavated shoots had been neatly stacked in the middle of the yard until it was decided what to do with them. Josh suggested making a fort while KariLyn proposed a pergola. Talitha wanted a tower to climb and look out over the neighborhood in search for other kids.

"And all this done in one day?"

"Yup," Steve said, barely able to believe it himself.

"How did you manage it?"

"Lila's horde of grandkids," Steve said with a smile. "The older ones were more than happy to make a little money. With them, my kids and Dean and Peter from the thrift shop, it was done by the end of the day."

"How much did it cost?"

"Ryan and Ellie took care of the cost," Steve said. "After talking to Lila about it, I called them Saturday evening with the proposal, and they arrived first thing Sunday morning with shovels, picks and the metal edging needed to contain the rhizomes."

"It was good of them to pay for it."

"They were grateful we could get it done so cheap."

159

Jack shook his head thinking about it, a smile growing on his sunny face. "It must have been a zoo here."

"It was," Steve said, "but Lila and her daughters spent the entire afternoon preparing a soul-food supper for everyone."

"You don't say?"

"Lila says it's called 'soul food' because it's good for the soul."

"Was it?" Jack inquired, always attuned to matters of the soul.

"One could argue the gain for the soul is paid for by the arteries. The kids loved it though."

"I'm sorry I missed out," Jack said.

"Of course, I got into trouble with Susan," Steve said, sucking in his lips.

"Oh?"

"She informed me that her children were not to be subjected to backbreaking labor, but the kids couldn't have had more fun. I don't remember seeing them so happy, and all three caked in dirt."

"Did Talitha help?"

"Oh yes," Steve said, smiling in spite of himself. "She made a point of climbing up each shoot to give it a kiss before it was dug up."

Jacked took in the redesigned bamboo hedge. "That's pretty high for a seven year old."

"The girl has a liking for heights," Steve said. "What can I say? She's a chip off the old block."

"Susan's reaction is curious though," Jack said, a finger tapping his chin. "If the experience was positive for the children—"

"Don't think this as about putting the children to work," Steve said, moving over to a lawn chair. "Susan always worked them hard. All three are expected to get top grades and medals at school. If I know her, and I think I do, she's angry at me for allowing the kids to associate with Lila's grandchildren."

"Susan's a racist?"

"No, no," Steve said, sitting down with the help of the cane. "She's too conscious of how she's perceived to waste time judging others."

"That's harsh."

"It's the truth," Steve said. "If Lila's grandkids were sons and daughters of, you know, the right sort of people, she wouldn't have minded at all."

"Was she always like that?" Jack said, looking perplexed.

"No," Steve said, running his fingers through his hair. "She wasn't always like that."

At one time Susan had been a sensible, pragmatic girl, and a beauty at that. She was fun to be around in those early years. Steve couldn't have been more proud to land one of the most sought-after girls on campus. Those blue eyes and that long, shiny free-flowing hair was a trophy he proudly showed off every chance he got. Whatever changed in her happened over years. There simply came a time when she no longer smiled, except on shopping sprees.

Steve changed the subject. "Talitha made fast friends with one of Lila's granddaughters, and Josh hooked up with one of the grandsons, Joseph, a football player like himself. KariLyn and one of the older granddaughters, Desarae, held a whispering campaign that lasted all day."

"What a beautiful name," Jack said, locking his fingers together. "What did the Light reveal to you about Susan, if you don't mind my asking?"

"Everything."

It revealed the blush that flowered on her cheeks that night he slipped the engagement ring on her finger and the year she couldn't stop crying. Steve remembered it was around the end of that year that her blue eyes started to freeze over.

"She's going to be really nasty, Jack. You can bet on it."

"When's the custody trial?"

"Next week."

"Have you considered having the court appoint a guardian *ad litem*?"

Steve looked over at the other lawn chair, surprised as always. "Someone impartial to make the wishes of the children known to the court when there's a dispute over their wants and desires?"

"Exactly."

Steve mulled over the idea. "I don't want this to become emotionally draining on the kids."

"Could you ask for a court appointed psychological evaluation of the children?"

"Yes, possibly, but what if Susan coaches them? Talitha's only a kid, remember."

"Unless the therapist is a complete dunderhead," Jack said, slipping off his shoes, "that strategy would quickly backfire. How's the money holding out anyway?"

Steve smiled, making it clear he didn't want to talk about it.

"Are you still seeing Melody?"

"Yes," Steve said, "but I cut back on physical therapy again to save money. I go twice a month now."

"Is it helping?"

Steve sighed. "I'm starting to wonder if the cane is going to be a permanent part of my life."

They both sat silent listening to the diminished chorus of bamboo leaves snapping in a breeze.

"Perhaps Qigong would help," Jack said. "It got you out of the wheelchair."

"I can't afford it."

"Lucky you know me then."

162

"What do you mean?"

"Let's just say I know people," Jack said, secretively. "Are you available one night out of the week?"

"I can make myself available."

"Good," Jack said, wiggling a toe poking out of a sock. "Have you managed to set a date to take the kids to Inchelium?"

Steve smiled. This time he had his own surprise to share. "Well, since Justice for the Earth will be representing the tribe with me heading the case, I'll have an excuse to spend time there and, hopefully, an excuse to take the kids."

"Congratulations," Jack said. "And how long were you going to keep that information from me?"

Steve continued to smile, letting the sun warm his face.

"Might be a good time to look into the spirit quest you missed out on as a kid," Jack said, mumbling a song as he turned his gaze to the sky.

******

"Next on the docket, Susan J. Forrest versus Steven S. Forrest, Your Honor," the court clerk called out. "Mr. Michaels is representing Mrs. Forrest and Mr. Forrest is representing himself."

Steve didn't recognize Susan's lawyer, but that wasn't surprising. Corporate lawyers tend to keep company with corporate lawyers, or that was what he and his associates always did. Family law was another world. With that said, Mr. Michaels seemed composed and confident despite the air of tension in the crowded room, each dejected soul waiting his or her turn to be called to the docket to tear themselves that much further from the people they once claimed to love. His composure was particularly impressive in light of the fact that his client was in absentia.

163

The judge looked up from the folder and stared over her glasses, her gaze coming to rest on Steve.

"Mr. Forrest, I see you're representing yourself," the judge said, apparently stalling a moment before deferring the case to a later date.

Before Steve could respond, the judge's eyes shifted to a buzz at the back of the room. Susan had arrived, late as always, strutting down the aisle, tall in her high heels and dazzling in an electric blue dress to set her eyes sparkling. She looked terrific. Even the people she passed, all dressed in their best attire, looked up at this vision of wealth and privilege. She seemed to fool everyone in the room but Steve.

"Is this your client, Mr. Michaels?"

"Yes, Your Honor."

"Very well, let's get started," the judge said, pulling off her glasses. "Mr. Forrest, I see you've added two last-minute requests, one for a court-appointed guardian *ad litem* to make the children's wishes known to the court and the other for a psychological evaluation of the emotional health of your children. If I'm reading this correctly, both are to be paid by you."

Susan had just sat down beside her lawyer, scooping her dress so it wouldn't crease beneath her. Her practiced smile froze as the judge's words sank in. Steve could hear the benches squeak behind him as people leaned forward, anticipating a show.

Susan looked to her lawyer and then to the judge and finally back to her lawyer. It wasn't clear who she was addressing when she finally spoke.

"Psychological evaluation!"

"Mrs. Forrest," the judge said, her glasses swinging from her fingers, "the absence of such outbursts in this courtroom is appreciated. Mr. Forrest," she resumed, turning to Steve, "would you explain your reasoning behind these requests?"

Steve pulled himself up by his cane. He didn't intend to make a show of it, but the lawyer in him got the better of him, and he winced strategically.

"Certainly, Your Honor," he said, clearing his throat. "As things stand, I believe my children's true wishes have not been heard, and, due to this, an independent evaluation of those wishes could only help to determine an outcome favorable to their welfare. It is also my understanding that custody proceedings strongly impact the future emotional health of children involved. Accordingly, it is my express wish to mitigate this potential negative influence on my children to the greatest extent possible."

Steve glanced at Susan as he sat down with a little grunt, but she had brushed a wave of hair to the side of her face, repositioning it to screen herself from his view as she spoke into her lawyer's ear. Mr. Michaels nodded and stood up to face the judge.

"Your Honor, my client has suffered considerable emotional abuse from her former husband throughout their marriage. She feels the requests raised are simply a continuation of such abuse."

Steve knew it was paramount to remain composed. An outburst from him could be misinterpreted and feed into Susan's claim, but it wasn't easy. It was an unjust attack as far as he was concerned.

"I see," the judge said. She looked from Steve to Susan and then down at the folder, slipping on her glasses. "Mr. Forrest, it seems your former wife feels these requests are an attack on her person, and not motivated by concern for your children."

A flurry of whispering could be heard between Susan and her lawyer. A moment later, Mr. Michaels cleared his throat to get the judge's attention.

"Yes, Mr. Michaels?"

"Your Honor, my client would like to interject that she has seen little concern for the children's welfare by her former husband at any point in their marriage."

"Mr. Forrest, how do you respond?"

It took all Steve's willpower to hold his tongue. Outrage flowed through his veins like acid. All of a sudden, he was his old self, ready to throw a bombshell into the proceedings to get revenge. If Susan was going to play dirty, he'd play dirtier. He'd make her pay.

"Well, Mr. Forrest?"

Steve saw it in a flash of recognition, and everything changed in an instant. It was a hideous, ferocious thing hiding behind his pride, his sense of injustice and his sudden, blind hatred of his former wife. He had finally met his ego, and once he recognized it, looked into its eyes and saw it for what it was, it popped like a balloon pricked by a needle.

"Mr. Forrest?"

"Yes?"

"How do you respond?"

Steve wasn't sure he could even form a sentence. He had just undergone a defining moment in his life, a firm step toward enlightenment, in one of the most inopportune settings imaginable.

"Your Honor," Steve said, struggling with his words, "all I can say is circumstances within the last four months have led to profound changes in my life. I can assure you these requests are motivated purely by my love for my children."

The judge stared at Steve for what seemed minutes. "Mr. Forrest, being that you decided to represent yourself, would you please approach the bench with Mr. Michaels?"

Steve floated over to the bench as light as a flame. Somehow he felt if the power went out and the room went dark, everyone would see him glow.

The judge pulled down her glasses and stared Steve straight in the eyes. "I know who you are," she said between her teeth so no one but Mr. Michaels could hear. "Is this a performance or am I supposed to believe this?"

"No, Your Honor, sorry, I mean yes, Your Honor," Steve said. What he blurted out next seemed perfectly reasonable at that moment. "I had a near-death experience…I saw a Light!"

The judge stared at him before responding. "As I understand it," she finally said, not looking amused, "a near-death experience is nothing more than hallucinations brought on by a shortage of oxygen to a dying brain."

Steve wanted to argue the point, but he stopped himself, realizing the mistake he made. He was in court and had to behave accordingly.

"Mr. Forrest," the judge continued, bending in a little closer, "based on your reputation, I have to take into account these requests are based on some attempt at an arcane manipulation of the law; and, I assure you, I won't allow that to happen here."

"But—"

"Please return to your seats."

The judge addressed the court as Steve and Mr. Michaels carved a path back to their respective seats.

"I'm going to reschedule disposition in this custody suit," the judge ordered, flipping the folder closed. "Mrs. Forrest, you are directed to confer with your counsel to come up with a reasonable argument to convince me why a guardian *ad litem* and a psychological evaluation of your children are unacceptable, especially since your former husband has agreed to pay the cost. The court clerk will set a date for your next hearing."

Susan buzzed past Steve in a flurry of metallic blue as the court clerk called up the next case. She turned her head just enough to flip him an eye of fiery malice.

167

******

Steve assumed he was rid of his ego, but it wasn't long before he caught a glimpse of it again. He was at work, deep in prep work on the Inchelium case, copying documents of toxins measured in Lake Roosevelt when he caught sight of Katherine throwing him a look of disdain. He wanted to confront her then and there, and he almost did. The bellicose words were on his tongue, ready to fire. He only just caught himself, realizing it was his ego trying to gain back control.

It felt like a setback until Steve realized it wasn't the banishment of his ego but its recognition that mattered most. His enemy was in sight, and maybe now he'd be mindful of his actions and deeds. He felt reasonably confident he'd be able to distinguish the self-serving tongue through the inflection in its tone and the sensation in his body. It would no longer have free rein to do what it pleased.

Steve wound his way through the confusion of Chinatown, entering the shop with the address Jack had written down. The room was split down the middle by a counter that spanned the length of the cramped, dimly lit space. Behind the counter was a wall of jars stacked on shelving one on top of the other all the way to the ceiling. They were filled with powders and seeds and tubers and what looked like bark, ranging the chromatic spectrum from red to yellow to green to blue and every shade of brown imaginable.

Steve got a little buzz from the bouquet of scents. He didn't even notice the stick-thin figure with the mop of black hair until it addressed him point-blank from across the counter.

"Welcome to Grandfather's store, Mr. Forrest."

"Michael," Steve said, the hair on his arms standing on end. "Good to see you again."

168

Master Feng's grandson stood in front of the wall of jars, his skin having taken on a kaleidoscopic hue.

"So this is what a traditional Chinese medicine shop looks like?"

"Yes."

"What's in those jars?"

"Prescription medicines Grandfather gives to his patients."

"Oh," Steve said, scanning the rows. "Do they work?"

"They are very potent medicines," Michael said. "Some have been in use for thousands of years."

Steve was startled again when he noticed a second figure standing in a doorframe behind the counter. Michael flipped open a section of countertop when Master Feng gestured Steve to follow.

Steve found himself in a long, narrow room with a wooden plank floor. It was highly polished and inlaid with the yin-yang symbol in the center. Several people were there, including Jack. At the back of the room others stood silent in a series of alcoves, likenesses in long, flowing robes. The half sized statuettes retained a dignity in pose as they gazed upon the living.

"What are those?" Steve said, pointing to the back of the room.

"Much revered masters of Taoism from ages past," Jack replied, standing with his legs slightly bent, breathing in through the nose and out through the mouth.

The others present were dressed in loose-fitting Chinese-style clothing. As Steve watched, they changed from a relaxed standing squat position to bouncing on their toes, arms jerking loosely at their sides.

"Master Feng has asked me to teach you '*wuji* standing,'" Jack said, talking softly so not to disturb the others.

"W*uji* standing?"

"It's the beginning stance for all Qigong," Jack said, limbering up. "Let's get started. Maybe later we can join the others."

Steve was directed to stand with his feet parallel to each other and shoulder width apart. Jack circled him, adding further instructions, some of which seemed peculiar.

"Now rest your tongue softly on the roof of your mouth."

They never did get a chance to join the others. *Wuji* proved more difficult than it looked. It took more than half an hour for Steve to achieve something that remotely satisfied Jack. He tried to maintain the pose, letting his arms dangle from their sides as instructed, but he was distracted by Master Feng.

******

"That was strange," Steve said as he and Jack passed a storefront with a paper dragon hanging on wires, staring out at them with cunning malice.

"One's first encounter with Qigong is always a culture shock," Jack said. "What did you find particularly strange?"

"The light moving over Master Feng's hands."

In the soft light of the room, Steve had detected a faint light radiating from the spotted old hands, a bluish glow flashing on the fingertips.

Jack stopped dead in the gathering dusk and stared down at Steve. "You saw a light?"

"Yes, moving over Master Feng's hands."

Jack continued to stare down at Steve with a growing look of surprise. "You can see *qi*?"

"That's *qi*?"

All at once Jack bounded forward with renewed energy. Steve had to hustle to keep up the pace. Soon they passed under the stylized arch that marked the boundary of Chinatown.

"I've read of others who've had a near-death experience talk of seeing auras and chakras," Jack said, three paces ahead, arms gesticulating. "It's not technically unheard of."

"It isn't?"

"Auras and chakras and *qi* are all forms of energy," Jack said, stopping to wait for Steve hurrying behind with his cane. "Will you be able to make it next Tuesday?"

"No."

"No?"

"I'll be in Inchelium."

"Oh, yes, the case," Jack said, looking disappointed. "Bringing the kids?"

"No," Steve said. "I don't dare ask Susan after what happened at court."

The two moved on at a more leisurely pace.

"Ask the children's opinion on the matter," Jack said. "Grandparents have legal rights too. If the kids want to see their grandmother, Susan may have little choice in the matter."

******

Steve set up shop at Steemus. Centrally located, the restaurant proved an ideal spot to gather information. He hoped the menu might also lubricate the lips of the locals, but he needn't have worried. Amassed in a couple of days was a thick pile of affidavits on health issues related to toxins found in Lake Roosevelt as well as all sorts of other information that could be used to move the case forward. Accuracy of information was guaranteed. Those who listened in to the ones being interviewed were quick to point out extraneous facts or add pertinent details.

171

Breakfast proved the most rewarding time of day for information gathering. Heads were as yet uncluttered by the day's events. The community was more disposed to answer questions with candor while slurping down the first coffee of the day. Lunchtime was better employed in verifying evidence obtained at breakfast. Steve would return at suppertime to listen to discussions taking place around him, by then too groggy from the day's grease-laden grub to get much accomplished.

By the end of the week, Steve relocated to Sally's kitchen table to sort out all the information. He discovered patterns. For example, those who swam or fished in the lake had a higher percentage of health problems than those with minimal contact. Symptoms ranged from rashes to malaise and from lymphoma to cardiovascular disease. Diabetes was a common complaint, but that could have been more a question of diet, making it harder to prove.

Steve and his mother spent the evenings chatting, just the two of them. They discussed everything. No topic was off limits.

"What's Qigong?"

"Part of traditional Chinese medicine," Steve explained. "It's a series of slow movements that enhance the flow of *qi*."

"Think it'd do my arthritis any good?"

They talked about the past, slowly working their way further back. It wasn't long before all the worst memories of his father's drunkenness came up for discussion. Sally didn't shy away from the topic no matter how upsetting it must've been for her. It wasn't easy for either of them, especially that first week, but what was initially painful became therapeutic. The result of their nightly discussions was a deepening understanding and the planting of a seed of forgiveness for the father Steve always thought he despised.

The nightly discussions took on a more spiritual tone as the first week drew to a close. Mostly Steve talked and Sally listened. She seemed particularly interested in the story of meeting his ego face to face, wanting to hear every detail. He hesitated telling her of the bluish light moving over Master Feng's hands, but she sensed he was keeping something from her and prodded him until he gave in.

The night before his last day in Inchelium, Sally suggested he go visit old Tom Louie. Steve hadn't heard that name since a kid. Frankly, he was surprised to hear the old man was still alive.

"How old is he now?"

"Not sure," Sally said, clearing the dishes. "No one is, maybe not even Tom. They didn't keep good records back then like they do now."

The next morning, Steve called the number his mother wrote down for him, mostly out of a sense of curiosity. It was picked up on the second ring.

"Free this morning, boy?"

"Yes," Steve said, not having as yet introduced himself.

"There's a nice tender two-point buck that'll be waiting up in the Loomis high country for me 'bout ten o'clock. Think you can get here no later than nine?"

Steve didn't know what to make of this. "Are we going hunting?"

"Nah, we're going to kill a two-point buck. Can you make it?"

"I don't—"

"Need help loading 'im in the truck…not so young no more."

Steve held onto the handset after the line went dead, not sure what just happened.

"Was that Tom you talking to?" Sally said, sweeping the kitchen linoleum.

"I think I'm supposed to meet a two-point buck."

173

"That what Tom said?"

"Wants me there by nine."

Sally leaned the broom against a wall and shuffled off to the bedroom. "I'll see what old clothes I can dig out of your father's," she said. "You'd better hurry. The back roads to Tonasket aren't as good as 'round here."

The drive to Tonasket wasn't too bad. It was when Steve turned off onto Tom's long, winding driveway that the trouble started. The Honda's pan thumped on rocks, and the tires kept spinning out on sand. Steve switched the gear stick from third to second, pressing on the gas, fearing he'd stall on the steep grade, all the while keeping an eye on the oil pressure warning light. When he cleared the hill he passed what was once a washing machine before parking close to an old beat-up Chevy pickup where a scattering of dog bones was strewn about.

Steve was on his hands and knees looking up at the pan when a voice called out.

"Hit a rock?"

Shuffling over was a stooped old man with a head full of liver spots, purple on the walnut skin. He wore a leather scabbard with buckskin fringe slung over a shoulder. Steve stood up, scratching at a tingling sensation in his lower belly.

"Well, c'mon then, we'll look at it when we get back," Tom said, moving towards the battered old pickup. "When a buck's ready to give himself up, you'd better be there to receive it."

Steve stared at the old pickup. "How long do you think this'll take?"

"Not more than a couple of minutes, but getting there's an hour."

Tom pulled open the door of the pickup and carefully placed the scabbard barrel end down. Steve stood by his Honda, stalling as the old man revved up the engine,

174

the pickup disappearing underneath a cloud of blue exhaust.

"Coming?"

Steve took a leap of faith. Hurrying, he got into the passenger side, feeling around for a seatbelt. Tom put the pickup in reverse, swung it around and started off. They barreled down the steep drive like skiers racing down moguls. Steve hit his head on the headliner twice. He held on as best he could after that, not knowing what he had gotten himself into, chasing down a phantom buck with a man almost too old to be alive.

******

Tom pulled over to the side of the mountain road at two minutes to ten. He reached down and slid the Winchester out of the scabbard. Easing the door open, he crabbed forward in a crouch with only his head above the hood. Slowly, he raised the rifle to the hood and sighted down the barrel.

Steve looked down to the clearing where Tom had the rifle pointed. He saw nothing but dog-hair lodgepole pines.

"Ten o'clock," Tom whispered.

Steve looked down at his watch. When he looked back up a buck had moved into the clearing, gazing up at the pickup with big black eyes. He would never forget how the buck turned to its side as if offering the greatest surface area for a fatal shot just before the rifle roared.

"Okay, let's get 'im," Tom said.

The old man laid the rifle on the seat of the pickup and pulled out a hatchet, tarp and skinning knife from the bed. Steve made his way down into the clearing where the buck lay wheezing, its side rising and falling in gasps. Tom squatted beside it, laying a hand on the heaving chest.

Raising his eyes to the sky, he began to sing, a plaintive wail rising to the crowns of the trees.

Steve stood off to the side, watching this Salish shaman singing a eulogy to a dying buck. The buck's shudders slowed, and then stopped altogether. At that moment Tom looked skyward, searching for something. Steve followed his gaze. Sixty feet above their heads a raven lit gently onto the swaying crown of a larch.

"That's good," the old man whispered.

A second raven flew in and landed next to the first.

"They're looking for the gut ball," Tom said, pulling himself stiffly to his feet. "Help me roll 'im onto his back."

Steve didn't want to touch it but bent down and did what he was told.

"Hold 'im right there now, and we'll get 'im gutted and ready to skin," Tom said. "Gotta work fast…meat don't last long in this heat."

Tom's skill with a skinning knife was immediately apparent. His strokes were sure and swift. In no time, he rolled the steaming, stinking gut ball out onto the needle-strewn forest floor. Steve brought a hand to his mouth in nausea, but it was stained in blood. He wiped his hands on his father's old trousers instead, determined not to disgrace himself.

Tom picked up the hatchet, and in no time had the anal canal disposed of.

"Soon as I get 'em legs chopped off, I'll start skinning, working to the belly to get the meat cooled off as fast as possible. You go find a straight stick 'bout this long and this big 'round," Tom said, using his bloodied hands to describe what he wanted.

Steve hadn't taken more than five steps when he almost tripped over the perfect sized stick, exactly what he was asked to find. He brought it back to Tom who took it from him and thrust it into the buck's chest, propping open the rib cage.

Together they dragged the buck onto the waiting tarp. Steve's job was to pull tight on the buck's skin as the old man sliced away. The skin peeled off like sticky tape. What was left of the buck gleamed in the sun.

"Okay," Tom said, dragging a sleeve across his spotted forehead, "leave the hide here and grab the buck's horn 'long with a corner of the tarp, and we'll pull 'im up to the truck. Got that?"

The buck might've freely given itself up, but moving its mass proved a difficult task. It took all Steve's strength to pull the dead weight up the hill. He was trying to take the brunt of the load to ease the old man's share of the burden while balancing on his cane.

"Okay, hold on," Tom said, wheezing, as he pulled down the battered tailgate.

Together they lifted and heaved the buck up into the bed and pushed it to the back. Steve leaned against the pickup to catch his breath while Tom strode off to retrieve the hide, coming back with it rolled into a neat bundle. He tossed it into the back with the carcass while Steve went to fetch the hatchet, skinning knife and sheath.

"There's a small stream down the road where we can wash off the blood," Tom said, looking satisfied with himself.

Steve looked at his watch as he approached the bloody hatchet. It was twenty past ten.

******

Steve marched into Justice for the Earth with all the affidavits, copies of photographs of skin anomalies and dead fish floating on the surface of Lake Roosevelt, which the people of Inchelium had the presence of mind to take over the years. He had with him an outline of potential

177

ways in which to move the case forward. It had all been organized into separate folders and neatly titled. He was proud of the work, but what would the partners think of it?

Steve long ago concluded that Brian was so dedicated to the environment and saving it from the hands of man that sometimes his passion overruled his sense, and he would ride roughshod over anyone who didn't frame the environmental debate in the same terms he did. Although not proud of it, it was a weakness Steve had utilized against him in court. All he would have to do was rile Brian and the man would always overplay his hand. The tactic worked every time.

Steve hadn't heard anything from anyone at the office that day. He sat at his desk trying to look busy while Brian and the others convened together out of earshot. It was only when he was heading out the door on his way home that he had gotten his answer. Katherine murmured 'good night' to him. Those two simple words confirmed that a mammoth change had taken place. He had passed the environmental test. His prickly coworkers had accepted him as one of their own.

******

Jack showed up the next day. Steve plunged into the story of the buck, having waited the whole week for the opportunity to tell it. Jack looked captivated holding a cup of Saturday morning herbal tea, drinking in every word.

"What did you do with the carcass?"

The bamboo was flourishing. New shoots had burst from the earth, safely inside the metal edging. It was a wonder how tall they were already, but underneath this backdrop the back yard was abloom in weeds, fighting for autumn dominance. The harvested shoots lay where they were stacked and were now starting to caramelize in the sun.

178

"We took it to a grocer friend of Tom's who had a cooler big enough to accommodate it. He said it'd hang there for ten days before he'd butcher and wrap it. Apparently, that's the time it takes for the meat to reach a perfect state of tenderness."

"Interesting," Jack said, blowing on his tea. "But how could he have known about the encounter with the buck before it happened?"

"He said he had a power dream."

"A power dream?"

"That's what I was told," Steve said, knowing he had Jack's full attention. "It's a certain type of dream Tom has when his totem visits, telling him things."

"Fascinating."

"I may have had one myself."

"Oh?"

It wouldn't be long before Steve and Jack would have to take their conversations indoors. The winter rains were blowing in from the ocean, and it was getting a little too cool to sit out on lawn chairs.

"That night, after I got back to Sally's, I had this luminous, unsettling dream unlike any dream I've had before."

"Continue."

"I was in the high woods again, but this time without Tom. I was standing on the very spot the buck was shot when it pranced up to me with pride, its black eyes sparkling. It spoke so softly, like...I don't know—"

"Bamboo?"

"More like the rustle of aspens."

"What did it say?"

"It asked me why I'd question its offering itself to a shaman. It said it was an honor to give itself as sustenance to such a man. It seemed puzzled why I didn't respond the way I should, with the person I truly was, to the bond between it and the hunter."

179

Jack took a slow sip of tea. "Totems are associated with Native American shamanism, if I'm not mistaken, spirit ancestors that guide their kin in life."

"That's my understanding."

"They're known to take the form of an animal, aren't they?"

"Yes," Steve said, recalling the stories he had heard as a kid.

"An individual can have multiple totems, but only one is the 'totem animal,' the one that bonds with the individual and stays with him or her through life."

"Yes."

"Do you have a totem animal?"

"No," Steve admitted.

"Then you couldn't have had a true power dream, not like Tom's, at any rate." Jack took another sip of tea before continuing. "What happened next in the dream?"

"The buck bowed its head with the most beautiful arch of the neck, and I touched its forehead. It bowed three more times, slowly, majestically, pawing the earth with its hooves. It faded away after that, and I woke up in a cold sweat."

"Did you talk to Tom about the dream?"

"I called that morning."

"What did he say?"

Steve had a suspicion that Jack knew exactly what Tom had said. "He asked me whether I'd gone on a spirit quest as a kid. When I said no, he recommended I prepare for one over the winter, that I should see him as often as possible and participate in several sweats."

"Sweats?" Jack said, excitedly. "You mean a ceremonial sauna performed in a sweat lodge?"

"Yup, that," Steve confirmed. "He also suggested I go up to the spirit rocks on Black Mountain before I attempt a spirit quest."

"Spirit rocks?" Jack said, like a kid being handed an ice-cream cone.

Steve had to smile. "About two-thirds up the trail to the summit of Black Mountain is a scree slope. Near its base against an old Douglas fir is this wall of rocks that generations of Indians have added to."

"You don't say?"

"I can tell you the place gave me the willies the one time I got to see it," Steve said, "but that was when I was a kid," he added, pulling the sleeves of his sweatshirt over his fists as he brought his knees to his chest. "Jack?"

"Yes?"

"When I first saw Tom, I got this tingling sensation—"

"Just below the navel," Jack interjected, "about two to four inches inside your body."

"How do you—"

"It's called the *dan t'ian* in Chinese and the *hara* in Japanese. Western medicine refers to it as the enteric nervous system. Not only does this system receive and process neurotransmitter signals from the brain, but it also generates its own neurotransmitters and sends them to the brain. In other words, it runs independently, a second brain, if you will. Of course, the discovery was greeted with gales of laughter from the East."

"Why?"

"Because it's long been known there," Jack said. "It's where the 'ocean of *qi*' resides in the human body."

Steve sat contemplating the information, his hands now buried between his thighs.

"Cold?"

"No," Steve said. "My hands have been bothering me for weeks."

"Since when?"

"Don't know…just before I left for Inchelium."

181

"Since your first Qigong class?" Jack said. "Describe the feeling."

Steve had trouble describing it, putting it into words. "It's like a buzzing pressure in the center of each palm. It gets stronger and weaker through the day, but it's always there."

Jack shook his head, smiling. "I can hardly believe it—all from just one class."

"What?"

"It takes us mere mortals eight or ten years to get to that point even with diligent practice," Jack said, shaking his head in disbelief. "The centers of your palms are the *lao gon* points in t'ai chi and Qigong. These points respond to *qi* flow into and out of the body."

Steve pulled his hands from his sleeves, looking at his palms, while Jack reclined back in his lawn chair and closed his eyes in wait.

"I stopped in to see Denise on the way home from Inchelium."

"Did you?" Jack said, smiling at the sky. "How's she doing?"

"She's tending bar in Ellensburg, living a Spartan life to save up enough to head back to Alpental when the snow flies, so she says."

"How does she look?"

"Sexed up," Steve said, unable to hold his tongue, "lots of cleavage and midriff showing."

"You don't approve?"

Steve snorted. "She shouldn't be wearing high heels at this stage in her recovery. She just got out of a wheelchair, Jack."

"How did she act toward you?"

"Warmly, but—"

"But what?" Jack said, turning to Steve.

"I don't know," Steve said, shaking his head. "It was like she was putting on a performance for the men in

182

the bar—me included—using her sexuality to draw attention."

Jack slowly got up from the lawn chair. He stepped off the deck. Circling the bamboo stacked in the middle of the yard much like a Tibetan lama circles a *stupa*, he locked his hands behind his back and spoke. "It's dangerous to psychoanalyze. Although what we see in others is indicative of something else, something deeper, these signs are not cut and dried facts. They're clues. People, unfortunately, don't fit into convenient psychological profiles. Let's not judge until we know more."

Steve nodded in agreement. "I think I'll try to stop in and see her when I can on my way back and forth from Inchelium."

"Good idea," Jack said, plucking a leaf from a weed and raising it to his nostrils.

Chapter Six

Days later, as Steve was leaving for work, the phone rang just as he was about to pass it on his way out the door. He remembered staring at it a moment, sensing trouble. The voice on the other end of the line made a simple request. Steve agreed and hung up. That day an escalating sense of apprehension grew inside him. By the time he left work, he was a wreck.

When Jack finally showed up the following Saturday—unannounced as usual—Steve had dark circles under his eyes.

"Tom Louie wants me to spend Halloween night alone at the spirit rocks!"

They couldn't sit outdoors, not on such a blustery day. Rain was slashing the windows, the bamboo thrashing wildly in the wind. It was as miserable outside as Steve was inside.

"How exciting," Jack said, pulling off his raincoat, undeterred by the deluge.

Steve stood leaning into the cane for emotional support, shaken by the thought of this looming ordeal he had agreed to embark on before thinking it through.

"What're you afraid of?" Jack said, hanging up the raincoat.

Steve stared at Jack in disbelief.

"There's an old Zen saying," Jack finally said, walking past Steve and into the kitchen. "Doubt and confusion are the beginnings of wisdom.'"

"I believe you used that one on me before," Steve said, standing by the kitchen door. "I appreciate your Zen sayings, Jack...I really do, but they're not always the most encouraging."

Jack grabbed a box of herbal tea from the pantry. Opening it, he breathed it in before placing it on the counter

184

and picking up the kettle. "Have I told you the translation of the Zen-Christian monastery I was ordained in?"

"Shinmeikutsu?" Steve said, having to speak up to be heard over the faucet.

Jack placed the kettle on the stove. "Which dial do I turn?"

Steve limped over and turned on the gas. "What's the translation?"

"Cave of Divine Darkness."

"And what's your point?"

"Well, first of all," Jack said, retrieving two mismatched cups from the cupboard, "you have to be familiar with the writings of John of the Cross."

"Who?"

"John of the Cross," Jack reiterated. "He was an independent-minded sixteenth century priest later canonized by, I believe, Pope Benedict XIII."

"John of the Cross is a saint?"

"He is, indeed," Jack said, crossing his arms and leaning his weight into the counter. "*Dark Night of the Soul* is a treatise of sorts he wrote of a journey a soul takes after plunging into a dark night. The point of the treatise is that several steps had to be taken before a union was reached with the Creator."

Steve moved to the kitchen table, another thrift-shop find. He pulled out one of the chairs, the backs of which were shaped like a crest. It was an old-fashioned cumbersome set that had stood the test of time. Through the windows, the mid-October torrent persisted, hosing down the city.

"The protagonist of the story had to undergo this terrible, depressing sort of cleansing process known in Christian circles as *kenosis*, an 'emptying out,' through apophatic or dark contemplation, before being permitted admittance to the presence of God."

"Why?"

185

"To shed that which held back admittance."

Steve shook his head, unable to grasp the correlation. "I don't suppose there's a Zen parallel to 'dark night of the soul?'"

The kettle started to sing. Jack lifted it off the burner and poured out two cups of steaming hot herbal tea.

"As a matter of fact, there is."

"Oh?"

"It's called 'dying on your cushion,' and it's quite similar to the Christian concept, but apophatic contemplation is not easily understood," Jack said, placing the cups on the table. "Think of it as a 'dazzling darkness.'"

"Dazzling darkness?"

"Yes," Jack said, sitting down beside his troubled student. "God is everywhere. He exists in the dark as well as the light. Does that make sense?"

"Yes."

"And God is found by not looking for him."

"What?"

"Don't understand?"

"No."

"Many don't," Jack admitted, dabbing his pinky in the cup to test the temperature. "In apophatic theology, God is not a common object to be found like a set of house keys."

"So God cannot be found?"

"Wrong!"

"How then?"

"Through apophatic contemplation or, if you will, Zen meditation."

Steve raised his cup and stared at the wisps of steam. "What was it in this treatise that held back admittance to the presence of God?"

"Ego, of course," Jack said. "I suspect the terror you've been feeling is rooted in your ego."

Steve stared down at the dregs floating on the surface.

"It fears being subjected to the 'dazzling darkness' of a night of contemplation at the spirit rocks. It fears being exposed. It fears most of all death; its death, not yours. Your ego's a liar. It will try to convince you that a threat to it is a threat to you."

Steve closed his eyes and searched for that devil inside him, the desperation it emitted. He realized that Jack was right. His ego was mounting an all-out assault in its attempt to stop him from spending Halloween night at the spirit rocks, and he was almost tempted to let it win.

******

Steve drove past a scraggly jack pine whose miserable whorl of branches looked like arms warning against advance. He passed it with a sense of doom, sporting the fluorescent orange vest Tom suggested he wear.

"Nuttin' flies faster than bullets through the backwoods in huntin' season," the old man said into the receiver. "You don't wanna be mistaken for a buck."

They were in almost daily contact that last week. Tom would call early in the morning as Steve was preparing to leave for work. As if secretly allied, Jack would show up at the door most evenings soon after Steve arrived home. Together, the two helped prepare him for the night at the spirit rocks. He needed all the help he could get.

Pintsized gangs of ghosts, zombies, witches and ghouls had passed Steve's house on their way to school that morning, stopping in front of Lila's. Her plot of grass had been transformed into a graveyard for the better part of a week, each cutout gravestone filled in with names and dates

187

so the neighborhood kids had to venture close to see if their names were on them.

By lunchtime, most of the kids had abandoned their bed sheets and rubbery masks, but as Steve headed out the door with the last of his gear, he had come upon a lone Indian no more than three feet tall. The little warrior stood gawking at him from the sidewalk, a plastic tomahawk in hand. The encounter unsettled him, staying with him as he drove up into the mountains.

Steve's heart raced in time with the gears of the Honda as he turned up toward the Black Mountain trailhead. There wasn't a car on the road except his. All the same, a gnawing feeling persisted. He felt a malevolent presence and kept looking in the rearview mirror, expecting to see a pair of menacing eyes.

The road climbed steadily higher. For a time Steve convinced himself he was lost, but he soon spotted the turnoff. He parked the car at the head of the trail and dragged out his pack, shrugging it on after stowing the car keys safely inside. Daylight was fading. It smelled like snow.

Trudging up the trail with the help of the cane, Steve rounded a bend and stepped out onto a bright splash of gold blanketing a thin layer of soil.

"Larch needles," he said to himself, risking a smile.

A flash of white made his heart skip a beat. Steve breathed only after recognizing the whitetail flags of the deer in the woods, waving as they raced away, their hooves thumping lightly on a thick bed of needles.

Steve followed a footpath into the trees. He wound his way through fragrant woods, humming an improvised tune. A scree slope met him on the other side, lit by the last rays of daylight, fading as he made his way up toward it. At its base stood the black, mangled trunk of a heavily scarred, ancient Douglas fir flanked by a wall of rocks that spanned from its sides like wings. It was just as he remembered it.

He got to work, pulling on a fleece sweater and then a parka, the fluorescent vest having been stuffed inside the pack. It was unearthly quiet. In the silence he spread out a tarp and secured it with rocks. Next, he unfolded a cloth chair and pulled out his half bag. Wriggling into it as soundlessly as he could, he kept an eye on the quickly fading woods.

Steve sat in the chair bundled in the half bag and mittens, staring up at the shrine erected by his forebears. The rocks had been placed with care, selected for size and shape, guaranteeing future stability. He could almost sense the ghosts of the people who built it, old and young, each having added a single rock.

"Maybe this won't be so bad," Steve muttered to himself.

A bird screeched in answer.

Steve had his long dead grandmother to thank for encouraging him to familiarize himself with bird calls. "Just a Steller's jay…nothing to worry about."

He caught movement high on the scree slope. It seemed to be made up of a number of shadows, one noticeably larger. Logic dictated it must be a buck trailing some does, but he couldn't fathom how they could move without making a sound on such a precarious slope of stones.

The mountainside faded until it finally disappeared altogether. Shortly thereafter a ghostly light from a gibbous moon washed over the spirit rocks. It flickered like a candle as clouds scudded across it. From nowhere, a breeze rushed up the mountain, adding to the chill. Steve pulled out a wool cap and dragged it over his ears.

Closing his eyes, Steve started to meditate, determined to stay in control. The minutes stretched out as he allowed his fears free reign, something both Tom and Jack had encouraged he do. He confronted them head on

189

and almost attained a sense of serenity when a deep, thundering clang shook the mountain.

It took Steve an hour to regain a level of composure, to focus on the reason he came up here in the first place. All the same, he couldn't work out what could've made such a sound. He finally decided it was none of his business, that the only thing he should be concerned with was surviving the night.

The hours passed in a state of angst. Steve didn't know what he was supposed to do. Neither Tom nor Jack had enlightened him on that particular point. He felt too cold to continue to meditate and had to remind himself of the many nights he had spent in freezing bivouacs. Finally, cramped in the chair, he fell into an uneasy sleep.

Steve suddenly found himself standing frozen in the half bag, bombarded by snapping noises he couldn't begin to explain away. The moon had disappeared. The sky was inky black. As he deliberated whether to blindly dig for his headlamp, the strange snapping sounds shifted behind him like a predator stalking its prey.

A second sound emerged from the night, a sound like nothing he could rationally account for. It could only be described as a heavy, abrasive skulking sound like an immense snake-like creature's skin rasping against the tangle of lodgepole pines that edged the woods below him. He was about to call out he didn't know what when his throat clamped shut. Something else had entered the arena of this living nightmare. It overpowered everything as it roared up the mountainside. All he could do was brace for impact.

When it hit, the blast knocked him flat on the tarp. Hail started to beat on him, and he covered his head with the hood of the parka, not knowing what else to do. He decided to try to make a run for it, but as he pushed up a lightning bolt flashed, and for a split second he caught sight of a coiling shape swirling in the hailstorm before him.

Steve screamed in terror. He fell back on his buttocks and kicked out of the half bag, bumping into his pack. Grabbing it by the straps, he swung it with all his strength, hoping to beat the apparition back, but the pack only glanced off the hail. As he tried to swing the pack a second time, an icy grip encircled his wrist.

Steve snatched his arm back and started to scuttle away on his elbows, tears streaming down his cheeks. Something bore down on him as he tried to get to his feet. He shot out his hands to shield himself, and his mittens flew off, exposing a bluish light flickering on his fingertips.

Steve forced himself to stand up straight, steadying himself on the rocks. He spread out his legs and let his arms fall to the sides, bending his knees ever so slightly, beginning the sweep of Qigong. Soon his breathing began to stabilize and his mind started to clear. He could feel a warming in his palms.

"I will not succumb to fear," he declared to the night.

The snapping started up again with renewed energy. Steve continued to sweep his arms the way he was taught, piecing together phantom words coming from the snaps. It seemed a debate was taking place. It was as if each rock stacked on the wall were offering an opinion. The storm abated as the snapping slowed. When Steve next opened his eyes, a shaft of moonlight had penetrated the clouds, and the spirit rocks were set aglow.

The voice spoke with hollow clarity. "Welcome, warrior brave, warrior son."

An overwhelming thirst came over Steve as he stood there, staring at the spirit rocks. He bent to his knees and scooped his hands together as if gathering water from a stream. He drank it up and could feel the *qi* washing over and into him. His whole body started to warm.

The spirit rocks dimmed as the first snowflakes fell. "Sleep now."

191

Steve retrieved his mittens and moved to the tarp, shaking out the hail.

"Tonight we shelter you from harm."

After laying down on the tarp, Steve stared up at the dancing snowflakes. Not one seemed to touch his face. His eyes closed at the exact moment the moon disappeared, and he fell into a deep sleep in the dazzling darkness.

******

Steve was thinking back to Black Mountain while he peeked out through the purple polka dot curtain panels Lila had sewn up for the living room windows—at the small flock of Canadian Jays that had tracked him down the mountain that morning, chirring softly, skipping from tree to tree, while black-capped chickadees, hanging upside-down, whistled from firs, disturbing the snow that had dusted the boughs in the night.

Steve made his way down in what could only be described as a hallowed enchantment that abruptly fractured when he turned a bend and came upon a big black wolf blocking the path. Before he had a chance to react, the wolf had turned into the trees, stopping once to look back before fading into the shadows. Even though he could vividly recall the snowflakes that dappled the guard hairs on its back and its ferocious predator stare, he started to question whether the encounter happened at all.

Tom thought it significant, regardless. When he called that week, Tom hadn't seemed interested in hearing details of what went down at the spirit rocks. He dismissed it like he already knew. The old shaman had been far more interested in hearing about the lightness Steve felt as he descended the mountain and the meeting with the wolf. After answering his questions, Tom wished him a good one and hung up.

Emotional tides turned the week following the spirit rocks. Steve's mind would wander on the most trivial things, like a puddle he had spotted in front of his house that kept resurfacing in his mind. He imagine how it would always reform when someone stepped into it or brushed it with a shoe, but, in the end, how it would vanish into vapor, becoming the air he breathed. He thought he could still pick up its blueberry-scented waft.

While flipping through the Lake Roosevelt photographs, Steve had come upon one of a school of fish, floating dead by the shore. It might not have been a school at all; the lake currents could have simply brought them together in death—a little toxic graveyard for the birds to scavenge. It was the pearl color of the collective stare that had gotten to him, haunting his dreams.

The day before his kids were to arrive it had suddenly occurred to Steve that he might be simply manifesting the emotions of the moody change in climate. The rubbery heaviness of his limbs seemed to echo the torpor of the autumn clouds, his tears the rain. He became so preoccupied in analyzing this new discovery that it hadn't occurred to him that he no longer needed the cane, mindlessly using it to probe carpets of colored leaves to and from work, curious to see what lay beneath.

The SUV moved down the street like a Hippo in a river. Steve made his way out the door determined to say nothing of the energy-cow Susan chose to drive their kids in. He could just imagine Talitha innocently ratting him out. Better to keep his mouth shut, he thought.

KariLyn was the first out. She ran up to her father and wrapped him in an embrace before he even got to the sidewalk. His son appeared beside him with a backpack slung over a shoulder. Steve messed up his hair.

"Hey, dad…what's up?"

Talitha squirmed her way into the middle of the three and jumped up and down with her arms raised to the heavens. By the time Steve picked her up and squeezed her in a big embrace—giving her a loud smacking kiss on the cheek—the SUV had already made its retreat. He caught only a passing glimpse of his former wife.

It started to rain.

"Okay, you three, let's get inside."

"Maybe Lila's got some fresh-baked, straight out of the oven cookies for us, daddy."

Steve smiled. "Not this time, pumpkin," he said as he carried Talitha to the door, "and we're not going to wait in the rain to find out."

"It always rains here," Josh said.

Steve regarded his son as he stomped up the stairs. "Did you want to play outside?"

"Can we go climbing again?" Talitha said, unable to hold her tongue.

The thought of it turned her into a squirming bundle of excitement in her father's arms.

"The climbing wall's inside," she reasoned. "We won't get wet!"

Steve plunked his youngest on the couch and pulled off her shoes. Once free of them, she sprang up and started jumping on the cushions.

"Can we, daddy?"

"What do you two think?" Steve said, looking at his older kids. "Would that be okay?"

"I'd like to have a family meeting first," KariLyn said, standing in front of the purple polka dot curtain panels with her arms locked around her budding chest.

Talitha stopped jumping. She dropped into a corner of the couch and peeked out over her knees. Josh ran his fingers through his hair, looking displeased. Steve noticed how he distanced himself from his older sister, having moved to the other end of the room.

"Would you rather put your stuff away first?"

"I'd rather have the meeting now."

Josh and KariLyn exchanged a stony glance.

"What's on your mind, Kari?" Steve said.

"Mom's seeing men."

The room seemed to darken. Steve took in a lungful of air, involuntarily feeding the spark he felt ignite in his gut.

"Is that so?"

"Yes," KariLyn said, nodding, "she's seeing different men."

Steve's grip tightened on the cane as he hovered in front of the corduroy lounger, looking from KariLyn's fixed stare to Josh, avoiding all eye contact. Talitha seemed to fade into the couch, her yellow sweater just another sunburst on the guacamole base.

"Your mother's allowed to date, Kari," Steve said as steadily as he could. "We're no longer husband and wife."

It was said for the sake of the kids. What Steve felt was another matter. Wasn't there a time-honored grace period divorced couples respected before kicking up their heels?

Josh broke the silence. "Anything else to blab about?"

"Don't rush me!" KariLyn snapped.

Josh's mouth opened before slowly closing shut.

"It's not just that, dad…the men she's bringing home," KariLyn informed her father, throwing out discretion, "are staying the night!"

"Just two!" Josh shouted. "You're making it sound like she's a—"

Slut

It was as if someone whispered the word in Steve's ear. He could almost feel the malevolent breath.

"I don't like it!" KariLyn cried out. "I can't sleep with strange men in the house."

"Mom can do what she wants!" Josh shouted from across the room. "It's her life!"

"She can go to a motel like all the other—"

Whores

"Shut up!"

KariLyn and Josh stood frozen in fear. Neither had expected their father to react so aggressively. Talitha's eyes darted around the room, focusing on nothing. The only sound was the rain pelting the windows.

"Sorry, dad," KariLyn whispered, desperately trying to hold back tears.

Steve stormed into the kitchen, away from his kids. He headed for the toaster, holding the cane like a bat. By some miracle it got hooked on the handle of the fridge and slipped through his fingers. He looked for something to steady himself against, his face flushed in fury. Finally, he rested his head against the freezer door to try to cool off.

"So the little parasite has returned."

Steve at once questioned himself. The dark presence he could feel was unlike the jackal he had come to know. This time around it felt different, more detached, like his ego had become an entity of its own, separate from him. It also seemed to have changed tactics, acting as tempter. One part jealousy, one part indignation and one part defense of the woman he still believed he loved was quickly distilled into a poison fed through his bloodstream.

The tactic was simple but effective. Get Steve so blindly infuriated that he would be tempted to hit his daughter, smack some respect into her, something he had never done. What was temptation but the desire to act on something that would soon be regretted? The act would have devastated him, turned him to mush; but that was the point, wasn't it? Once weakened, the creature would reassert control over him.

KariLyn appeared in the doorframe. Strands of her long brown hair pasted on her teary face.

"Sorry, dad."

Steve pushed off the freezer and pulled KariLyn towards him. They hugged for a full minute before walking back into the living room, holding hands. Josh was sitting on the couch beside Talitha, his arms around her little shoulders.

"Okay," Steve said, "we're going to start fresh. Take your bags up and unpack. When you return, we'll have a real family meeting."

KariLyn dragged her bag up the stairs in silence. Josh followed, grabbing both his and Talitha's, calling his little sister up the stairs with a flick of his hair. Once alone, Steve sat in the thrift shop lounger, having planted his feet firmly on the floorboards, taking the opportunity for a little timeout meditation.

The presence lingered. Steve could sense its smirk. He tried to locate it, but it wasn't playing under earthly rules. Either it moved at a speed he couldn't detect or it was able to exist in two places at once. A trickster by nature, it seemed to be standing by the purple polka dot curtain panels, in the doorframe to the kitchen, on the stairs…everywhere.

KariLyn returned. Without moving from the lounger, Steve gestured for her to sit on the couch. When Josh appeared with Talitha in tow, he asked them to sit beside their sister. Owing to the couch's size, Josh was able to distance himself from KariLyn without disobeying his father's directive. He pulled Talitha beside him like a shield.

Steve looked at his children in silence, reading their body language. Josh appeared restless, angry, perhaps a little frightened. It could be the way he manifested dread. Talitha looked like a squirrel searching for the closest tree to escape into. Defiance was the only way he could describe KariLyn's expression. She knew she was causing a rift with her siblings but was determined to stand her ground.

"I'm sorry," Steve said. "I didn't mean to react so harshly."

"That's okay, dad, we still love you, don't we?" KariLyn said, looking over at her brother.

Josh made a point of not meeting her eyes.

"Kari," Steve said, "I'm sure your mother isn't trying to hurt you. What she's doing is meeting her own emotional needs. Try to keep in mind she's as much an injured party as any one of us."

"I want to live with you."

It took Steve a moment to respond. "What about school?"

"I'm fifteen, dad. I can take a bus."

Steve turned to his other two kids, giving himself a moment to think. "Josh, how do you feel about this?"

"All we do is fight," he said, his lip jacked in bitterness. "Kari and mom yell at each other all the time. It might do us all good if she moved in with you for awhile."

Steve sat silent, thinking what best to do. "From what I gather, Josh, you're okay with Kari moving in with me."

"Yes."

"But you want to remain with your mother."

Josh shrugged. "One guy mom brought home was a phony, one of those that try real hard to be nice to kids, but we only saw him once. I don't think mom liked him much either. Anyway, I need to stay close to school to get to and from football practice."

Steve got up and knelt in front of Talitha, buried under her brother's arm. "What do you want, pumpkin? Do you want to stay with mom or live with me?"

Talitha took her thumb out of her mouth long enough to express an opinion. "I want us all to live together like before."

Steve smiled. "Well, if we can't do that, would you prefer to stay with mommy or come and live with daddy?"

"I want to stay with Josh."

Steve pushed up with the cane and looked down at his kids, each possessing unique, special needs.

"Are the three of you still in contact with your guardian *ad litem*?"

"Yes," Josh said. "She seems nice."

"Do we have to go through court?" KariLyn said, looking a little apprehensive.

"I'm afraid so, honey, but it shouldn't be difficult. I believe all you have to do is call and tell her what you want, and the court will rule on it. I doubt there will even be a hearing."

"Can I use the phone, dad?"

"Don't you want to take a little time to think it over?"

"No," KariLyn said. "My mind's made up."

"Then of course you can," Steve said, his eyes following his daughter as she got up from the couch.

"Daddy?"

"Yes, pumpkin?"

"Can we go to the climbing wall now?"

******

It was a dreary, overcast, blustery day that ended the week, a week during which most people would have popped open a bottle of champagne to celebrate. A godsend arrived in the mail, a severance package, and a decent one at that. The lawyer in Steve had no illusions regarding this unexpected gesture of generosity. His former employers must have weighed their options or—in business terms—authorized a risk assessment of potential liability, and decided their former employee had a case against them after all. Compensation was offered lest a suit be filed.

Steve knew it was a ploy. By accepting the package, they could then wash their hands of him forever. He would never be able to take future action, and he knew it. It took him less than a minute to make a decision. He cashed the check and paid his bills, walking away from his past life as a hired assassin. With what was left, he was in a better position to one day offer a down payment on the house if Ryan and Ellie agreed to sell, something they hinted they might be willing to do for the right price.

To top it off, Susan accepted her daughter's decision and offered no resistance to her moving in with her father—a sign of just how much their relationship must have deteriorated in recent months. The move proved beneficial to all concerned. Susan had Kari off her back, and Steve had his oldest daughter back in his life, eager to help out and be of use. It felt as if the house was coming alive for the first time.

To add to the week, a friendship quickly developed between KariLyn and Lila, whose way of "making do" seemed to appeal to the teenage girl. She proudly wore the first thing she had ever created with her own hands: a long shirt stitched on Lila's sewing machine, patched together with her collection of thrift shop scraps. The zigzag pattern of earth tones suited KariLyn's lean figure—its simplicity reminiscent of a mismatch of Native American designs.

All in all, it was a very good week, yet the sense of tranquility that it ought to have provided didn't materialize. Steve couldn't seem to shake the shadows swirling around his head. Assistance finally arrived in the form of a giant. KariLyn had just stepped out to Lila's when he heard a cheerful knock at the door. The kettle was on and cups were out before Jack had a chance to take off his coat and make his way into the kitchen.

Jack was far more interested than Tom had been in hearing about the spirit rocks. No detail was too small. He lapped it up with his herbal tea. They were on their third cup when Jack took a break from his questions, sitting back in his chair.

"Fascinating."

Jack sat silent awhile, contemplating all he was told. Steve waited, turning his attention to the room. The light switches had been set with dimmers. Initially, he thought it an extravagance for a kitchen, but he came to appreciate the moody olive quality it gave the room. He especially loved the sheen of the gray granite countertops at different times of day. At night the stone shone a subtle shade of jade.

"What do you think it was that challenged you at the spirit rocks?"

"It's hard to say," Steve said, swirling his cup to make the tea leaves spin, "but, if I had to guess, I'd say whatever it was, it was an expression of all the people who ever placed a stone on that wall. I suspect if you add a stone to the spirit rocks, you leave a little part of your spirit there."

Jack deliberated on the theory. "An entity that is the product of the combined spirits of generations of Indians," he said, looking up at the fireside glow of the pot lights in the ceiling. "What a beautiful thought." His eyes lingered on the ceiling as if he were staring at stars. "Explain why you think Qigong helped you overcome this test."

"What do you want to know?"

"Was it that it helped you to overcome a state of extreme anxiety or was there more to it than that?"

"I'm not sure," Steve said, shaking his head. "I couldn't tell you why they suddenly switched from attacking to protecting me, but, if you ask me, it was because I stood up to the challenge they threw at me."

"Continue."

"Using what I'd learned of Qigong, I was able to calm myself enough to engage fully in what was happening. It gave me the confidence to confront it, but whether it was Qigong which turned the assault around, the focus it provided me, something else entirely or a combination of everything, I really don't know."

"And the lightness you felt the following morning as you descended the mountain?"

"What about it?"

"Did it last?"

Steve reflected on the question. "I can feel it slipping away," he said, hesitating as he continued. "Something happened last week that really put a damper on any feelings of lightness."

"Oh?"

Steve would have put the kettle on to stall for time, but he knew a fourth cup of herbal tea was overkill. He could already feel the slosh in his stomach. In truth, he felt ashamed, deeply ashamed. He wished he hadn't brought it up.

"What happened?" Jack said, cupping his hands on the table.

"I almost hit my kid."

Jack locked eyes with Steve. "Which kid?"

"KariLyn," he said, tearing his eyes away only to look down at his cup. "If I hadn't walked away from her, I would've slapped her face."

"Why?"

Steve took a deep breath and spent the next twenty minutes trying to explain just that. He spoke of how the room seemed to dim when he heard words of contempt spill from his daughter's mouth, words that seemed to offend him in ways he had trouble understanding; how he wanted to punish that mouth, slap some respect into it.

"What do you think possessed you?" Jack said. "Ego?"

Steve took a sip of tea and winced as he swallowed what had by now turned cold. He put the cup down a little too hard. "I don't know. I thought so at first, but I'm not sure anymore. It felt different, disengaged somehow."

"Describe to me how you felt just prior to this yearning to hit your daughter."

"Anger, maybe…hurt…I don't know. I was just possessed by this sudden, overwhelming temptation to hit her."

Jack pulled his hands back from the table and folded them around his chest. "Temptation?"

"Yes, temptation."

"I think I may know what it was…have I ever told you the story of the Buddha and Mara?"

"No," Steve said, not in the mood for another Zen anecdote, but he took the bait, posing the requisite question. "Who or what is Mara?"

"A demon."

Steve had learned to always take Jack at his word. This time, however, he waited to see if the room would break out in laughter.

"A demon?"

"Mara is known as the 'Evil One' in Buddhism, or the 'Tempter.'"

"Are we talking about the devil?"

Jack's eyes shifted as he considered the implications of the question. "Christianity and Buddhism differ on the subject of evil. The latter is more accepting. While Christians disdain evil in all its varied forms, Buddhists are encouraged to embrace it."

"I don't—"

"Think of it this way: The Buddha had to get in touch with what we in Zen call his 'shadow side' in order for him to reject Mara and realize enlightenment. Mara is therefore vital to the story of the Buddha. There couldn't be one without the other."

"This shadow side sounds a lot like ego if you ask me."

"And for good reason," Jack said. "Many Buddhist scholars believe Mara and ego are one and the same."

"Are they?"

"It's hard to say," Jack said in that noncommittal way of his, "but they both have the same objective."

"Which is what?"

"Absolute opposition to enlightenment," Jack said, tapping a finger on the table. "As the story goes, the moment Gautama planted himself under the Bodhi tree with the intention to remain there until he was able to see clearly into the human condition, Mara did everything in his power to stop him, even marshaling vast armies that shot flaming arrows at him."

"What did the Buddha do?"

Jack couldn't help but smile. "He continued meditating, turning the assault into flower petals that rained down around him; and by the grace of the earth goddess that he called up by touching the soil beneath him, calling on her to testify to his acts of goodness, he achieved enlightenment under the Sacred Fig."

"Mara was defeated?"

"Mara cannot be defeated," Jack said, pointedly. "Only in *Nirvana* is it powerless. Here, on earth, it has influence over all who've not realized enlightenment. Buddha was even visited by Mara long after he became the Buddha."

"Really?"

Jack bent into the table. "One day, Ananda, the Buddha's cousin and devout attendant, saw Mara approach. He tried to stop it, but he was tricked. Mara simply asked that its presence be announced to the Buddha. Ananda had no choice but to comply for he knew he couldn't speak for his master. To his disbelief, the Buddha agreed to see it. He called out, 'I see you, Mara,' and invited it in for tea. The demon immediately started to complain to the Buddha how difficult life had become and how everyone despised it. 'You have no idea how hard it is to be Mara,' it said. The Buddha responded by saying, 'Oh, I know what you mean.

My life is hard, too. Everyone expects so much of me just because I'm the Buddha.'"

Steve sat in anticipation. "That's it?"

"That's it."

"Zen stories always end before they even get started."

Jack, weighed down with herbal tea, held his stomach while he laughed. "But don't you see? The Buddha invited Mara in for tea."

"No, I don't see," Steve said, baffled like he always was.

"Of his own free will the Buddha agreed to face his shadow side," Jack said. "By inviting it in for tea, he accepted it as part of his reality, and by accepting it, he triumphed over it. He was in perfect balance."

"You think I need to embrace my shadow side like the Buddha did his?"

Jack brought his fingers together, tips to tips. "Yes, I do, and I think it may be time for you to take a further step into the unknown…if you're willing, that is."

"How?"

"In December, the Zen Center of Seattle is having a three day Zen *sesshin*."

"A what?"

"A *sesshin* is a period of intensive meditation or *zazen*," Jack explained. "Two of the three days will land on a weekend, by the way. So it shouldn't affect your job…interested?"

"Do you think a novice like me is ready for such a thing?"

"I think so," Jack said, "since this will be a short one as *sesshins* go. Typically, I wouldn't recommend an intensive to a practitioner that hasn't been persistent in personal practice for at least three years, but your particular case is…exceptional."

205

"Do I have to stay the night?" Steve said, thinking of his daughter alone in the house.

"No, but you'll have to get up in the middle of the night to arrive on time; and you won't get home 'til late. By Sunday, when it concludes, you'll be close to exhaustion, both emotionally and physically, I can assure you."

"I suppose that's intentional."

Jack's face lit up with a smile. "Welcome to Zen intensive!"

******

While Steve drove through the deserted streets, slickened from rain, he reviewed what he had learned in group meditation the week prior. Jack had persuaded him to participate in preparation for the intensive that he was now making his way to at this ungodly hour in the morning.

Jack took group meditation as serious as Tom had the spirit rocks. His instructions were meticulous; no detail was too small. Steve thought all the prep work a waste of time until last week's meditation session concluded, when he came to the conclusion it was one thing to meditate on your own and another to meditate in a group setting. Details were as nitpicky as the Law.

Last week's meditation session took place in a dingy single story brick building of dubious origin. There was nothing Zen-like about the exterior, being as drab and lifeless as the other buildings that surrounded it. Once inside, Steve took the plunge and pried off his shoes, leaving them with the others on the shelves in the sparse and uninviting entrance hall where drywall screws accented the gypsum boards that for some reason had never been painted.

Steve took a moment to appraise the shoes to try to get a better sense of the type of person he was likely to meet when someone approached from the shadows, silent in socks, beckoning him forward. The stranger stopped at the entrance to a large room, bowing from the waist before stepping inside with his left foot first. Steve mimicked the movements before entering the *zendo* (or meditation hall), being directed to a chair facing the wall. Left on his own, he waited for the three bells that would signal the beginning of *zazen*.

As instructed by Jack, Steve paid close attention to every detail, such as the way the participants bowed when the bell was rung two additional times, ending meditation; how the others present stretched their bodies before methodically turning to the right, standing in front of their cushions and chairs. When a clacker sounded, all turned to the left. When the clacker sounded a second time, the group responded by moving together in a very slow, circular walk. Jack referred to this as "*kinhin*" (walking meditation).

Kinhin ended when the clacker sounded two additional times, signaling that all should quickly return to their seats for the beginning of service. A gray-haired woman sitting in the chair beside Steve reached under her cushion and pulled out a binder. He followed her example, pulling out the one under his. Only after the others started to chant the logograms had he recognized what sounded like Japanese. Thankfully, chants followed in English, so he was able to take part.

When service ended, Steve made a point of sticking around. He joined the others in the common area, sipping tea. There he met Joyce, the gray-haired woman who sat beside him in the *zendo*. She extended a warm hand and introduced herself just like a normal person would. Steve clasped it gratefully.

"You're new here, aren't you?"

The others listened as Steve explained he had come in preparation for the upcoming intensive. When asked whether he had ever participated in one before he replied that he hadn't. The reaction was conspicuous if silent.

Clearly, he was been pegged as a novice that had no business participating in an intensive.

This was what Steve was thinking back on as he waited at a red light under the buzz of streetlamps, smiling to himself as he recalled what had happened next. Joyce asked if he had a teacher, and he replied he had; that it was his teacher who instructed him to participate in the meditation session in preparation for the intensive the following week.

"Oh," Joyce said a little skeptically. "What's your teacher's name?"

A ripple ran through the room when Father Jack Sheehan's name was mentioned. Suspicious and disapproving eyebrows immediately melted and a couple of people even nodded their heads in approval. All of a sudden Steve was accepted into the group.

Joyce was equally impressed. "If Father Jack thinks you're ready then who am I to disagree? Do you need an *oryoki* set?"

An *oryoki* set, as Joyce explained, is a three-bowl eating system developed in Japan for eating in a *zendo*, and particularly useful during an intensive (the reason Joyce brought it up).

"You can rent a set here with instructions for ten dollars?"

Joyce took care of Steve. He was grateful for the knowledge she willingly shared, informing him of such things as *dana*, which was a voluntary payment one gifts a teacher to support his or her continued teaching practice. He, of course, had never given Jack a dime, but he doubted his teacher would accept *dana* if it were offered.

Dokusan, as it was next explained to him, is a one-on-one interview between student and teacher.

"It's encouraged that all go to *dokusan* once a day during intensive to discuss with a teacher any issues that may arise," Joyce said. "You'll see a wooden sign hanging in the *zendo* that says '*dokusan*' on it. During *kinhin*, you turn it out as a signal that you require a *dokusan* session with a teacher at the next sitting."

Steve must have looked puzzled because Joyce chose to elaborate.

"This is how it works: During your next *zazen* session, you'll hear a high-pitched bell calling *dokusan*. The person nearest the door goes first if they requested it, and then people take turns clockwise around the room until all have had their turn."

Joyce placed a reassuring hand on his arm. "Don't worry, we all screw up. I know there are a lot of details, but they are only put in place to make sure people are present and paying attention."

The people scattered around the room nodded in empathy. By the look in their eyes, each and every one must have screwed up at one time or another.

"Wait 'til you start *oryoki*," Joyce added with a wink. "You can't imagine all the niggling little details, but when you look around—with discretion of course—you'll find that no two people do it exactly the same."

Steve remembered feeling better after that.

"Do the best you can…let all the rest go."

That was Joyce's chief advice.

"It's easy for little mistakes to become issues that'll fester and interfere with meditation. Many of us have beaten ourselves up from the mistakes we've made, but one comes to realize that that only detracts from the experience."

It ended up that Joyce was the very person Steve needed to hand his application to for the following week's intensive (as well as the check to pay for it). She was the self-proclaimed unofficial secretary and "bottle washer around here," as she put it.

"Don't forget," Joyce said as Steve was leaving, "*zazen* starts at four-thirty sharp, but you should be here at least fifteen minutes earlier."

She made a point of looking him straight in the eye so there would be no misunderstanding.

"*Zazen* waits for no one."

In spite of the hour, cars lined the road that fronted the Seattle Zen Center. This forced Steve to park several blocks away, arriving at the door of the building with less than twenty minutes to spare. Like the previous week, he pried off his shoes and moved down the hallway, following a light. He was conscious of his limp but resolute in not bringing his cane.

The common area was lit by a single candle of a size typically seen flanking church altars. Two dozen people were silently gathered in the room. There was even a hushed lineup in front of the coffee-tea area.

Steve stepped into the lineup, desperate for caffeine. He could see into the *zendo* from where he stood. It was lit by a single candle of a similar size. At the back of the common area, through a pair of glass doors, he could make out an inner courtyard where a man in a black robe stood inside a small alcove, lit by a single compact fluorescent light bulb that gave off a frosty glow. Before his turn came up at the coffee pot, the man in the alcove pulled down on a rope attached to a thick rectangular block of wood. He then raised a wooden mallet and gave the block a mighty whack.

Steve's eyes were acclimatizing to the candlelight when he spotted Joyce sitting on a couch, looking up at him with a smile. He gestured out at the courtyard, raising his eyebrows questioningly. Joyce grinned as she got up and moved over to where he stood.

"That's the *han*," she whispered, "the traditional way of signaling that *zazen* is about to start. Just watch me. When I line up at the door to the *zendo*, you should too."

"All right," Steve whispered back, aware that people were looking on disapprovingly.

Jack warned Steve that he would be expected to remain silent during the intensive's entire three day duration. That in itself was intimidating. He doubted he had been silent for more than three hours at any one time in his life. He would just have to keep his mouth shut, take cues from the others and do the best he could.

As Steve was finishing off his coffee, the *han* was struck. After a couple of seconds, a third strike was heard, followed by a fourth. They came in shorter and shorter intervals in a stuttering crescendo until it stopped altogether—its echo reverberating in his brain. The room responded when two final whacks ensued. People got up from their seats and started to put their cups away. Joyce placed hers in a tub of dirty dishes and got in line behind the others. Steve stepped in behind her.

******

Steve could pick out the remnants of wrapping paper scattered through the living room. The shiny pieces of fanciful fragments glittered under the lights strung around the tree, the only lights on in the house. Although he didn't realize it, he was immersed in an open-eyed, automated meditative state of consciousness precipitated by fatigue more than anything else.

It had been strange and wonderful to watch Jack preside over Midnight Mass. Steve had to stop himself from laughing out loud when he first noticed how the chasuble and stole Jack wore only reached to his knees. Evidently, the Catholic Church didn't think it expedient to spend its money on fitting priests with religious vestments tailored to their varied widths and heights.

Steve didn't know why Jack made him promise to attend Mass with the kids. Talitha—at first excited to be

211

allowed to stay up so late—had started to drift after concluding her examination of all the statues and religious iconography that the church had to offer. His other two remained composed if bleary-eyed, old enough to be respectful of the ritual they were invited to participate in.

One of the questions his kids raised on the way home was why the Sanctus bell was rung by an altar boy when Jack raised the host and chalice. The old Steve would concoct an answer to any question he didn't have an answer to. Back then he believed it was better to falsify an answer than to expose himself as deficient in any way, especially in front of his kids.

The new and improved Steve tried to answer questions without being swayed by an inflated ego. He hazarded a guess, that the Sanctus bell was rung to call attention to the importance of the priest offering up the body and blood of Christ. KariLyn wasn't convinced. She had her own opinion on the matter, believing the bells were rung to call to God.

Steve had been invited out to dinner by a group who participated in the intensive on the Sunday it concluded, earlier that month. Worn out as he was, he had decided to go. It proved a good decision. Three days of silence made everyone talkative. The result was that every question he raised had been answered with eagerness; and he raised many, especially concerning the foreign words used.

To place hands in "*gasho*" in the Japanese sense of the word was to put one's hands together and bow from the waist. A couple of those who joined the party at the restaurant were quick to point out that in American Zen its meaning leaned more toward a sense of thankfulness or gratefulness.

Joyce added that some practitioners believe that when one raises one's hands alongside one's head at the conclusion of a full prostration, it signified the person was raising the feet of the Buddha (the Buddha within).

212

"It's meant to teach humility as well as an interconnection to all things," Joyce said. "Bowing in this manner signifies the embodiment of not only the existence of all things, but one's interconnection and interdependence to them...their true natures. When you utter '*gasho*,'" she added, using a French fry as a pointer, "you're giving thanks and offering your gratefulness."

"Full prostration," a man named Peter offered between bites from a plate of vegetarian salad, "is using one's own body to show appreciation, veneration or commitment to the three pillars of Zen: the Buddha and his teachings, the *dharma* and the '*sangha*' or spiritual community one meditates with."

Steve took the opportunity to delve deeper into the meaning of *dokusan*. He had his reasons. On day two of the intensive he was quick to turn the wooden sign out during *kinhin* to discuss with the resident teacher what he learned in service the day before. It was a knockout speech on how the "father superior" voice within us all is apt to make us feel that we are not good enough and, as a result, won't be able to make it through intensive. All he got from the teacher in response to his question was he should "love the water more than the pitcher."

"The saying is a quote from the Sufi poet, Rumi."

While Joyce filled Steve in on the meaning of Sufi—one of at least two mystic branches of Islam—a debate broke out on what the teacher could have meant by the quote. Most concluded that the teacher meant that Steve shouldn't get too attached to his spiritual path but instead let it flow naturally in the way God's absolute, unconditional love flows through all of us.

"The spiritual flow is what we should love most," Joyce said, "not the path that got us in touch with it."

The table roared with laughter when Steve compared the intensive to a lobotomy.

"Wait 'til you try a *Rohatsu sesshin*, a seven-day intensive," someone said to renewed laughter.

Over coffee, Steve raised another question that was troubling him. "Why does Japanese culture play such a big role in Zen practice?"

Everyone had an opinion. Apparently, it was a hotly debated subject in American Zen. It soon became obvious that more traditional practitioners were for it and less traditional against it.

"The Japanese added accretions of their own to Zen Buddhism," Joyce offered in explanation, "and what they introduced evolved to become what is now part of Zen tradition."

"However," interjected a middle-aged woman, "there are many who believe that cutting out Japanese additions and Americanizing Zen for Americans wouldn't lessen the Zen message. Personally, I believe it might even provide a superior message."

"You think, Gertrude?"

"It's a better course of action since Zen points directly to experience and not to the technical aspects of its theology."

"But the devil's in the details," Joyce was quick to point out. "For instance, how does one react to the sound of the *han*?"

The question resulted in silence.

"That block of wood that's whacked to signal the start of meditation?" Steve said, trying to get the terms right.

"Yes, that."

Joyce decided to modify the question when she didn't get an answer. "Look at it this way: Would you prefer the *han* be replaced by a buzzer?"

The question achieved the desired effect. Everyone jumped on it, speaking out, even those with a mouthful of food.

214

"The *han* is a mystery of Zen!"

"At some larger monasteries," an older man named Walter said, raising his voice to be heard, "the beginning of meditation is announced by a huge bell called a *densho* that produces a sound completely different to the *han*."

The words had the effect of once again silencing all, allowing Walter to continue uninterrupted.

"When I took part in an intensive in one such monastery, the sound of the bell made me cry the first time I heard it."

"I send my heart along with the sound of the bell," Gertrude murmured, tears attesting to her words.

"As I do mine," Joyce added, also becoming teary-eyed.

"You know," Walter said, in case anyone present wasn't aware, "those are the words a monk is taught to silently chant when he rings the bell."

The whole group had sat reflective until Walter cried out what Steve would soon learn are the words engraved on *hans* throughout the world.

"Great is the matter of birth and death! Life is fleeting, soon gone, gone! Awake, awake each one! Don't waste this life!'"

Everyone in the restaurant turned to look, not sure what to make of this spirited party.

Joyce turned to Steve, nodding knowingly. "Certain sounds stimulate the brain in ways unknown. Perhaps chanting in Japanese is one such sound."

Steve dragged himself from the lounger before he fell asleep. He turned off the Christmas tree lights and started up the stairs to bed, hands feeling for the banister in the dark.

******

215

Steve came upon a cluster of crocuses that hadn't been there when he left for work that morning. The purple petals dotted the sides of his walkway like Lila's purple polka dot curtain panels did the windows that faced them. He bent down to pick one for KariLyn, but stopped, thinking better of it. He decided to let the little flowers have the front yard, thinking he might get a couple of pots and plant something out on the back deck now that spring had finally arrived.

Steve might have seen the crocus blooms as a sign if he had known that Jack would come to call that evening after such a long absence. He last saw Jack officiate over Midnight Mass. But Tom Louie had kept him busy of late, insisting he participate in a minimum of three sweats before thinking of attempting a vision quest. Steve already survived one and was eager to discuss it now that his teacher had finally materialized.

Jack's complexion sobered Steve. The eyes shone as bright as ever but the skin that framed them appeared sallow and thin. That wasn't all. He appeared stooped, and the sprightly step heavy. For the first time Jack was stamped with age. Timeless was the way Steve would have described him in the past. On this day, however, that perennial, robust quality had noticeably diminished, and the man's true age could be more easily seen.

Steve brewed a pot of green tea twice the normal strength—doubling, he hoped, the antioxidants and the other benefits claimed of the beverage.

"I went on my first sweat!" Steve said, a little too enthusiastically.

"Tom has you preparing for your vision quest, then?" Jack said, smiling at Steve from the kitchen table.

"Yes."

"What was it like?"

Steve made his way towards the table with a steaming cup of concentrated tea in each hand. "Well, when I first crawled into the sweat lodge, I thought there was no way I'd be able to stand the heat and humidity."

"How did it look?"

"The sweat lodge?"

"Yes."

"It was a dome-shaped structure built low to the ground, made from stone and wood and earth."

"Was it just you?"

"No," Steve said, setting down Jack's cup. "It was crowded, but I couldn't tell you how many were inside, even in such a tight space."

Jack hugged the heat from the cup before bringing it to his lips. He took a long, slow draught, pressing Steve to continue with a flash of his eyes.

"I started to get used to the heat, at least for awhile. When more rocks were piled on and water thrown onto them, I ran outside naked and dived into the river like the others. It almost stopped my heart when I hit the water."

"I'm sure it'd do the same for mine," Jack said, quietly. "Anything else?"

"It's hard to explain," Steve said. "I dropped down into this state where I was at one with the heat and humidity. All conversation in the sweat lodge stopped after a period of time, and the others started to sing with beat of the drum."

"How did you feel after it was over?"

"I had that feeling of lightness again," Steve said, "almost as if I was floating in space, with that buzzing and pressure in my *dan t'ian*—that same feeling I got coming down from the spirit rocks and after Zen intensive."

Jack looked out the darkened windowpane. "The different elements that frame your spiritual path seem to be reinforcing each other," he said, looking at his haggard reflection. "It could mean you've found and are walking your path with heart."

"I guess."

217

"Has Tom spoken anything more of your spirit rocks experience?"

"All Tom wants to discuss are external details."

"What external details?"

"Things I saw, felt and heard around me."

"Like what?"

Steve thought about it. "When I told him I'd seen what I thought were deer moving high up on the mountainside moments before night set in, he pressed me for details, wanting to know if it was exactly three muley does and one big buck."

"What else?"

"He wanted to know which way the wind blew when the spirits circled behind me, and what exactly did the spirit voices sound like." Steve said, taking a sip of tea. "He imitated the sound after I'd described it."

"The sound of the spirit voices?"

"Yes."

"How'd he do?"

"It made my hair stand on end."

Tom used his tongue to reproduce the snapping sounds as expertly as a hunter would mimic a duck's call.

"He said it was a great honor that the spirits spoke to me and an even greater one that they'd called me their warrior son by name," Steve said. "That seemed to impress him."

"I could imagine."

"Tom also said he'd soon be providing me with specific instructions for my vision quest."

"When's that supposed to take place?"

"Late April or early May was all I could get out of him," Steve said, a little smile curling his lips. "He's as noncommittal as you can be sometimes."

Jack smiled back. "Did Tom mention anything about an animal totem?"

"No," Steve said, "Jack?"

218

"Yes?"

"Do you think I'm destined to add my Christian upbringing to the list of factors that frame my spiritual path?"

"That's for you alone to answer," Jack said. "It's your path, not mine...why?"

Steve took a moment to think his answer through. "Not that they sound anything alike, but the Sanctus bell that rang at Midnight Mass reminded me of the *han*."

"And did the Sanctus bell and the *han* have any parallel to the drum in the sweat lodge?"

That hadn't occurred to Steve, but now that Jack mentioned it, all three seemed intrinsically related.

"Have you tried to meditate on it?"

"On what, exactly?"

"On the illumination of your own unique spiritual path," Jack said, "the connections you make between Christianity, Zen Buddhism and your birthright."

"Native American spirituality?"

Jack looked back at the darkened windowpane. "The last words the Buddha said to his disciples on his deathbed were, 'Be a light unto yourself.'"

He paused a moment to take a sip of tea, again using both hands to lift his cup. Steve was about to take the plunge and ask about his health when he was diverted by a question.

"Tell me," Jack said, "did you feel at unity with the congregation at Midnight Mass?"

"Yes," Steve said. "When the Sanctus bell was rung, it called to me as much as it did the rest of the congregation."

"What about the intensive?" Jack said. "Did you feel a connection with the other participants?"

"Definitely."

"And your Indian cohorts in the sweat lodge?"

Steve nodded, grasping the point.

Jack's eyes held Steve's. "Never underestimate the power of the *sangha*."

"The spiritual group that meditates and prays together?"

"Yes, and remember what Jesus said, 'Where two or three are gathered together in my name, there am I in the midst of them.'"

******

"A vision quest is a rite of passage, a journey of self discovery."

Tom's voice came and went. Steve thought he glimpsed him once outside the circle of rags tied to the stunted, wind-blown spruce and junipers, joined by the tobacco ties Steve had made: the markers that designated the sacred circle where many a youth had hunkered down for days, waiting—famished and bleary-eyed—for the visions to come.

Steve no longer needed to squint or strain his eyes to see, for three days of fasting had sharpened his senses. He could pick out the shadows of deer passing under the trees far down the mountain; hear rodents digging under the earth. Even the thin air of the summit started to flicker. He sat watchful in his sleeping bag, sometimes wearing it as a cloak as he paced slowly around the inner circle, peering out at the world beyond.

Jack had come by to see him, sporting a guacamole shirt covered in yellow sunbursts. At first Steve thought it a hallucination, but he became confused even though he knew hallucinations were caused by altitude and lack of food and sleep. No one needed to tell a mountaineer such a rudimentary fact.

Steve tried to focus on what he knew to be real, such as the drumming of the ruffed grouse on his way up the mountain—following the map Tom had drawn—and higher up the deep grunting of a Blue Grouse from a stand of alpine spruce. When he neared the summit, he encountered large patches of snow and refilled his water bottles with meltwater, risking sickness. His partial immunity to Giardia had likely been rendered null and void after leaving reservation life so long ago.

But Steve didn't feel sick. He wasn't nauseous. It was only that some things—everyday things—weren't as clear while other things had never been more so. But he had to make an effort to focus. Hadn't Tom in their last telephone conversation said to Steve that he would be with him in spirit, praying for him around a fire he would keep lit in Tonasket until the vision quest concluded?

That may be so, but rationale wasn't set in stone anymore. It didn't need to be; it wasn't central to the course of a vision quest. Memories were another matter. Steve was deluged by them, some of which he never knew he possessed; like that time he opened his eyes to find his father crying over his crib, his breath reeking of alcohol. A key had been turned inside him, and it had unlocked what had previously been stockpiled deep in a cerebral crypt.

Outside the circle of sun-bleached rags were a scattering of dwarf junipers, kinnikinnick and the gorse that each morning promised to burst into yellow. Steve had befriended a wind-tortured stand of spruce that watched from a distance. They established camaraderie of sorts, together experiencing the joy in the high altitude sunshine and shivering when the wind passed over the snow cap and transported its glacial chill down on them.

There hadn't been anything particular to do but meditate, but he wasn't idle. Tom's instructions were meticulous, and Steve had followed them precisely before entering the circle three days earlier: taking out the smudge of sweet grass and the matches as instructed, lighting it in a shielded hand and waving it back and forth three times in each cardinal direction, intoning the chant Tom taught him, stumbling over the Salish words.

Steve sipped mountain water, amused by the ease he felt when considering where he was. He even had inexplicable fits of laughter as if his ancestors, those children before him who had passed their days inside the sacred circle, were giggling in his ears. The laughter would cease when the shadow of the mountain lengthened over the carpet of trees below. Nighttime was a serious matter on top of a mountain.

Each night the moon would wake him if it caught him slumbering. Once, Steve saw Tom looking down from its silvery face, reminding him that he must try to stay awake. The cold helped as did the rumbling in his stomach, which he satisfied with icy sips of water. Even so, this third night was proving to be a struggle of mind and body. He had never been so tired.

Halfway through the night Steve's lids slipped over his eyeballs, and he couldn't will them open as he had done before. He suddenly found himself struggling to stay conscious, berating himself that if he didn't open his eyes that very moment the whole effort would be for nothing. But his body wasn't listening; it had mutinied, shutting itself down muscle by muscle. He could feel himself sway back and forth when he heard a bark.

With bloodshot eyes, Steve followed a shadow racing up the mountainside, red eyes ablaze in the night. It sat on its haunches just outside the circle.

"What are you?"

"A wolf," Steve said after the shortest of pauses.

"And what does a wolf do?"

Steve didn't need more than a second to answer. "A wolf takes care of its own."

"We hunt together and we howl together," the wolf said, "and the clan raises its pups as one."

"The deer bowed to me," Steve blurted out, speaking of the dream of the buck that Tom shot dead as if it hadn't been a dream at all.

"The deer knows to respect our kind."

The wolf then laid his huge head on his forelegs, its snout just outside the sacred circle. Two ears pricked the air, responding to the soft soughing breeze passing through the spruce boughs still standing watchful in the moonlight. Never had Steve seen an animal of such unequivocal power. He was smitten, but he knew why the wolf had laid itself down, and what he had to do.

Steve climbed to his feet and pulled off his mittens, digging into a pocket for Tom's notes. He let the sleeping bag fall from his shoulders as he shuffled to the eastern edge of the circle, beginning to chant the words illuminated in the starlight. When he moved to the southern edge, the wolf was again sitting on its haunches, only inches away. The brilliance of its eyes registered the greeting being offered it.

A harp-like thrill ran through Steve's body as he moved to the western and then to the northern compass points of the circle to complete the greeting ritual to his totem protector. At its close, he turned back to the east to face the wolf, but it had gone. Even when he strained his eyes he could detect no movement in the alpine meadows silvery light. It would be a power dream where they would next meet.

Steve started to shiver. He grabbed his sleeping bag and zipped it up before sitting down on the hardened earth to wriggle back into it. As he lay there, a northern saw-whet owl began a chant, a tooting whistle, calling out the long-awaited alpine spring.

Chapter Seven

Steve chugged down the dregs of the coffee he picked up at a twenty-four-hour drive-through, keeping an eye on the road. He felt an aching compassion for the girl behind the window, stuck working the graveyard shift alone. She couldn't have been much older than his daughter, fast asleep at home.

Being the weekend, KariLyn would probably sleep 'til eight, still a good three hours away. He left a note—a lie—telling her he had to drive up to Inchelium to settle a work matter that couldn't wait. He hoped she would buy it.

Steve felt uneasy about leaving his daughter in the middle of the night. He wished Josh was there to keep her company. That decision, however, had yet to be finalized. It had been two weeks since the bombshell hit. Except for KariLyn—suspiciously Zen about the whole matter—the news rocked the family.

But was it a surprise? Even though Susan had always been careful to hide that side of her persona, Steve knew that deep down she was a fool for love. Hidden away in a drawer under her lingerie was the romance novels she would never admit were hers—and what about the master indifference she would act out when handed the obligatory roses each Valentines? In some ways, mother and daughter were a lot alike, perhaps the cause of KariLyn's neutrality.

The news still ate at Steve's emotions. There hadn't been time to adjust, to think it through and come to terms with what it meant. He first had to deal with the changes it kicked off. Josh had already contacted the guardian *ad litem* and made the request to move in with his father. He couldn't even begin to imagine what Susan felt about the upheaval she was causing.

KariLyn was Steve's only source of information on Susan's fiancé. Jeremy, according to his daughter, had a stockpile of money. Josh let slip to her that the engagement ring was twice the size of their mother's old one—the one Steve slipped on Susan's finger all those years ago; the one that cost a month's wages, now tossed in a jewelry box or, for all he knew, on display at a pawnshop.

Josh said that Jeremy bought a large plot of timberland near Chesaw with its own log cabin, and that was where the newlyweds were to live. Steve knew Chesaw was north of Wauconda Pass, up near the Canadian border. It was about as isolated as you could get in the Lower 48, roughly twenty miles east of Tom Louie's shack in the woods.

Something had changed. The old Susan would never have agreed to live in the backwoods (her name for anywhere outside Seattle), but that hadn't always been the case. He and Susan would go hiking before they were married, spend days canoeing, skiing or passing a Frisbee in a park. When the kids were little, they would even go camping, letting the kids run naked.

Last weekend was spent on Mount Adams with the kids as planned. Susan finally agreed to relinquish Steve's climbing gear, locked up in a storage facility. She fought against giving it up, but he insisted, and she finally gave in. He expected to be hit by a cold front when she arrived with the kids; but as Josh and KariLyn pulled out their gear, Susan uncharacteristically sat giggling on her cell phone, her left hand dancing on the steering wheel. The engagement ring sparkled in the windshield.

Steve asked the most benign question he could think of in the most leisurely manner he could manage on the drive to Mount Adams with the kids. He had been backhanded by the answer he got.

"The wedding is in August…next month?"

Steve used the climbing retreat to try to clear his head, to get a better gauge on all the changes happening around him. He picked Mount Adams because he used it in preparation for larger expeditions in the past. It was relatively safe as mountains go, having all the characteristics of a good hike without life-threatening glaciers or cliff faces—at least on the chosen route. It was also high enough to impress the kids without being beyond their capabilities.

Steve started to feel better once they reached the mountain. He remembered how the seasons regressed as they climbed: June had turned to May and May to April where flowers were still in spring bloom. They camped at the "Lunch Counter" at 9,000 feet, a place he had often camped before, under the soaring false summit to give the kids the impression of being on top of the world.

It happened at the strike of sunrise, soon after Steve awakened. Crawling quietly out of the tent so not to wake the kids, he made his way to a flat stone not far from camp, teetering over scree at the base of the snowfield he intended to glissade on their way down the mountain. Settling into sitting meditation, he waited in anticipation for the sun, but fate had something else in store. In place of the sun appeared the colossal shadow of the mountain, darker and denser than the night, swallowing him whole in a single gulp.

The event likely lasted less than a minute, maybe only seconds, but it felt like an eternity to Steve. It started in a flash when the halo of the sun burst into flames around the contour of the false peak. From tip to root the mountain unfolded its shadow, spreading down and stretching to the west over the green carpet of treetops, like the mountain was a stylus and the earth a sundial.

Body and mind simply dissolved; and somehow, inexplicably, Steve became the mountain. He was momentarily its weighty soul. For the short time it lasted, he felt the immense age and vast wisdom of the standing peak—awareness itself, witness to the mysteries of time.

And now this...awakened by a phone call in the middle of the night. Steve could feel claws gripping his chest and wondered if he reached the age where he would have to start worrying about his heart. He drove on, the radio off, keeping a lookout for deer.

Piecing together the crazed phone call in his head, trying to make sense of it, Steve approached a circle of fluorescent lights on the side of the freeway. He flicked on the blinkers, drawn to the prospect of coffee and maybe a donut for a little sustenance. He would need it in the coming hours.

Ahead of him, there was still an hour's drive to Ellensburg. Ready or not he was going to have to be on his game once he arrived at the Kittitas County Jail. There was serious business to attend to—as serious as it gets.

******

Steve waited for the deputy's steps to exit the holding cells, staring down at the wreckage on the cot. Deputy Garcia appeared to be a decent man. Arriving to find the immediate situation secure had been a relief.

The figure stirred, grabbing for support that wasn't there. As it rose, a rank mass of congealed curls got pushed to the side, revealing a pair of eyes without a glint of sparkle and a puffy face stained in yesterday's cosmetics.

"That you?"

Steve's senses were in overdrive. The odor was like something that had gone bad in the fridge. He pulled open the folding chair Deputy Garcia provided and sat down a little way off, sitting with the backrest facing front so he could breathe into his folded arms to give himself time to adjust to the stench.

"Yes, Denise, it's Steve," he said, talking softly so he wouldn't gag.

She was as sorrowful a figure as when he first saw her under the reckless and domineering care of Judy

227

Copeland. The tight mini and the gauzy blouse were all the more tragic.

"What happened?"

Denise extended a filthy claw of broken nails. It was as if she were trying to hook onto Steve's wrist, dramatically misjudging the distance between them. He stopped himself from recoiling, debating whether he should move the chair closer, but making the decision that it wasn't yet time for hugs. He needed information if he were going to be of service.

"I shot a man, Steve," she slurred, letting her arm slowly sink in despair.

Denise's eyes seemed to be brushing Steve's hair, unable to focus. He took the opportunity to visually examine her, trying to draw initial conclusions as best he could. He couldn't detect the presence of alcohol in the bouquet of fetid scents. The dilated pupils must be the result of narcotics.

"The bastard tried to rape me."

There was a pattern to the smearing of cosmetics. Steve could make out smudges of blush and foundation on the cheeks and forehead.

"Did you kill him?"

Denise slouched in a daze, her head sinking forwards, making it difficult for her to concentrate. Steve had the impression that if he nudged her with a finger she would slump back down on the cot.

"I don't...I think I...passed out."

The words were becoming unintelligible. She was fading. Steve knew he would lose her in a minute. He knew he had to act fast.

"Did he beat you up?" Steve said, scanning her arms and legs for bruising.

Denise's head rose, and she leaned forward, squinting, staring at Steve's lips as if he were speaking Chinese. He manufactured a smile.

228

"Get some sleep," he said. "We'll talk later."

It took a moment for Denise to register the words, but she seemed to finally sort them out, falling backward and to the side in one fluid motion, allowing gravity to return her to the fetal position Steve found her in.

"Were her pupils dilated when she was brought in?"

Deputy Garcia didn't have to think. "Yup," he said, pouring a coffee. "Did you notice the smearing on her face?"

Steve smiled, a real smile, impressed. "Were the buttons missing on her blouse when you booked her?"

"The three top ones," the deputy said. "They were missing when she arrived, but I don't think it'd take much to rip a button off that blouse. Lucky she was wearing a bra."

"Yeah, lucky," Steve said, although he knew a black bra under a sheer white blouse would work against her in court.

"I didn't book her, by the way. I'll ask the booking deputy if he did."

"I'd appreciate that," Steve said, taking the Styrofoam cup being offered him. He lifted it in a small gesture of thanks before downing half in one loud gulp.

"You're going to represent her?"

"Looks like it," Steve said, swirling the liquid into a vortex to mix the sugar better.

Deputy Garcia offered Steve a seat before sitting behind a desk. On it was a picture of the man out of uniform with a small boy, both with fishing rods in hand.

"You don't seem wildly enthusiastic about the prospect of it."

"Is there any way to get her cleaned up?"

"Trudy's shift starts at eight. She'll dump her in the shower clothes and all, if she has to," the deputy said as he handed Steve the paperwork he had asked for. Deputy

229

Garcia then sat back in his swivel chair and flung his feet up on the desk.

"Ask Trudy to save her blouse, skirt and undergarments as evidence," Steve said, scanning the papers one by one. "Make sure they don't get washed."

"Will do."

"Any witness to the shooting?"

"Leo Benning."

"Who's Leo Benning?"

Deputy Garcia looked past his glossy shoes and straight at Steve. "Not the type of person a defense lawyer would be too happy about, if you want my opinion."

"Why?"

"Want to know Benning's nickname?"

Steve got a sinking feeling. "Let's hear it."

"Leo the Liar."

Steve stared over the paperwork, past the pair of well-worn soles and into the deputy's eyes. "Got any good news to share?"

"Only that the lazy S.O.B. we got for a prosecutor will probably wring as much out of Leo as possible to get another conviction for his growing collection."

"Collection?"

"Around these parts," the deputy said with a smirk, "convictions get you re-elected."

"Who's the prosecutor?"

"Nick DiMonte."

Steve made the connection immediately. "A man about my age?"

"I'd say so," the deputy said. "Know him?"

"We went to law school together."

The deputy's face hardened. "Everyone has his own opinion, friend, but it's mine the man's a lazy S.O.B.," he said, cracking his knuckles before folding his hands behind his head.

"Yours and mine both," Steve replied, closing the folder. "Where can I get breakfast around here?"

"Shirley's," the deputy said, once again at ease, "just a block down the road that way," he added, gesturing with the toes of his shoes.

"I'll be back in a couple of hours," Steve said, getting up and heading for the door, the stack of paperwork secure under an armpit. "Don't forget to tell Trudy to set the clothing aside for evidence."

"Will do."

******

Nick DiMonte, as Steve soon discovered, wasn't the only college mate to have made a home in Kittitas County, but that piece of information wouldn't reveal itself until later that morning. Steve had gone through the paperwork at Shirley's, doing a brisk business with rumors of the shooting on everyone's lips. His head started to throb from all the coffee and scandalous talk around him, vilifying his client as a monster.

Events that led to the shooting were sketchy (and would remain so for some time). In one version, the deceased, a man named Jason, may or may not have tried to take advantage of Denise's need for a "fix." The buzz at Shirley's was far more cynical and one-sided. It was generally agreed that the shooting was a result of Denise's inability to raise enough cash to support her cocaine habit.

"No one wants to pay for sex with a whore that smells like piss," one woman openly declared, crumbs flying as she scarfed down toast.

There was no denying the basic facts. All the proof of Denise's decent into drugs and prostitution had been evident on her person. The stack of police reports removed any doubt Steve might have had.

By the time Steve returned to the jailhouse, Denise had gone into withdrawal. She kept asking when she could go home, bent over double, holding her stomach. Sweating badly, swearing like a sailor, she cursed out Steve—the one man willing to help her—when told she would have to stay put.

Trudy managed to get her cleaned up, but Denise had been so disoriented by the effects of withdrawal that she started to deny knowledge of the man she earlier claimed she shot. Steve had little choice but to give up trying to extract information. He went back to Deputy Garcia's office empty handed. That was when it was suggested he contact Randy Forsythe, a substance abuse counselor at a government supported drug and alcohol treatment center in town.

"Randy Forsythe?"

"Yup."

"A man about my age?"

******

Steve banged on the door of the building, eyeing the empty parking lot. He stuck his face up to the glass, fully aware it was Saturday morning. A lanky figure appeared just as he was about to give up and head back to the police station.

The lock turned and the door swung open, and Steve found himself face to face with his onetime college roommate.

"So what brings the boy wonder to the thriving metropolis of Ellensburg?"

They shook hands in the lobby after Randy relocked the door, awkwardly exchanging pleasantries, not having seen each other since Randy decided that law wasn't for him and transferred into social work. Steve got right down to it, stating his business as he followed Randy down a corridor, stopping in front of an open door.

"I see you're still as neat as ever," Steve remarked after entering the office.

They had shared a room in their freshmen year before Steve established himself with the more stylish upwardly mobile crowd. Steve liked him—everyone did— but Randy wasn't made of the right stuff for the young movers and shakers at the law school they attended, those who would go on to bigger and better things. Randy involved himself with the radicals from the get-go, always promoting the types of things that didn't impress law firms scouting for talent.

In the year they lived together, Steve didn't bring a single person back to their dorm room. He didn't dared, knowing the chaos and disarray would have reflected on him. If Randy put something down, there it would stay. If he ordered a pizza, the grease-stained box would become an art piece on permanent display, propped up on the back of the couch with the others.

Randy moved stacks of papers from a chair for Steve's use. The ensuing air turbulence caused piles of folders and paperwork on the desk and shelves to shudder. Collapse was averted by Randy pressing down on the most vulnerable piles, smiling an apology. He then pushed out a chair for himself, speaking in an even tone so not to set anything off.

"If you want my advice, Steve, keep her in jail. She'll hit the streets before you can sneeze, searching out johns to get her fix. Cocaine isn't cheap, and I doubt your client has a credit rating with her dealers."

"She killed someone," Steve said, feeling the effects of lack of sleep. "She's not going anywhere."

Randy acknowledged the fact with a twitch of a brow. "At least her addiction will finally be dealt with," he

233

said. "You can't get drugs into Kittitas County Jail, not past Trudy, at any rate."

"Know Trudy?"

"Everybody knows Trudy…everybody knows everybody. This is Ellensburg, old friend."

"If everybody knows everybody, how did Denise go under the radar?"

"She didn't…everyone knew," Randy said, nudging a pile of papers out of the way with an elbow, "but she's a grown woman; she has rights to privacy like everyone else, and you just can't go detaining people for drugs and prostitution without evidence—and trust me when I say addicts are skillful at not getting caught. I have the gray hairs to prove how difficult it is to try to get them clean."

"Not an easy job, I guess."

"No, but at least I don't have your pressure-cooker position," Randy said. "Don't think I could handle the stress of corporate life."

Steve smiled despite himself. "Things have changed, old friend. I now work for Justice for the Earth."

Randy sat staring, open mouthed and wide-eyed, blinking like a kid. "You?"

"I have a plan," Steve said, moving forward with the matter at hand, "but I need to get her out of jail and in here with you. Can that be done?"

Randy twisted his lips from side to side, seemingly unable to come to a decision.

"What if I get the court to commit her here instead?" Steve said. "You have a lockup in this facility, don't you?"

"We like to call it a 'safe room.'"

"Well?"

"We could give it a try," Randy finally said. "Tell the judge you can't get the cooperation you need from your client to fairly represent her until she's dried out and determined competent. It's a long shot, but you never know."

Papers went flying as Steve shot out a hand to shake on it. He got what he came for. It was a start.

******

Crocuses sprang from the soggy earth around the front walkway for the second year in a row, dotting the spring sod purple. It was a reminder for Steve to put a long-drawn-out plan into action. Not that there was ever one by and of itself. He had only sought to repair the damage caused by ripping up the bamboo and exposing the soil to the rains—a nice way to thank Ryan and Ellie for their generosity.

The weedy confusion of the backyard echoed the way Steve felt since the previous summer: overrun, prickly and low to the ground. Life had taken its toll on him, driving back and forth from Ellensburg, having to deal with a client who refused to be persuaded to take on a lawyer experienced in criminal law all the while being the sole acting parent of two of his three kids.

Steve didn't have anything grand in mind, he just wanted to move the bamboo stack in the middle of the yard and perhaps plant some grass seed at his own expense, but thinking about the possibilities proved therapeutic. It relaxed him, and once relaxed, his creativity started to stir. He spent hours sitting on the deck as soon as the weather allowed it, trying to decide how best to proceed.

The answer came in a flash of inspiration. What Steve needed was a boulder, and he knew where to get one for free. All it took was three weekends of backbreaking labor to dig out the one in Lila's backyard.

It was a monumental task, but it got done with the help of Josh, two of Lila's sons and a couple of her grandkids. Once a pit had finally been dug around the

235

boulder, they hauled it out with ropes and a rented "come-along," rolling it on bamboo shoots in the manner the ancient Egyptians moved the stones they used to build their pyramids.

It was finally set in place back and to the right of where the bamboo was stockpiled. There was no logic to placement other than the spot felt right. Steve spent hours gazing at the stone once in place, having settled itself into its new home by the weight of its mass. He would circle it, sensing a bond.

Given that the bulk was hidden underground, Steve didn't know what to expect until he put shovel to earth and liberated it from its slumber, having rode south long ago in the belly of a glacier. It had three ridges tapering up to a peak. The surface remained encased in soil until the spring rains polished it to a shine, revealing all its detail.

Steve was struck by the similarity to Chomolungma, by the three protrusions on one of the ridges that looked like little steps, one after the other, close to the tip. The deep fissure on its broad face brought to mind the Great Couloir. Somehow, he even got the direction right, north facing north. The likeness was uncanny. It inspired him to do more.

After Ryan and Ellie gave the green light, Steve, using the reserve bamboo rollers, built a simple gazebo-like structure at the far end of the yard so he could sit out and contemplate the stone in the rain. He bound together three panels with hemp twine, one for the base and two smaller ones for the slope of the roof planes—cut to measure with a saw Ryan left at the house. What remained of the bamboo was used as posts to prop the roof to the base. The whole structure was set on a foundation of river rocks to raise it above the soil.

******

236

"So you decided to create a Zen garden?"

Steve just stepped out onto the deck, holding two glasses of lemonade. Ice cubes clinked in the glasses as he stood looking out on his little project. "Did I?"

Jack held his chest, restraining any outburst of laughter, sitting on one of the kitchen chairs brought out for his use. It had become a bit too much for him to wiggle in and out of low-lying lawn chairs.

"You even built a temple out of the bamboo," Jack said, barely able to contain himself. "Don't tell me you didn't know what you were doing?"

"It's a gazebo."

"In the shape of a *tera*?"

"What's a *tera*?"

"A Japanese Buddhist temple."

Steve could see some similarity now that Jack brought it to mind. "I just wanted to create something useful," he finally said, handing over a glass.

"You know," Jack said, after taking a cautious sip, "it can take a lifetime to create a Zen garden."

"What exactly is a Zen garden?" Steve said, placing his glass beside the lawn chair before settling down into it.

"It's an idealized, often abstract landscape set in miniature, designed for meditation or contemplation; but there're no set rules that govern design, only common elements."

"Like what?"

"In the ones I've visited in Japan, white sand would typically be spread out and raked to resemble rippling water," Jack said. "Stones like the one you found are commonly placed at points within the sand to suggest, for example, islands in a sea."

"This one's a mountain."

"Is it?"

"I call it my Chomolungma Stone."

"Do you?"

237

"I'm going to drive up to the mountains and see if I can find some evergreen saplings to transplant," Steve said, eyeing what he had accomplished thus far. "I also need more river rocks to make a path."

Jack nodded, sweeping his eyes over the construction site. "Water is also an important Zen Garden element."

"Is it?"

"Ponds with *koi*—a Japanese carp—swimming just under the water's surface are popular in Zen garden design."

Steve rejected this option outright. "No ponds for me. This garden is all about mountains. Maybe an icy pool of water trapped in a crevice in the rocks...yes, a place where birds can bathe."

"Make it your own whatever you do, something unique to you."

Neither mentioned the glossy black Cadillac parked in front of the house. Inside, the driver, conspicuous in a black scapular, appeared content. Steve was worried about his friend and was thankful to find he was being looked after. He had enough on his plate as it was.

"How's Denise?"

Steve sat up to cough out the ice cube shard he swallowed. "Her arraignment has been postponed until competence to stand trial is reevaluated," he said, ending the discussion there.

There was nothing else to say on the matter. Randy's updates weren't encouraging. Denise would stare out the window, locked in the safe room, day after day, turning inward on herself. Steve's visits didn't prove helpful either. He wasn't able to reach her as he had in the past.

"Are you familiar with Sufism?"

"What's that?" Steve said, distracted by his thoughts.

"It's a mystical dimension of Islam," Jack said. "Practitioners, called Sufis, believe that to repair the heart it must be turned from all else but God. A core teaching states that the true purpose of human life is to become aligned with the subtle forces of grace so they can then be channeled into the physical world."

"And how does this relate to me?"

"By the simple act of wishing blessings on Denise, you can channel the subtle forces of grace into the physical world of her ordeal and, perhaps—in the aftermath of the trial—into the rest of her life."

Steve sighed, unable to withhold his frustrations on the matter. "It seems like every time I take a step forward, I take two steps backward."

The kernels of ice that hadn't yet melted chimed against Jack's glass as he took a slow draught of lemonade. "As much as this is about Denise, it's also about you," he said, smacking his lips. "Think of this as another test on your journey towards enlightenment."

Steve's eyes fixed on the Chomolungma Stone. "You know, Jack, me and Denise…we're connected. We're both mountain people."

"Yes, I believe you are," Jack said, nodding. "It's where you both seek gurus."

"Gurus?"

"Naturally, mountains aren't really where you'll find your true guru; but for now I think it's safe to say that in your case as well as in Denise's, mountains are a fertile ground for both your spiritual growth."

"How?"

"Are they not symbols, like pyramids, of man's attempt to know God?"

"But—"

"Eihei Dogen, the founder of Japanese Zen, said, 'There are those who, attracted by grass, flowers, mountains, and waters, flow into the Buddha Way.'"

239

"I became a mountain," Steve blurted out, not having yet broached the subject of what happened to him on Mount Adams.

Jack listened in silence, taking in every word, asking a question only when requiring a specific detail. The story concluded in silence.

"What?" Steve said, never having known Jack to be silent on matters of spirituality.

Jack shook his head. "No, I'm sure I haven't...I'd have remembered."

"Remembered what?"

Jack sighed, a smile brightening his haggard face— the color of aged marble.

"Tell me."

"I was at *Rohatsu*," Jack finally said, "in Japan, on the eighth of December—the day Japanese Buddhists observe the enlightenment of the Buddha. It was my fifth *Rohatsu*, so I had no expectations. I was just letting the experience happen, and on the fourth day something did, something unexpected."

Steve stared at Jack. "Go on."

"I entered *zanmai*.

"You entered what?"

"*Zanmai* is a state of unknowing where all one is aware of during sitting meditation is the bell that begins it and the bell that ends it," Jack said. "My teacher noticed, and to my surprise he suggested that I take a walk on the afternoon of the sixth day. Since one isn't supposed to leave the monastery during *Rohatsu*, the proposition was unusual; but I agreed, and off I went."

"What happened?"

"I strolled down the streets on the outskirts of Tokyo, letting my feet lead me where they would. Eventually, I passed a public bathhouse, and something compelled me to go inside."

"Go on."

"I entered through the male side, and just stood there, fully dressed on the edge of the pool, looking down at all the heads bobbing in the water and the men sitting on the deck in towels, their legs swishing the pool."

"And?"

"I spied a naked boy standing on his tiptoes on the pool's edge, facing away from the water, his eyes focused on nothing. I felt the mischievous delight he was conveying in the thought of letting go. The grin on his face made me grin. I felt his joy."

"What happened?"

"As I watched, he slowly began to fall backwards, his arms hanging at his sides," Jack said, oblivious to a butterfly circling his head like a halo. "When he hit the water, pandemonium broke loose inside me. Suddenly, I found myself in two places at once. I was standing by the pool where I had been and, at the same time, falling backward into the warm water with complete release, exactly as the boy had done, feeling the deliciousness of it all."

Jack hugged the lemonade to his heart, his eyes closed.

"That's it, isn't it?"

"No," Jack said, blinking at the sun. "Standing by the pool, I immediately began to roar with laughter at the deep and powerful interconnection I felt with the boy— with the universe around me—sobbing over the power of the experience. I collapsed where I stood, unable to stand. My legs just gave out from under me. Naked men surrounded me; rushing over to see what was wrong, but nothing was wrong...all was right."

Something told Steve that Jack had just shared something deeply personal; something few people had had the privilege of hearing.

"Did you know I was a competitive swimmer in my youth?" Jack said, turning to Steve.

"No."

"I've always had an affinity for water. Perhaps water is for me what mountains are for you."

******

The springy, nutrient-rich soil the bamboo had fostered had quickly lost ground to the rains. Steve wasn't put off. It reminded him of subalpine soils where only the hardiest plants thrive—those that appealed to what he had in mind. What was needed was a means of transport, and that was once again provided by his good neighbor.

The old utility trailer was propped on its side, leaning against the back of Lila's house, resting on a couple of boards to save it from rot. Steve was in the habit of forcing the wheels during breaks in the Chomolungma Stone excavation. He spent time examining the plywood sides and underside, determining whether it was roadworthy. Deciding it could be brought back, he offered to fix it up at his expense if allowed to borrow it, and a deal was struck. A wire brush, a bucket of paint and a grease gun was really all he needed to bring it back into service.

The first outing with the trailer took place early on a Saturday morning in August. Steve hauled it all the way to Ellensburg after one of Lila's sons—the electrician of the family—rewired it to get the turning signals working again. He decided to drive up to Kittitas County after being told that a young woman had attempted to arrange bail for Denise. He thought he better get over there to see what was going on. While there, he would call on Randy and get caught up.

Steve was told that Betsy, the young woman, worked dayshift at the Starlight Tavern, the same dump Denise worked at before her fall from grace. Betsy was working the lunch shift when he arrived, too busy to stop and chat. He waited at a corner table with a bowl of nachos

242

he barely touched. The men she was serving were pirates by the look of them, plundering the greasy fare with their fingers, talking with their mouths full, shamelessly ogling the overworked barmaid.

Betsy was a young, buxom girl with blond tresses at odds with the mousy brown roots of her natural hair color. Strappy high heels that had seen better days clicked a rhythm on the wood plank floor as she moved from table to table. Her clothing didn't fit right, especially around the midriff. It may have been that she had outgrown them, but Steve thought otherwise. She had that look of a new mother back to work too soon.

Betsy was standoffish at first, but the lawyer in Steve could always get people to relax and open up. It was his specialty, what he had been known for (other than his famous courtroom bombshells). He never had the trouble that other lawyers did: talking down to people or coming off as phony. No person was too humble for him to adjust his mannerisms when information was needed. He could relate to all kinds, having himself been a troubled kid from an Indian reservation—the son of an alcoholic.

Steve learned through Betsy what he hadn't been able to coax from his client, that Denise acquired the gun a good month prior to the shooting to protect herself from the very man she shot. Betsy also pointed out that almost every cent Denise made went to drugs those final months. Often short on rent, she had to borrow to make it up. She would even choose hunger if in need of a fix, but despite this, she had the presence of mind to save enough to buy a gun.

"That's how much she feared that brute, Mr. Forrest."

Steve knew that Denise was to start counseling sessions the following Monday. It was to be an eight week program, the first couple of sessions a one-on-one before being introduced into group therapy. Randy made it clear that he would have liked her placed in a three- or six-month

243

program, but eight weeks was all they could get. Nick DiMonte made sure of that.

On the drive back, Steve turned off the freeway. He scoured for stones at the base of a scree slope while keeping an eye out for any plant that had the misfortune of seeding in an avalanche cone. Only mountain plants would do for his Zen garden. Even so, he made the decision that he was only going to take those under threat that needed his help to survive.

Steve didn't want to risk unthreatened plants to lower altitudes. Mountain plants have adapted to longer winters, higher winds and reduced oxygen, growing slower than their lowland cousins. These stunted specimens of endurance were adept at surviving, using boulders as shelter from lashing winds, cunningly growing outwards under cover rather than upward into harm's way.

It took the better part of a week for Steve to lay out the stones, every one having a specific function in the evolving design. Many were used at the base of the Chomolungma Stone to replicate the terrain surrounding Everest. Working from memory, it was a tricky business, more like a jigsaw puzzle than anything else. Others were set around the base of the Temple like the shrines he had seen in Tibet that looked out from high up on cliffs.

A scraggly, stunted fir saved from a stranglehold of rocks was carefully transplanted about halfway between the Chomolungma Stone and the Temple, set back close to the bamboo border but far enough away to provide the equivalent amount of sunlight it would receive under natural conditions. Each morning he stepped out into the backyard to appraise it before heading off to work. It seemed to take.

Just as Steve was planning a trip to Mount Adams—this time to rescue plants he noticed trapped in the scree slope he and the kids glissaded down—he received a telephone call from the last person on Earth he thought would want to contact him. The conversation was brief. Susan simply asked Steve to take Talitha off her hands, offering no explanation. He was puzzled by the request, but he agreed before his silence could be interpreted as a refusal.

It was arranged to meet at a point convenient to both. Steve mentioned Ellensburg, and Susan agreed. He decided to make a weekend outing of it. Saturday would be spent on Mount Adams in Yakima County with Josh and KariLyn. They would then drive north to Kittitas County to pick up Talitha in Ellensburg the following day. The outing was foremost a rescue mission. The plan was to stop at several points on their slide-down Sunday morning to save any plants in distress. Josh reluctantly agreed, having preferred to try to best the time he previously set.

Steve awakened early that Sunday morning, well before sunrise, plenty of time for him to find his way through the dark. He crossed the scree slope and made his way up to the spot where he sat months earlier, gazing up in the direction of the false peak, waiting for dawn. Goose bumps prickled his skin in anticipation, but when the time came, the sky was streaked in pink and salmon. The shadow of the mountain didn't throw its cloak over him as it did before. It was a more gentle transition to day this time around.

Dawn's hallowed minutes passed uneventfully while Steve sat dismayed. He looked up at the false peak questioningly, and it stared back down at him, providing no answers. As the day brightened, mountain birds started to call out the morning in a chorus in direct opposition to his growing disillusionment.

A mountain bluebird landed in a streak of blue. It immediately started to give Steve a talking to, pecking the earth to emphasize its point. He watched how the blue of its feathers, stretched out to intimidate, grew electric in the budding light. Having had its say, the bluebird flew off in the direction of the tent where his two kids were still fast asleep. He looked down at it, realizing that in a couple of hours he would have all three with him again.

Steve drove north, trying not to jolt the booty under the tarp that was used for transport. It was a bonanza. There was yarrow, woolly Pussytoes, mountain Arnica and silver Crown. Particular care had to be taken with the whorled leaves of the Heather and Heath. Although the Bear Grass he rescued would have to be periodically burned to produce strong new growth, he expected little trouble with the Moss Campion, happy to hug the ground for warmth. The pygmy Bitterroot usually found at higher altitudes was a special find.

Steve watered them from a jug brought along for that purpose after temporarily transplanting them into recycled plastic pots (using mountain earth), weighted down with the stones harvested from the slope, hoping that that would appease them after the shock of the bumpy ride down.

As prearranged, the family met at Shirley's, where Steve had breakfasted on his first trip to Ellensburg. Susan looked exquisite, her outfit appropriate for someone living in such a remote location, but beautifully put together. She always had a flare for adapting to her surroundings (as he hoped the mountain plants would to theirs). As they sat down to lunch, however, it dawned on Steve that her sun-kissed cheeks were a little too rosy to be real.

It was all surprisingly pleasant if not cozy and warm. Susan got what she wanted and was in an agreeable mood. The veneer cracked only when Steve asked about her new husband. She became standoffish, stabbing at her salad. After excusing herself to visit the washroom, she returned only to say she had to go, laying down enough money to pay for them all as well as a generous tip for the waitress. Kissing her finger, she touched the forehead of each of her children—insisting they call collect—before making a measured exit out the door.

Steve didn't have time to reflect on what happened. He had to get the booty back as quickly as possible. Each plant would have to be transplanted that day if it were to survive. He made a quick stop to see Randy and get updated on Denise, leaving the kids in the car. The arraignment was set to take place when Denise completed the drug rehabilitation program eight weeks hence. Before that happened, he needed to assure himself that his client was of sound mind for the ordeal ahead.

******

Talitha adjusted to her change in address with ease. Upon arrival, she raced up the stairs and bounced on her bed so everyone would know she was there to stay. That first night, when all three were asleep in their rooms, Steve stopped in front of her room and smiled. Using what was likely an old tube of her mother's lipstick rescued from the trash, Talitha printed out her name in cherry block letters on a piece of paper she taped to her door.

Within a week, Talitha was registered at her new school, and come September, she had charmed her new teachers who took it upon themselves to get the spritely little girl caught up with the class. She got herself invited to all her classmates' birthday parties and spent several nights at sleepovers. The backyard was the only matter of contention.

Talitha was disappointed that her father didn't use the bamboo to build a tower like she wanted. When Steve explained he was creating a Zen garden, she didn't looked impressed, noting there weren't any trees to climb or build a tree house in, just "bendy bamboo" as she put it and "prickly old plants" that stabbed her fingers.

After bringing Talitha out to the Chomolungma Stone, Steve told her it was the tallest mountain in the world, reproduced in miniature. He then escorted her to the Temple and explained it was built in honor of houses of meditation like those on Tibetan mountaintops.

The months preceding the holidays were especially busy. Not only did Steve have a full-time job and a house full of kids, but he was deep into preparatory work on Denise's trial. Most evenings were spent slogging through paperwork and working out a plan of action, all the prep work required by a good lawyer. He had no such influence over the nights.

Steve was having dreams unlike any he had had before. One in particular kept recurring: figures frozen in theatrical stances on a circular stage, bodies in arabesque and other positions suggestive of dance—lit so brightly all else was draped in velvet oblivion. Even though he couldn't see them, he could feel the faceless multitude gathered in the dark, gazing up at the stage with him, interconnected in heightened anticipation of the dance about to start. The dream always ended with the first beat of a drum.

When a *Rohatsu* (a traditional seven-day intensive) was announced for the first week of December, Steve signed up without first thinking it out. He managed to get the week off work with all the hours he banked the preceding year. Brian was surprisingly supportive and wouldn't hear of him offering to work through the holidays. Lila, having gotten wind of Steve's predicament, offered to move into his house for the week and act as chaperone to his kids. She countered his protests by saying it would save her a fortune in electricity (later admitting she was dying to try Steve's fancy new kitchen appliances).

Steve hoped Jack would make an appearance before the intensive, but he started to lose hope as the day approached. On the eve of it, he realized that he would have to go it alone; but once he accepted that fact, he felt that that was exactly what Jack intended. With a small suitcase packed with a change of clothes, a toothbrush and his oryoki set, he drove off in his Honda in the wee hours of the morning of the first of December.

Steve was greeted with smiles and little nods of recognition upon arrival at the Zen center. It was a full house. After the _han_ was struck, he got into the lineup to the *zendo*, psyching himself up for the seven days of silence ahead of him.

The trouble started soon after, at the end of the first meditation session when Steve stood to do a *gasho* bow with the others, just before *kinhin* (walking meditation). Something inside him went haywire. He simply couldn't stop himself as he bowed to everyone he met in the hall. He bowed to the chopping board and vegetables before he chopped them in the kitchen; he bowed to the server before and after he ladled food into his bowl; he even bowed to his oryoki set after setting it out.

So much deep bowing made Steve's old injuries flare up. He spent a sleepless night in pain in spite of the ibuprofen he took. At *teisho* the following day when the resident Zen master made a formal presentation to the congregation, he sat hunched over listening. Something the master said had resonated deep inside him. He found himself whispering it to himself despite the vow of silence he took.

"All things are equal, all things precious."

Later, during *zazen*, after turning the wooden *dokusan* sign and waiting his turn to meet one-on-one with a teacher, Steve sat mute, unable to express what was troubling him. All he knew was he was in crisis.

"All things are equal, all things precious," the teacher said, repeating the words of the master.

Steve blubbered something unintelligible.

"Before enlightenment, we chop wood and haul water, but after enlightenment…ahhh! We chop wood and haul water."

"I don't understand."

"Describe a Zen monk for me."

Steve thought about it before answering. "A Zen monk is one who is dedicated to enlightenment?"

"I beg to differ," the teacher said. "Simply put, a Zen monk is nothing special."

Steve stared at the dancing eyes, trying to grasp the point.

"Enlightenment illuminates truth, including the truth of the person inside us, both our virtues and our faults. When that happens, we find ourselves not set apart but on equal footing with all other things. Thus, all things are equal, all things precious."

"All things are equal, all things precious," Steve repeated.

"Do you think you're the first person we've seen compulsively bowing at an intensive?"

"You knew?"

"Of course we knew," the teacher said. "Why do you think the master said that at *teisho*?"

"He said it for me?"

"You've come to a realization in your journey that many have come to before," the teacher said, raising a finger to make a point, "but be aware, Zen isn't a self-improvement course. If your goal is to make yourself a different and, perhaps, a better person then you won't see and accept yourself as you are, will you?"

"I guess not."

"Accept yourself, faults and all, equal to and as precious as everything else in this world."

The throbbing in Steve's lower back diminished. He got up stiffly, bowing to the teacher and exiting *dokusan* to join the others. Throughout the remainder of the week, when inclined to bow, he did just that.

******

Recovery for Denise was a slow, arduous process. It meant dealing with her addiction and the prostitution that fed it. It also meant she had to come to terms with killing someone (however justified her action) without the benefit of hiding behind a veil of drugs. Only she could know what stared back at her when she looked in a mirror.

It was more than six months since Denise had had a fix, but that was due to confinement. Steve had to face the fact that if she had had the opportunity, she would have likely opted for the escape it offered. She was still struggling with recovery, and the thought of standing trial only made things worse. It terrified her, threatened to compromise the delicate emotional state that Randy carefully nurtured.

Steve went through Denise's meager wardrobe with Betsy who took it upon herself to store it at her place after her friend was evicted in absentia. Every article of clothing she owned was unsuitable for trial. Lila offered to whip something up on her sewing machine, using her collection of thrift shop fabrics, but Steve only to think of his curtains to politely decline the offer.

Denise needed a simple conservative outfit. Betsy came up with a navy blue skirt and matching blazer (her funeral wear) that didn't fit since giving birth. She also provided a pair of sensible black pumps she knew Denise would fit into, her friend having borrowed them in the past. Entering a ladies boutique to buy a blouse at his own expense, Steve was forced to use hand gestures to communicate the size required to a prickly old sales lady who took pleasure in his helplessness, rolling her eyes, asking questions she knew he wouldn't be able to answer.

251

Steve drove the three hours to Ellensburg after leaving work early to make it to the fitting scheduled three days in advance of the trial. The skirt had been a little long as were the sleeves of the blazer. The blouse, however, fit perfectly, and his heart warmed to the old sales lady at the boutique. As per Lila's instructions, he inserted pins to determine the length of Betsy's bequest, and before he drove off to work the next day he dropped off both skirt and blazer to be hemmed by his gracious neighbor.

A dress rehearsal of sorts took place the day before the trial. Steve felt harried by the drive to Ellensburg, knowing he would be doing it all over again the following morning, but everything needed to be ready. Criminal law was uncharted territory. Too many things could go wrong.

Denise's hair was pulled back into a simple ponytail as she modeled for Steve who stood back to appraise his client. She gained weight since the summer. Her face was no longer junky gaunt, but without makeup she appeared younger than her age, a teenager almost, which worked against the outfit he had carefully picked out, the impression he wanted to convey to the jury.

"Do you have mascara?" Steve said.

"No."

"I'll ask Betsy to drop some off."

"I don't want to wear makeup," Denise mumbled.

"Just a little," Steve said, "so you don't look like a kid."

Denise was fidgeting, clearly uncomfortable in what she was being forced to wear. "I look like a lawyer."

"You look smart."

Steve was concerned by her visible discomfort, the way she pulled at her skirt, how she kept fiddling with the buttons on the blazer. She looked as though she was on the verge of tears. She needed to relax.

"Good," Steve said. "Now we're going to practice breathing techniques."

"Breathing techniques?"

"Yes, breathing techniques, and how to meditate on your fears—techniques to help you deal with scary situations."

Denise's eyes met Steve's for the first time. "You're trying to make a Buddhist out of me?"

Steve saw the comment for what it was: an attempt at humor, a positive sign—the first that showed that Denise might be able to handle the stress of a trial. "One can only hope," he said, receptively, giving a little smirk.

Steve didn't get home until early evening, later than expected. His mind was on the trial as he slowly drove down the street. That was when he spied two figures smooching on his porch, and all thoughts of the trial evaporated in the blink of an eye.

Steve, releasing the pedal to allow the car to glide, watched as KariLyn pushed herself away and fumbled for her keys. He parked in the driveway, taking his time to get out.

"Hi dad," KariLyn said, "home late?"

"Yup, who's this?"

"Ezra," she blurted out, unable to suppress a girlish gush despite the anxiety at getting caught.

The teenage boy showed no sign of offering a hand or a nod in greeting. He eyed Steve lazily, unconcerned that his jeans were hanging off his hips, exposing boxers bunched up around a studded belt that offered no support. A tattoo was just visible under the sleeve of a loose-fitting t-shirt—frayed and proud of it. Everything about the boy's demeanor was lax except for his hair, shellacked to a gooey fluster that called to mind diverging winds.

"Nice to meet you, Ezra."

Ezra's eyes closed as he smiled.

******

253

The following morning Steve was on the road before the kids woke for school. Family obligations were divvied up, encouraged by a small allowance. Josh was commissioned to collect Talitha in the afternoon for the duration of the trial while it would be KariLyn's responsibility to make sure her little sister got her homework done and was fed a sensible meal.

Brian long knew that Steve would have to take time off work to represent Denise. He was ethically against it, however, and was vocal in his disapproval.

"You're not a criminal lawyer."

The criticism was justified, but Steve didn't see a way around it. Denise didn't have the money to pay for a toothbrush let alone a decent lawyer, even if she were open to it.

"Someone has to help her."

Steve was also aware that the hours he banked in overtime over the preceding year wouldn't cover both the time off he had taken for the intensive in December and the trial in March, especially if it were to drag on for any length of time; but being lawyers of conscience—people accustomed to making ethical decisions—the partners of Justice for the Earth agreed to support him in the end. He heard Katherine swung the vote in his favor.

The scent of pine and spruce helped to calm Steve's nerves as he wound his way through the Cascades, breathing in the mountain air. It invigorated him on the long drive east, keeping his senses brisk. He arrived early, before the trial was to start. None of the key characters had yet arrived at the courthouse. He took the opportunity to hunker down at the defense table to go over his notes one last time.

Steve jumped as a briefcase was slammed down across the aisle. Nick DiMonte had arrived, still irate that the defense had objected to the misogynist collection of rednecks the prosecution attempted to assemble at jury selection. The years seemed to have only exaggerated the surly features of the man, the overhang of the forehead and the bulbous brown eyes with the pointy lashes that made him the poster child of all things vile to the girls at the law school they had attended. Life for DiMonte had always seemed an insult his pride couldn't bear.

Steve decided to give it one more shot, but his old nemesis wouldn't take the bait when he looked over and smiled, prepared to stand and cross the aisle to shake hands. The opportunity was lost a moment later when a door opened and Denise was led in. She had put on a little makeup as he suggested, and even though her hair was again pulled back into a simple ponytail, she looked like a young woman and not a kid who had ransacked her mother's closet.

The courtroom quickly filled up. The press made sure that the story didn't die in the minds of its readership. Back in August, the local papers had it splashed all over the front pages. One such headline read "Junky Prostitute Guns Down Family Man!" The paper soon had to admit that the only "family" in "family man" was several illegitimate children that never received a dime in child support.

It wasn't long after that that the press got wind of the long history of battery and aggravated assault charges laid against the deceased (courtesy of Steve). Several of these women even agreed to stand witness for the defense after Steve won them over to the idea—something DiMonte fought against.

Steve had high hopes for Deputy Garcia's testimony. He was pretty sure DiMonte wouldn't be able to intimidate him. Betsy was going to be a key character witness. Randy was also scheduled to testify, being Denise's counselor and privy to her emotional state of mind.

Steve's biggest problem was Leo Benning (aka Leo the Liar), the only person to have witnessed the shooting (which had gone down on a street corner in the middle of the night). What he had to prove beyond a reasonable doubt was that Denise was a victim of attempted rape, regardless of her status as prostitute and drug addict.

"Hey, kid, how you doing?"

"Not too good," Denise whispered.

"Just relax," Steve said, encouragingly, rubbing her shoulder to stop her from fidgeting, "and don't worry. I'll be with you the whole time."

Conversation in the courtroom was cut off when the court clerk stood up to announce the judge who walked in from a door behind the judge's bench. The courtroom became silent as the judge settled into the chair, setting a stack of folders down and pulling out a pair of glasses from a case.

Steve's mind immediately focused on the two loud bangs of the mallet. It brought to mind a *han* signaling the start of *zazen*. He smoothed out the thrift shop tie Lila had sewn for him (insisting he wear it for luck) while the judge addressed the courtroom.

"This court is now in session."

******

The residents kept a respectable distance, peeping from behind shrubs, peering down from the windows that overlooked the garden. No one was allowed to get too close under the Professor's orders. He stood guard with his walker a little way off, blocking access to the path that led to the bench. The birds were under no such restrictions. They chirped and cawed and cooed in the trees, having come back to nest in this little inner city sanctuary after the plastic bags were removed from the branches.

Steve stared down at the tear-blot stains on his dress shoes. It was upon arrival at the Green Lake Retirement and Nursing Home that he finally surrendered to his

256

feelings, emotions so consuming that he couldn't even bring himself to speak. What he desired most was time alone here, in this garden, where he had spent so many hours reflecting on his life. It was where he returned after hearing the verdict.

The trial started out well. DiMonte's opening statements only served to distance the jury, their faces expressing little appreciation to his brusque manner. Like any good lawyer, Steve knew not to treat jurors like a herd of sheep. He respected their individual personalities. During his opening statements, he only approached those whose body language appeared receptive. Others he granted their personal space.

After opening statements concluded, the prosecution first called the sexual assault nurse examiner to the stand. The SANE testified to assessing Denise sixty-two hours after the shooting, when the drugs wore off and she was deemed fit for such an examination. Nurse Tanaka was a plain-speaking professional accustomed to providing evidence in court proceedings. DiMonte was careful not to interrupt as she read through her findings, wanting her out of the way as quickly as possible.

According to the SANE, Denise had bite marks to the left shoulder and on the soft tissue of the upper left breast that matched the dental records of the deceased. Fingernail lacerations were found on the lower left back. It was inconclusive whether the wounds were obtained at the crime scene even though the lacerations had occurred approximately fifty to seventy hours prior to the time of the examination. Nurse Tanaka explained that the pattern of slight bruising visible on Denise's face was likely the result of a large hand that grabbed and pushed on the cheekbone and forehead in a backward and downward motion.

"Did you find evidence of rape?"

Nurse Tanaka stared at DiMonte before responding. "Everything I just said is evidence of rape."

DiMonte raised his voice for the benefit of the jury, ignoring the SANE's look of disdain. "Evidence of a possible attempted rape, you mean?"

"Yes."

"Did the accused have bruising on or around her genitalia?"

"No."

"Was there any evidence of semen on the accused, that is, semen matching the deceased?"

The look on Nurse Tanaka's face made Steve smile. "No."

"So, it's your professional opinion that the accused wasn't actually raped, that a rape never occurred?"

The SANE took a moment to answer, staring unflinchingly at the prosecutor. "It is."

"Thank you."

The rest of the day and the following morning were dedicated to forensics and expert witnesses. The medical examiner provided the results of the autopsy. The deceased died from a single bullet wound received at point-blank range to the middle area of the torso, just below the chest, causing massive internal bleeding.

"Death occurred within minutes."

The smoking gun was a Beretta 950 Jetfire, a "pocket pistol" designed for self-defense, as was confirmed by the firearms and ballistics expert.

"The .25 ACP cartridges are not powerful by any stretch, but the pistol is lethal if a shot is well placed at close range."

DiMonte kept a tight leash on Leo Benning, called to the stand first thing on the afternoon the day after forensics concluded, clearly worried that the only witness to the crime was apt to exaggerate or make things up. Scripted in short sentences, one after the other, the courtroom listened to Leo's description of how Denise called over the deceased from across the street, and when he didn't comply, she made her way across to him.

"Swaggering like a hussy, using language ya'd never heard from a chick before."

The witness stated on the record that the accused started to become aggressive when the deceased, Jason, refused her offer of sex.

"He had to fight the chick off!"

In Jason's attempt to break away, Leo believed his friend may have ripped some buttons off the blouse of the accused and bit her to force her to let go, but he found it impossible to say definitively, owing to the dark conditions. However, Leo conveniently recalled that Jason pushed his assailant backwards from the face in a last attempt to break away from the assault. It was at that point the pistol had been fired.

"All's I know is that's when I heard a bang."

Leo's primary purpose was clearly to fill the holes in the story the prosecution knew the forensics and expert witnesses would expose during the first days of the proceedings. When Steve stood to cross-examine the witness, he took note of the curl on the silvery lips. In the hope that Leo would continue to betray his character, Steve positioned himself in such a way the man's face was in full view of the jury.

"Why do people call you Leo the Liar?"

"I object!" DiMonte shouted, shooting up from his chair.

"Sustained," the judge said. "The statement will be stricken from the records. You'll refrain from using such tactics in this courtroom, Mr. Forrest."

"I apologize, Your Honor," Steve said, knowing the damage was done. He let the jury know that the man in the witness box was a celebrated liar, likely having committed perjury on several counts. Before continuing, he offhandedly glanced at the Bible that Leo had sworn on to see if a handprint was branded on the cover. "How tall was Jason?"

"Don't know."

"You don't know?" Steve said, folding his arms around his chest. "How much did he weigh?"

"Couldn't tell ya."

"Allow me to enlighten you," Steve said. "The deceased was six feet two and a half inches tall and weighed two hundred and fifty-three pounds, according to the autopsy records. Could you take a guess at the height and weight of the accused?"

The curl on the lip dried up by then.

"She's five foot two and currently weighs one hundred and eight pounds. She's gained about ten pounds since August," Steve added, shifting position to make eye contact with the jury, "since she's been in rehabilitation to tackle her addiction."

"What of it?"

"Well," Steve said, turning back to the witness, "it seems unlikely that a man who's over six feet two and two hundred and fifty-three pounds would have to fight off a woman who's barely five foot two and less than one hundred pounds, don't you think?"

"She had a gun."

Steve pretended to clear his throat to allow time for the statement to resonate. "But neither you nor the deceased knew she had a gun until the shot rang out. Isn't that correct?"

Steve watched as Leo's eyeballs shifted to the prosecution table.

"I have no more questions, Your Honor."

Betsy was called up midweek, deliberately coinciding with the prosecution's game plan, kicking into full force. DiMonte was able to turn the evidence around to his advantage. From that point forward, he focus on the fact that Denise obtained a gun a month in advance of the

260

shooting as proof of premeditated murder. He had Betsy on the stand all morning and the better part of the afternoon, lobbing questions at her only to challenge every answer, making her appear flighty and unreliable, determined to destroy her credibility as an upcoming witness for the defense.

Before the trial was even under way, the prosecution tried to amass a series of grandmotherly types from Ellensburg to be used to engender sympathy with the female jurors, fearing female-to-female empathy. Steve alone had understood the logic behind the tactic. No man had ever been spurned by women as many times as DiMonte. In college, he would approach women with fists clenched, using the same lines that failed him in the past. He became an untouchable as far as the female student-body was concerned. Women instinctually despised him.

Steve argued against it, of course, formally requesting a motion of denial, but the judge allowed for one prejudicial witness, which the prosecution flaunted shamelessly. This self-proclaimed Ellensburg society-queen testified of her indignation of this "ticking time bomb" that roamed the streets of the place she had spent her sanctified life, preying on the town's husbands and sons. Steve was mindful in his cross-examination. Any hint of harassment and he could've lost the jury, which had been DiMonte's plan all along.

After the prosecution rested, Steve called for a motion to dismiss even though he knew it would be denied. It was a formality to express to the jury that the defense felt the prosecution failed in its attempt to prove the defendant's guilt beyond a reasonable doubt. The days that followed were dedicated to the Beretta 950 Jetfire to try to refute what the prosecution established, that the alleged crime was premeditated and must therefore be murder.

Steve had to first establish Jason's history of abuse and, in particular, abuse towards women. There were reports dating back to his teenage years. Police were called to his residence for allegations of domestic abuse on numerous occasions. One woman who worked at the bar where Denise worked even had a court order against him. The problem wasn't a lack of evidence or witness willingness to testify; it was the prosecution's incessant pretrial motions to deny the admissibility of this history since the deceased wasn't the one on trial.

Steve was aware of the danger of putting Denise in the witness box. A lawyer never allows the person they represent to sabotage him or herself. First year law students could tell you that. The prosecution would take every opportunity to deconstruct whatever Denise gained in therapy, but as the trial entered its second week, Steve started to see it as the only way in which they could get around the problem of concealment of a dangerous weapon. Even so, he held off making that decision until the end.

The defense was somewhat successful in introducing uncertainty into the prosecution's case. Through Deputy Garcia, Steve was able to establish a sense that the sequence of events leading up to the shooting remained in doubt given that it could only be corroborated by a single witness. Betsy did much better the second time around when recalled to the witness box. She was able to convey the fear Denise lived with. Randy proved invaluable. The jury listened intently to his testimony concerning the desperation brought on by drug addiction.

"I call Denise Fairwood to the stand."

No one expected this, least of all the prosecution, but once Steve spoke the words there was no turning back. He had prepared Denise as much as possible. At first she refused to testify (hysterical at the thought of it), but he was insistent, asserting there was in actuality two surviving witnesses to the crime, and if she refused to testify to what really happened, Leo the Liar's version of events would forever be taken as fact.

"Please state your name for the court," the judge said.

"Denise Fairwood."

"Speak up, please."

"Denise Fairwood."

"You may choose to place your hand on the Bible if you wish."

Unlike Leo before her, Denise didn't hesitate, placing a hand firmly on the book, looking up at the judge, her eyes glossy with fear.

"Do you swear or affirm to the best of your knowledge that the statements you are about to give will be the truth the whole truth and nothing but the truth?"

"I do."

"She's your witness, Mr. Forrest."

"Did you shoot Jason Barnacle?"

Denise swallowed hard before answering. "Yes."

With that out of the way, Steve backtracked to her first encounter with the deceased. He let the story play out from the first time Jason fondled her as she was laying out drinks to the moment she pulled the trigger. The jury heard how Jason introduced her to cocaine; at first supplying her free-of-charge until she got hooked, then demanding money he knew she couldn't repay.

"He said I could pay by having sex with him."

"And he made it clear he would continue to supply you with cocaine if you continued to have sex with him?"

"Yes, but he made me have sex with other men too. He said he'd cut off the coke if I didn't."

"And you got hooked?"

"Yes, and that's when the beatings started."

In his testimony, Randy already established the characteristic downward spiral of drugs and prostitution. Get a girl hooked on drugs and then use her as a sex slave while demanding a percentage of her income. Denise's therapist was quick to point out the high frequency in

263

which prostitutes get beaten in Washington, and when DiMonte tried to challenge the statement with an objection, Randy shot him down by citing the statistics.

"Why didn't you go to the police?"

"I couldn't."

The question was only a reminder for the benefit of the jury. Randy previously explained (under Steve's directions) that it was typical for prostitutes to shun any police intervention since the police, in the point of view of a prostitute, were seen as aggressors. He affirmed that this behavior was especially prevalent for prostitutes harboring serious addictions.

"So you bought a pistol legally to protect yourself?"

"I was so scared of what he'd do, what he said he was going to do."

"Do you understand you need a permit to carry a dangerous weapon?"

"Yes."

"But you carried it in your purse anyway?"

"Yes."

"Why?

"My apartment had a lock on the door…everywhere else I was a target."

Like a conductor of a symphony, Steve looked down at the floor for a beat of time. "What happened that night?"

In Denise's version of events, it was Jason who called her over and when she didn't comply, he crossed the street with Leo in tow. That was the low point in her addiction. She was in such a state she couldn't even run away. All she could do was tremble as Jason ripped her blouse open and started to bite her breasts.

"I tried to back away but he grabbed me by the back and pushed me towards him, rubbing against me, telling me no one wanted to have sex with a dirty little whore like me. That's when he started to pull me into an alley."

"What did you do?"

Denise started to lose her composure by then, her eyes darting around the room. "I pleaded for him to stop, but he and Leo just laughed at me, mimicking my pleas."

"Go on."

"I stamped a heel on his foot. It made him mad. I knew I was in trouble, big trouble. I could see the rage in his eyes, even in the dark. I knew I was going to be beaten and raped right where I stood."

"What happened next?" Steve said, pressing on before losing her.

"Jason clamped a hand over my face to force me to the ground. He had such big hands…I couldn't breathe. I couldn't see. All I could do was fumble with the zipper of my purse."

"And you shot him?"

That was the moment that swung the verdict. The story being laid out seemed to have an effect on Denise as it had on everyone else in the courtroom. Up to that point, the courtroom was as silent as a *zendo*. Looking back, Steve now thought it was Denise's own emaciated voice that made her angry with herself. She faced her lawyer; her eyes narrowed in latent fury, her lips tightening, turning red, before forcing them apart to answer the question.

"I missed."

Steve remembered staring in astonishment, and Denise staring back, defiantly meeting his look of shock. Every time they went over her testimony it was all he could do to get her to speak up and stop fidgeting, but out of nowhere she had gotten her backbone back, and at the worst possible moment imaginable. He was relying on her wounded exterior—the beaten face of a helpless victim—to generate sympathy with the jurors.

"You missed?"

"Yes, I missed…I was aiming for his balls."

******

"Steve?"

Randy's voice jolted Steve out of his trance. He stared down at the old pair of shoes that had stepped into his field of vision.

"It's all settled."

Steve looked up and saw Denise behind Randy. Both were smiling. They looked like a dream from behind his tears.

"It'll be minimum wage," Helen said, "but they'll provide her a room since she'll be working the graveyard shift."

Steve nodded, too grateful to do more. When the verdict was read that afternoon, the words "not guilty" seemed to have been issued as much for him as they were for Denise. He felt a sudden, intense and overwhelming sense of gratefulness for his trials and setbacks. He understood, suddenly, that it was these difficulties that would lead him on the circuitous path to enlightenment—that if his path were made easier his journey would be fruitless. He realized mostly, in a flash of understanding, that he wasn't alone on this epic journey of his. A higher power hovered near.

"Let's get you inside and out of the chill," Helen said. "We've got something to tell you."

"That's right," the Professor said. "We've got ourselves a new delicacy on the menu. They call it green tea. I can't get enough of the stuff."

Part Three: Toward the Transcendent

"Value the water more than the pitcher": Rumi

Chapter Eight

The wedding was a blustery affair. Every time bouquets were righted they were knocked over again by a gust of wind, petals flying like confetti. The ceremony should've probably been moved indoors, but the Professor was adamant. He insisted that he be married on the exact spot where he first stole a kiss from his bride.

Talitha sat on Steve's lap while Josh graciously offered the last available chair to his older sister only to hoist himself up a tree and perch on a branch. Steve gestured his son down, but the Professor, standing resolute by the trellis with the minister (a cousin brought out of retirement to perform the ceremony), called out to leave the boy be.

Helen looked magnificent when she appeared in a knee-length skirt and matching jacket, holding tightly to a spray of flowers. She was a vision in tweed. The invited guests (mostly made up of the residents of the nursing home) weren't able to keep silent. They applauded as she made her way up the path crammed between wheelchairs, walkers and the cafeteria chairs set out willy-nilly where space allowed, holding onto their hats and kerchiefs.

It must have taken a whole can of hairspray to make Helen's hair stay in place, but it did the job. She looked radiant. The wedding was the most exciting thing to happen at the Green Lake Retirement and Nursing Home since Copeland was ousted. Months of preparation went into it. Suits and dresses were taken out of funeral storage. Med schedules were adapted to accommodate the festivities. No one wanted to miss the cake.

There wasn't anything to dampen the mood—not even the wind—and no nervousness to speak of in the bride and groom. When it came time to kiss the bride, Helen acquiesced and allowed the Professor to remove her cat eye glasses after she removed his clunky old bifocals and tucked them into his suit pocket. An audible peck to the lips was followed by a loving hug, the newlyweds blinking blindly at their guests. Everyone hollered approval.

Steve had a telephone message waiting for him when he arrived home with the kids. He listened to the message and punched in the number left for him to call back.

"Why'd you move back to Seattle?"

A long pause followed. Susan never liked questions.

"Things didn't work out."

"What things?"

"We're too different," she said, bringing the topic to an end. "I have a favor to ask."

"Okay."

"Could you meet him?

"Who?"

"Jeremy."

Steve felt a stillness start to gather inside him, at odds with the apprehension he suddenly felt stir.

"Why?"

"He's struggling."

"Financially?"

"Spiritually."

"Oh," Steve said, taken by surprise. "In what way?"

"In an annoying way," Susan said, impatiently. "Look, I thought you'd be the person to ask since you're into that type of thing."

Steve took a little breath to stall for time. He wasn't sure he wanted to meet this Jeremy character, but the stillness that settled deep inside his *dan t'ian* rose like a fountain, and he heard himself say, "I'll be glad to help."

268

******

Steve eyed the other patrons crowded into the little round tables at the coffee shop, trying to spot a person that fit the varying descriptions his kids provided. The only real physical description of any worth came from Josh.

"He's tall."

KariLyn spoke of the man's blond hair and gallant build like he was a knight at medieval court. Talitha—bless her heart—tried her best, but being the little girl she was, the more she tried the more outlandish her description became.

"He looks like a frog that's been kissed into a prince."

Despite his misgivings, Steve knew immediately when the man finally stepped through the revolving doors. In the end, Talitha wasn't far off in her description, and neither were his other kids. The man was indeed tall, blond and gallant looking, and the broad mouth was a little froglike.

Jeremy looked mostly like money, and not in an ostentatious way. It was partly the clothes he wore (top-of-the-line if slightly disheveled) and partly the casual way in which he held himself. Their eyes met in mutual recognition, and a signal was exchanged to hold up a moment.

Jeremy headed for the barista behind the counter, holding up the mug he walked in with. Steve had about a minute to scrutinize the man, younger than expected—someone who lived in the woods but owned his own Starbuck's mug. He found himself quick to be critical and spent the remaining seconds cleansing all negative thoughts, forcing a smile as Jeremy circumnavigated the tight little tables without spilling a drop from his mug.

"Do I look familiar?" Jeremy said, sitting back in a chair and crossing one leg over the other.

269

Steve was a little startled by the comment. "Have we met?"

"I was the person to your right, across the room, at *Rohatsu*."

"You were at *Rohatsu*?" Steve said, astonished. He didn't expect to have a history with the man. All the same, he got his wits about him, asking the first question that popped into his head. "Been meditating long?"

Jeremy gave a rueful smile. "Not long enough…just a year in spotty personal practice, then more regularly up in the woods. To tell the truth, I didn't think I was going to make it through the first day of *Rohatsu*. I felt like running out screaming."

Steve sympathized. He knew through experience that one should work up to *Rohatsu*. Jeremy probably jumped in too far too fast and found himself over his head.

"Do you have a teacher to guide you?"

"No."

Steve broke the ice by talking about his teacher. Jeremy sat absorbed, listening to every word. As time went on, Steve started to feel more at ease with this person he didn't think he'd even like—this enigma who married his former wife in a whirlwind romance. He felt comfortable enough to ask more personal questions.

"Are you Christian?"

"Baptized," Jeremy said, indifferently, "but I've become a little disenchanted with the inflexible dogma of 'Big Brother,'" he added, using his fingers as quotation marks much like Susan did.

Steve smiled. "My Zen teacher is a Catholic priest."

It took a whole mug of coffee and half a refill to answer all Jeremy's questions on the subject. He had a hard time coming to terms with the apparent conflict of interest.

"I've my doubts, Steve," Jeremy said, shaking his head. "It seems to me that that would cause an internal struggle in the best of men."

270

"Doubt is an integral part of the Zen path," Steve said, elucidating on what he had learned from others. "Great faith, great doubt and great perseverance are one set of what's known as the Three Pillars of Zen, each given equal weight."

Steve stopped himself from commenting on the pad and pen Jeremy took out of his jacket.

"I was told to think of the Three Pillars as a three-legged milking stool. If you cut off one of the legs, the stool falls over." Steve waited as Jeremy finished scribbling notes. "What prompted you to try Zen?"

"Dissatisfaction," Jeremy said, looking up from his pad. "I guess my interest in it grew at the same time I decided to buy the property out in the woods."

"Near Chesaw?"

"Yup, up near the Canadian border," Jeremy said. "I bought it before I met Susan. Everything came to a halt while we courted and ended up getting married. After that, I decided to sell the place and give up on the idea of a solo retreat, but Susan talked me out of it."

"She did?"

"Does that surprise you?"

"I'd say," Steve said.

"She thought it would bring us closer if we meditated together."

Steve choked on the coffee he was attempting to swallow. "Susan practices meditation?"

Jeremy smiled. "I think she thought it romantic, the idea of it anyway," he said, looking up at the ductwork, "but it went south fast."

Steve managed to mask a smirk in a muffled cough, taking advantage of the napkin at hand. He wasn't sure where the sudden spiteful burst came from, and he swept his eyes over the other patrons half believing he would catch sight of a chimera-like shadow flickering in illusion.

"Neither of us realized how hard it'd be to keep up personal meditation practice. It seemed to me that sitting still and being quiet wouldn't be a big deal, but the deeper we got into it the harder it became, and the more our relationship deteriorated from our disappointment in not being able to stay with it."

Steve's *dan t'ian* started to warm in understanding. "Are you familiar with 'spiritual materialism'?"

Steve hadn't been either until it was raised in conversation over lunch with the others at the restaurant after the conclusion of the last intensive he had attended. It seemed to apply, so he gave it a shot.

"The term was coined by a Tibetan Buddhist teacher who settled somewhere in Colorado."

"Trungpa Rinpoche?"

Steve stared in disbelief.

"I believe spiritual materialism refers to how people try to possess their spirituality in the same way they possess a car or a house, rather than inviting it in and surrendering to the great patience required to commit the time and effort for that to take place."

"You sure you don't have a Zen teacher?"

"I've been building a collection of CD recordings of Zen masters," Jeremy admitted. "If you're interested, I'll be glad to lend you a few."

******

"Just a bout of the flu, Steve…nothing for you to worry about."

Steve handed Jack a mug of streaming hot rooibos—an herbal tea rumored to ward off disease. He knew the remark was meant as a joke, but there was nothing funny about Jack's appearance. His teacher lost weight since his last visit, too much weight. More worrying was the purple discoloration around the eye sockets, a

272

deeper, darker purple than the polka dot curtain panels inside the house.

Steve could no longer play along. "We both know it's not the flu."

Jack rested the mug on the little thrift shop table set beside the kitchen chair brought out for his use. "As Buddhism teaches, all things arise, abide and pass away."

"Shouldn't we discuss this?"

"What's to discuss?" Jack said. "I'm not going to be here forever. Anyway, my eventual departure might benefit you in the end."

Steve breathed in the nutty flavor of the tea before taking a sip. "Don't say that."

"Why not?"

Steve plunked down on the deck in answer, refusing the comfort of the lawn chair. "There's nothing beneficial about losing a friend and teacher."

"Have I ever told you the story of the dying master?"

Steve looked over at Jack in amazement. "Do you have a Zen story for every occasion?"

There was something in the way Jack grinned that sparked the old vitality.

"A mournful group of students gathered around their dying master. 'Whatever will we do without you?' they said, tears streaming. 'You have nurtured us for many years.' The master looked up from his deathbed and said, 'you may well be better off without me.' The students gloom turned to incomprehension on hearing his words. 'How can that be?' The master only smiled. 'All these years I sat by the riverbank ladling out river water for you. After I'm gone, perhaps you'll finally notice the river.'"

"I suppose the meaning is to value the water more than the pitcher."

273

"Simply put, yes," Jack said. "By the way," he added, gazing down from the deck, "your Zen garden is doing nicely."

Steve smiled with pride. He was hoping Jack would notice.

"Is that little wall of stones around that little fir tree supposed to symbolize the spirit rocks?" Jack said, pointing to the middle back of the garden near the bamboo hedging.

"Yes."

"And the heather edging close to the Chomolungma Stone has taken too," Jack added, "like a miniature forest approaching the steps of a colossal mountain."

"That was the intention," Steve said, reflecting back on all the trouble he had had in creating the effect.

"How's the *tera* holding up in the rain?"

Steve looked lovingly at the Temple. "The sound of the rain drumming on the bamboo is a wonder to listen to, but Jack," Steve said, turning back to his friend, "are you sure we shouldn't invite him to join us for tea?"

"Brother Peter? No," Jack said, "he'd only decline. He's under strict orders to drive me back to the rectory. Anyway, I'm sure he's happy to spend a little secular time listening to the radio in the car, catching up with the world."

"I suppose."

"So how was the wedding?"

"Gusty," Steve said, "but nice all the same."

"And Denise?"

"Too busy with the residents to get into trouble."

"The kids?"

"Susan took them for the day," Steve said, swirling around the scotch-colored brew, still debating if the taste agreed with him. "You know, Jack, it amazes me that they never seem to be around when you come to visit."

Jack only smiled. "And you and Susan are becoming friends, you said?"

"Yes, but in a way we never were. It's like we're returning to something new, if that makes any sense."

Draped in a blazer now two sizes too big for his frame, Jack regarded his pupil for a stretch of time. "Have you and I ever discussed the Ox Herding Pictures?"

"Once," Steve said, "the one where the ox disappears out a window and into the Absolute. What exactly are they?"

"Ten pictures illustrating the ten stages of Gautama Buddha's progression towards enlightenment."

"Like the twelve Stations of the Cross?"

"The Passion depicts the events of a single day," Jack said. "The Ox Herding Pictures represent a lifetime's journey."

"Why an ox?" Steve said, kicking off his sandals.

"The ox is a metaphor for enlightenment," Jack said, going over the pictures in his mind. "The first depicts Gautama's aimless wandering in search for an answer to his spiritual dissatisfaction."

Steve immediately thought of Jeremy, recalling how he used the same word only days earlier.

"The second is the discovery of the ox's footprints, which Gautama follows."

"What's the third?"

"Gautama glimpsing the ox's backside."

"Really?"

"Gautama perceives the ox but is yet unable to see it," Jack elucidated.

"What about the fourth?"

"The fourth depicts Gautama catching up to the ox, and the fifth depicts him taming it after a long struggle."

"And the sixth?"

"Gautama's great joy as he rides the ox," Jack said with a smile, "playing a flute without a care in the world while the ox leads him home."

"And the seventh is when the ox disappears, right?"

275

"The Ox doesn't disappear; it transcends, and all becomes still." Jack looked up at the sky as he spoke. "The next, the eighth, is often left blank."

"Why?"

Jack closed his eyes and let the sun warm his face. "It represents the Buddha's transcendence with the ox. All is empty. Enlightenment is realized."

"If enlightenment is realized, what's the ninth?"

"The sound of cicadas."

"Cicadas?"

"The Buddha has returned to the source—the world in other words. He has achieved enlightenment, and the cicadas sing."

"Then why is there a tenth?"

"The tenth shows the Buddha re-entering society with a huge grin and many gifts for others, though his hands are empty. His gifts are from the heart. He's said to be 'entering the marketplace with helping hands.'"

Steve looked at his toes, counting each one off as he ran through the pictures in his head. "Where am I in this series?"

Jack's eyelids popped opened. "Do you mean which picture represents the current state of your path to enlightenment?"

"Exactly," Steve said, hoping he wasn't staring at the backside of an ox.

All the loose skin hanging from the sickly old face transformed into a sunburst of creases and folds. Jack started to laugh but pulled a hanky from a pocket when a coughing fit hit.

"So you and Susan are returning to something new?"

"Yes," Steve said, watching Jack wipe blood from his nose. "It's odd; I can't explain it. I don't know where this is going."

"It's not odd at all, and it's perfectly explainable," Jack said, a little hoarse. "Many in Buddhism believe that opening ourselves to our true natures and participating in Zen practice take a spiral course, much like a whirlpool. We eddy around as we move upwards toward the Light, revisiting the same stages in our lives but with greater and greater understanding."

Steve was startled by a figure in black that appeared by the side of the house.

"Isn't it time we return to the rectory, Father?"

"So soon?"

Brother Peter stood his ground, his arms folded behind his back. While Steve helped Jack down the steps, he noticed how the young cleric seemed to regard the garden with a look of puzzlement.

******

Steve stared transfixed at the half moons and stars, the ringed planets and the spaceships puttering between them. So bright was the moon and so low in the sky that the print of Lila's curtains had transferred like a stencil to his bedroom walls. It kept him awake as his mind drifted back to what had happened that day.

By midmorning, Steve had the trailer hooked up and was all ready to drive off and spend the day harvesting the mountains with Talitha, but just as they were about to lock up the house, the phone rang, and the plans for the day got shelved.

"Daddy drove right through a stop sign!" Talitha blurted out, running to her mother with arms flung wide.

Susan was wearing tight-fitting black slacks and a cream-colored ribbed sweater under a soft suede jacket. The outfit was classic Susan except for one important difference: running shoes, and not new ones at that. They were a little scruffy at the toe caps.

277

Susan, having caught Talitha in her arms, smiled as Steve approached.

"The other two were out," Steve said for lack of anything better to say.

Susan plunked down her daughter and took her by the hand. "Busy with their friends."

Steve's body seized when his former wife slipped her free arm into his and started to lead him down the Burke-Gilman Trail, a place they hadn't walked together since early in their marriage. Talitha pulled away and ran ahead.

"Sometimes it's hard to give the three of them the attention they need all at the same time," Susan mused, reflectively. "Other times they don't seem to need anything at all."

"They're growing up."

"Jeremy's quite taken with you, you know?"

"Is he?"

"Uh-huh."

"Well, we've gotten to know each other," Steve said. "He comes over occasionally with Buddhist tapes for me to listen to."

"Sounds exciting."

"It's not what you think," he said, accepting the friendly taunt for what it was. "They're lectures by acclaimed Buddhist teachers."

Susan looked up into his eyes. "You know, when he talks about you, I don't recognize the person he's talking about."

"I've changed."

"I've noticed."

"What have you noticed?"

Steve had stopped, waiting for an answer.

"What do you mean?"

"How have I changed?"

Susan took a moment to think it over. "You seem more hesitant."

"Dad!" Talitha yelled from up the trail, pointing down to the water's edge. "What kind of ducks are those?"

Hours later, lying in bed under the cinematic backdrop on his bedroom walls, Steve recalled how bent around Susan to see, and as he did, he had caught the perfume of her hair—a scent he could still describe in detail. At the time, though, his voice got caught in the lump in his throat as he shouted back the answer.

"Common goldeneye."

People on the trail turned to look at what sounded like a duck call, but Talitha stared straight at her parents. In her little hooded raincoat—a hand-me-down from her sister—she appeared like a miniature icon in gold, but whatever had gotten into the little girl lasted only a moment. She soon ran off again, weaving through strollers.

Susan didn't seem to notice the strange glint in her daughter's eyes. "Not too far," she called out before leaning into Steve's ear. "You're a birder?"

Steve could still feel the heat that rose in his cheeks.

"I've tried to acquaint myself with some of the local bird community," was all that he said at the time.

"Have you?"

"I'm trying to understand the natural world a little better, if you want to know."

The natural world was out in force on the Burke-Gilman Trail. Song birds were running through their repertoire in the trees while ducks quacked contently in the canal, just out of reach, calling out from the water's edge. Only the squirrels seemed preoccupied. Several with prized nuts in their jaws zipped across the trail and flung themselves up trees, spiraling out of sight.

"So, you and Jeremy listen to Buddhist tapes together," Susan said, rerouting the conversation. "Do you discuss them afterwards?"

"Yes, always."

"Do you discuss other things?"

"Like what?"

Susan flipped back her hair in that old college way of hers.

"Do you talk about me?"

They continued arm in arm, listening to the bird songs. Rain fell in a fine mist, but they hardly noticed. Talitha cartwheeled and got her hands muddy, but neither parent scolded her. It was a day to remember, one of simple bliss.

The half moons and stars, the ringed planets and the spaceships fluttered in a waft of air that sifted through the windows, calling Steve from his reverie. He refocused his attention on the celestial shadow play dancing on the walls. The heavenly scene started to fade as the moon sank to the horizon, and he closed his eyes and waited to dream.

******

"Smells great, Kari," Steve said, striding into the kitchen.

KariLyn was wearing her most recent creation. She made such pretty clothes on Lila's sewing machine, but this oversized, cumbersome tunic baffled her father. It fell heavily to her knees. On top of that, the fabric choice was unbecoming. The camouflage print made her look like she was trying to disappear.

All the same, Steve was relieved. He had been concerned over KariLyn's health. Tuesday morning found her unable to get out of bed. He considered calling a doctor, but his daughter talked him out of it, telling him it was a girl thing and it would pass. That night KariLyn looked much better, but she seemed to relapse the following morning.

Nevertheless, standing over the stove, stirring the spaghetti sauce, KariLyn was a specimen of beauty despite the sack she wore. There was a shine in her long dark hair and complexion that had nothing to do with the steam from the pot.

"Feeling better?"

KariLyn didn't answer. She continued to stir as if she didn't hear.

"KariLyn?"

"Dad…we need to talk."

Steve never heard her speak in such a tone. He felt a pressure build around his chest.

"Okay, Kari, what's up?"

KariLyn's head sank to the point where she was staring down into the pot, clasping the spoon like a crutch. A muffled sound came from her like she was trying not to cry.

"KariLyn?"

"I'm pregnant, dad."

A shadow passed before Steve's eyes. His hands formed into fists; his nostrils flared, but he wasn't the man he used to be. He had journeyed far. Recognizing this transformation for what it was, he breathed in from his *dan t'ian*, regaining a sense of balance.

KariLyn continued to stare down into the simmering sauce, unable to face her father.

"Are you sure?"

Any possibility to the contrary was obliterated by the silence that followed.

The shadow stayed close. Steve could sense it watching, waiting for an opportunity to strike. He ran his fingers through his hair to give himself a moment to think, but every passing second made the weight of the revelation grow heavier. He couldn't even form a coherent thought. He decided to trust his heart.

"I love you, Kari, more than you will ever know."

281

KariLyn burst into tears. Steve could see her knees start to wobble. He stepped up and wrapped his arms around her from the back. She spun in his arms and buried her face in his chest. Tears flowed like a mountain spring.

Standing there, holding his daughter, Steve realized that Lila must have known. That was why she dropped by, insisting on taking Talitha for the afternoon.

"A girl's never too young to learn to bake," his neighbor said, enticing the little girl with a cookie as she led her away.

Lila probably would've insisted on taking Josh along to learn the art of cookie making if he wasn't out playing football with friends. Steve wasn't angry, which surprised him. He was relieved KariLyn didn't suffer her secret alone.

KariLyn spoke through her tears, "I was such a fool!"

Steve was soon to discover why the shadow lingered close, why it didn't dissipate. Ezra dumped his daughter the moment he found out he got her pregnant. He wouldn't even answer her phone calls. KariLyn kept on trying until Ezra's mother picked up instead.

"She called me a whore!"

Father and daughter only let go when the sauce started to boil over and smolder on the stovetop. KariLyn wiped her eyes on a kitchen towel and turned down the heat.

"Does your mother know?"

"No."

Dread bled into Steve. It wasn't a week since that magical day spent on the Burke-Gilman Trail. He actually let himself believe that karma was finally kicking in. The challenges he was forced to face never seemed to end. Was he still only glimpsing the ox's backside?

"Would you rather I call instead?"

"Yes," KariLyn blubbered, still drying her tears.

Steve could feel her sense of relief.

******

Josh's first reaction was to hunt down Ezra and avenge his sister's honor, but it didn't take long for him to heap all blame on her instead. For awhile, he wouldn't even look her in the eyes when home, and that first week he wasn't home much more than to shower and sleep. He took his frustrations out in football, arriving after dark, still in uniform, muddy from head to toe, exhausted from practice.

Her brother's reaction confused Talitha. Accordingly, the house became deathly quiet those first few days. A shadow descended on the household. Cracks formed in the fabric of the family that Steve didn't know how to mend. Dialog was only initiated after Talitha climbed up on her father's lap and looked him in the eyes.

"Where do babies come from?"

It set off an avalanche of questions that Steve had to deal with in a manner that coincided with his changed ideals. He answered each delicate question to the best of his ability, taking into account his daughter's youth; but she was at that tricky age where imagination and reason met in the middle. She knew when something was being held back from her.

KariLyn spent much of her time with Lila—a comforting maternal figure. She would come home with fabric swatches for her father to consider, asking his opinion. Steve thought them all a little too garish for a newborn, but he didn't say so. He was only too happy to comply.

Thankfully, Steve's stripped-down insurance covered the cost of an obstetrician. With the medical issue taken care of, he felt it necessary to deal with future legalities. Ezra might not want anything to do with the baby

283

now, but he would still have parental rights down the road and could potentially cause trouble.

Beyond anything, Steve dreaded the call he knew he had to make. There was no getting around it. He stalled as long as he could, but after almost a week he finally picked up the phone to relay the news.

"Hi, um, Susan..."

She went ballistic. He dutifully held the handset away from his ear while she screamed, blaming him. She went back into the past and pulled up everything she could think of to prove him incompetent, strengthening her judgment that he was the cause of this calamity. He suffered it in silence, tears rolling down his cheeks.

Steve spent long hours meditating in the Temple those first few weeks, looking out over the garden—an unfolding record of his journey to date. Its incompleteness stared back at him. There was the Chomolungma Stone where his journey began, and, following the beginnings of a circular river stone path, the dwarf fir and the little stone wall that flanked it—his miniature representation of the spirit rocks where he called upon his ancestors.

Steve was undecided how to incorporate the vision quest into the design, whether it should be as simple as a circle of stones. He was in doubt on how to proceed because the vision quest felt incomplete to him. His guardian spirit had yet to visit him in a power dream as promised by Tom Louie.

The phone rang about three weeks after Steve discovered he was going to be a grandfather. KariLyn answered it, which was unusual; but Susan hadn't called since hearing the news, and his daughter's dread of confrontation must have started to wane. In the corner of his eye, Steve could see her rolling balls of cookie dough with the handset wedged to an ear.

"This is she."

Steve was sitting on the corduroy lounger, listening to a CD Jeremy had lent him. His friend had discovered something new. Advaita was a branch of Hinduism that taught that the phenomenal world, though real on a relative level, was merely the manifestation of the one abiding reality, the absolute ground of being, known as "Brahman" (or sometimes the "Self" with a capital "S"). That's how it was explained to Jeremy, and that's how Jeremy explained it to Steve.

"Yes, I remember you...would you like to speak to my father?"

Steve glanced into the kitchen while the guru continued to tackle the topic in a thick Hindustani accent.

"Long ago Advaita sage say one who realizes Self knows he is Self, and nothing exist but Self."

KariLyn was wearing her most recent creation. It wasn't that oversized, cumbersome tunic with the camouflage print. This one was a simple, loose-fitting summery dress of a light fabric and autumn print—a perfect reflection of the day. It looked beautiful against her flushed skin.

"I'm doing well, thanks," KariLyn said, moving toward the stove.

Steve had to shift position to keep his daughter in view.

"Advaita teach realization of Self come in single moment, not long years study or practice."

Steve was anxious to come to grips with this Hindu philosophy that Jeremy had become enraptured with, so much so that he was preparing to journey to India to live with one of its leading gurus.

"Sometimes people point and snicker," KariLyn said, "but I've learned to handle it."

Steve got up and moved closer to the kitchen, leaning against the doorframe. He was hoping Susan would call, that mother and daughter would reconcile and perhaps the two of them could salvage the friendship they only just initiated; but whoever was on the phone, it couldn't be Susan.

"I know I'm a good person, but I made a mistake, a big one."

Steve hoped that Jeremy wasn't making a mistake either. According to his friend, Advaita (or "nondualism") had a completely different take on enlightenment, and that was what Steve was having trouble getting his head around. In realizing enlightenment, an Advaitin didn't need to go through the process that Zen demanded because enlightenment existed in the here and now. This was puzzling to someone who had by now spent hundreds of hours in meditation and participated in several grueling intensives. In Advaita, enlightenment wasn't achieved through meditation but by reading the teachings of sages and by many hours being in the presence of a living master.

"My mantra?"

"Who're you talking to?" Steve said, sticking his head into the kitchen.

KariLyn looked over her shoulder, raising a cookie dough-caked finger to her lips. Not to be disturbed, she walked out onto the deck. Steve moved to the sink to get a glass of water. Through the window he eavesdropped on the conversation while the guru talked on, having lost his audience.

"So a mantra is words heard inside the head?" KariLyn said, slowly pacing the deck, her dress rippling in the breeze, "but the words I mostly hear in my head are 'I'm a fool.'"

Sunlight sparkled on everything it touched. Steve, sipping water, gazed out at the golden highlights in KariLyn's hair. It reminded him of Denise.

"Yes, it's a little critical for a mantra," KariLyn said. "You're right; maybe it's time I come up with something new."

Steve was about to ask who it was on the phone again when a gust of air rushed over the bamboo and flooded into the yard. Karilyn's dress billowed like a sail at the exact moment a grin blossomed on her face.

"Just this is good enough?" KariLyn said, smiling. "That's my new mantra?" She stopped pacing a moment to think it over. "I don't know…it's a bit silly, under the circumstances, don't you think?"

"Just this is good enough," Steve said, mouthing the words behind the screen, thinking it a bit bland.

The conversation continued. Steve watched as KariLyn came to life, tossing her hair from her face while moving freely up and down the deck, breathing in the air, looking at peace for the first time in months. Steve waited, swishing water in his mouth.

"Okay," KariLyn said, "It won't hurt to try…thanks for calling," she added, hanging up.

"Who was that?"

KariLyn was caught by surprise, holding onto her budding stomach. She hadn't seen her father in the window.

"Father Jack," she said, squinting to see through the window screen, using the phone to shade her eyes from the sun. "He was the priest who presided over Midnight Mass, the one we went to a couple of years ago. Remember?"

It took a moment for Steve to respond. "Yes, I remember Father Jack…did he ask to speak to me?"

"No," KariLyn said, stepping off the deck. "He called to speak to me."

Steve took another sip of water. His eyes followed his daughter as she made her way to the Chomolungma Stone, hands clasped loosely behind her back. She circled it before moving to the dwarf fir, bending down to touch the little stone wall that flanked it. A moment later she rose and moved across the yard, stepping up into the Temple and out of sight of her father who stood by the sink, swallowing the now tepid water stored in his mouth.

"Just this is good enough."

Steve spent a couple of minutes testing the mantra on himself before heading back to the guru he abandoned in the living room. He couldn't help but think it sounded like a cheer.

******

Steve felt the presence of his ancestors in the guise of the starlight, and it stirred his heart. The moon was a wonder on its own. From the mountaintop where he sat, gazing up, it looked like a giant pearl inlaid with gilded craters, reminiscent of Japanese *shippo-yaki*, or enamelware, depicting the seven treasures mentioned in Buddhist texts, such as lapis lazuli and amber, from which the lotus ponds of *Nirvana* are said to be made. It seemed to sparkle, reflecting the light of the stars.

All was in bloom. The gorse was a vivid yellow and the red berries of the kinnikinnick were ripe to pick by the grouse Steve could hear chattering under the spruce down the slope, a male drumming his wings as if it were the middle of the day. A saw whet owl tooted in a lodgepole pine, unseen, stopping at times to listen for mice huddled together under the earth, safe like everything else in this land of dreams.

But this was no ordinary dream. It was like nothing Steve had ever experienced. The sun-bleached rags tied around the junipers—the markers that designated the sacred circle—shone like silk. No, this was no ordinary dream. It was the sacred domain of his guardian spirit.

Steve gazed out beyond the circle, but he found himself easily distracted. It took discipline not to stand up, step out and explore, but staying put had its own distractions. He couldn't smell a thing until he thought to try, then everything offered its scent at once. The earth smelled of yeast, the junipers gin and the kinnikinnick berries an aromatic port. He closed his eyes and breathed it in, his head swirling in the delectable scents.

"What are you?" the wolf asked.

Steve hadn't heard it approach. The beast just appeared, sitting on its haunches outside the circle. He locked his eyes to the red ones staring into his, feeling a sense of trepidation.

"I am a wolf."

"From where did the wolf arise?"

Steve stared uncertain, anxious the bond would sever. The wolf didn't blink. Its eyes were a brighter red than the aromatic berries of the kinnikinnick, redder than rubies even, another of the seven treasures mentioned in Buddhist texts. All the same, it expected an answer, and trepidation soon turned to foreboding.

"From where did the wolf arise?"

As if by enchantment, the craters on the enameled moon reformed into a stylized landscape in jewel tones, one that Steve recognized at once. He smiled at the moon in thanks before addressing his guardian spirit.

"Where my journey began," Steve said.

"You were called home to be reborn."

Steve tried to grasp the significance of the statement. Finally, he looked up to the stars for help. The eyes of his ancestors met his, but their lineage, whether man or beast, he couldn't tell.

"What does a wolf do?" the wolf said.

Steve, knowing the answer, felt a sense of relief. "A wolf takes care of its own," he said.

"We hunt together and we howl together," the wolf said, "and the clan raises its pups as one."

Steve was about to repeat the words when the wolf growled for silence. As if in sympathy to the change in mood, the stars dimmed and the dreamscape grew fainter.

"You called me late in life," the wolf said.

"I was lost," Steve pleaded. "I needed to find my way to you."

"Now you call me to guide you on your journey, your resurrection on the slopes of our ancestral land."

"I do," Steve replied.

The wolf stalked around the periphery of the circle before sitting back down on its haunches.

"I am the spirit totem that guides you," the wolf said, "as I am the spirit totem that warns you."

The wolf bared its teeth, and its fur bristled. It became terrible to look upon, a murderous predator only inches away. Steve started to feel afraid. It was not the meeting he anticipated.

"Tonight I am the spirit totem of shadows," the wolf snarled. "I bring you fear to overcome."

The scent of the earth, the kinnikinnick and the junipers soured. An unbearable rot filled the air.

"What fear?"

With those words the wolf leapt up onto its hind legs and brought its forelegs crashing down. The explosive boom resounded down the mountain, stretching into a ghoulish moan. Stars flickered and extinguished like candlelight, leaving the moon alone in the sky, now as white as a ghost.

"What does a wolf do?" the wolf demanded.

"It takes care of its own," Steve said, feeling his heart pound.

Lifting its head, the wolf let out a spine-chilling howl at the moon. The kinnikinnick berries burst and bled over its leaves; the yellow flowers on the gorse furled and the junipers withered.

Beyond all reason, the horrific call triggered an instinctual reaction deep inside Steve. Putrid air filled his lungs, and he let out a howl of his own, harmonizing his call to the alarm being sounded by his guardian spirit.

******

Steve sat bolt upright, wide-eyed and panting, his bedroom lit by the moonlight spilling in from the window. Folded over the chair were the jeans where he had left them before crawling into bed, and on the dresser were the coins from his pockets, reflecting the ghostly light. He combed his fingers through his hair, relieved to be home.

The dream was no less chilling than the worst of his childhood nightmares. Unlike those now jumbled in time, the power dream was crystal-clear, branded on his memory for life. It was almost too real, so much so that it somehow leached its way into wakefulness. A sour effluvium hung heavy in the air. In the here and now, the infusion of kinnikinnick berries and juniper had the distinct taste of blood.

"Who's there?" Steve called out, his eyes on the door.

The knock was barely a scratch, more like a bird stirring in its nest.

"Daddy?"

Steve leapt from the bed. He pulled open the door and peered into the dark, his heart pounding again, the thick scent of blood as alarming as smoke. It took him a moment to realize he was standing in a puddle. Looking down, he could just make out a pair of eyes. He dropped to his knees in panic.

"What's wrong?"

"I'm bleeding…badly."

Steve reached up the wall, nervously feeling for the light switch, cursing in the dark the time it was taking to find it. Once he did, he was blinded.

"Something's wrong, dad," KariLyn whimpered, looking up at her father. The light in her eyes seemed to flicker like a candle in a breeze. "I think the baby died."

The door across the hall swung open. Steve glanced up at his son, standing in his boxers in a daze.

"What's going on?"

"Call your mother and tell her I'm taking Kari to the hospital."

"It's the middle of the night."

"Call your mother!"

Steve tore himself away. He pulled on his pants, grabbing the t-shirt he wore the day before. Josh hadn't moved. He stood staring down at his sister.

"Get your sister's purse; we need her ID cards...Josh!"

The bark jolted the boy from his stupor. He sprinted into KariLyn's room and ran back with her purse, throwing it at his father like a football. Steve caught it and hung it around his neck. No one saw Talitha until she started to cry.

"I need you to take care of your sister, okay?" Steve shouted over the little girl's wails.

Josh's face was white as a ghost. "Okay, dad."

"And call your mother."

"What hospital?"

"What hospital?" Steve said, struck dumb. He didn't know; he hadn't thought it out, but he knew he had to come to an immediate decision. "UWMC!"

Steve struggled down the stairs with KariLyn cradled in his arms, one step at a time, his old injuries protesting the load. He could feel the blood soaking into his pants, urging him to quicken his pace, but he took each step with care. His feet were greased in blood, and he wasn't about to risk a fall. By the time he reached the bottom, he knew there wasn't a moment to lose, no time to put down the precious cargo and get into his shoes. He would have to manage barefoot.

"How you doing, honey?"

KariLyn's eyes were glazed. "Scared."

"It'll be okay," Steve said. "Nothing bad will happen," he added, defiantly. "You'll see."

KariLyn slumped against the window next to her father as he flew through stop signs, trying to stay calm. It was the amount of blood that frightened him most. There was blood everywhere, even on the steering wheel. The odor was making him nauseous, and he cracked open the window for air.

Shadows passed over his eyes that had nothing to do with the night. He found himself flooded by irrational, rambling fears. For a moment he was convinced the fetus was still inside her, turning black; then, a moment later, he was certain it was lying on the floor for Talitha to find, traumatizing the little girl for life. The perversion inside was getting to him, working against what he was trying to do. It was like flies buzzing around his head.

"Tonight I am the spirit totem of shadows," he said to the night. "I bring you fear to overcome."

Voicing the words of his spirit totem helped him understand what was feeding the pestilence inside him. It was the unenlightened one, of course—Mara, taking opportunity to pounce as it always would. Its power seemed to diminish once he recognized its presence. To distance himself further, he pressed on the gas when he hit the Ship Canal Bridge.

UWMC was further than he realized. He would've already arrived if he drove instead to the Harborview Medical Center, but the University of Washington Medical Center was where all three kids were born, and that meant something to him. It meant life.

"We're almost there, honey…almost there."

Steve turned into the hospital and sped up to Emergency, coming to a screeching halt. At first he tried to rouse KariLyn, caressing her hair, whispering words into her ear, but she barely responded. He kicked open the door and ran around to the other side, pulling her out and running into the building with her in his arms, calling out to a couple of orderlies. In no time, she was on a gurney, disappearing behind a pair of swinging doors.

Steve was directed to Admittance to fill out forms. He unraveled KariLyn's purse from his neck and laid it on the counter. It was soaked in blood.

The staffer, a young woman no more than five feet tall, looked up at Steve in sympathy.

"There's a washroom where you can clean up."

Steve stood looking at himself in the mirror. His hair was a muddled mess. Red streaks marked his face where KariLyn must have laid her fingers as he carried her down the stairs. Both forearms were gloved in his daughter's blood. The reflection staring back at him looked like an Indian warrior from the losing side of a battle. He started to cry, but immediately turned on the faucet to clean up, washing away his tears. This was no time to fall to pieces. There were forms to fill out.

******

Steve was pacing adrift in the waiting room when Susan arrived. One look at her made him grateful he took the time to soak his t-shirt in the sink and try to wring out the blood. The fabric was clinging to his chest, clammy and uncomfortable, but the source of the staining was no longer obvious. It looked tie-dyed in tea rather than his daughter's blood. His blue jeans better masked the evidence.

"How is she?" Susan said, rushing up out of breath.

"I'm still waiting for news."

Susan's face contorted. She threw her hands over her mouth, but her eyes crinkled with tears, betraying her anguish. Steve didn't think, didn't hesitate, didn't even take into account this woman was another man's wife. Present conditions and past conflicts were momentarily forgotten. Graced by this sweet armistice he stepped up and enfolded her in his arms. She didn't resist. They held tight to each other, saying nothing for minutes.

"What happened?" Susan finally whispered in his ear.

"She may have miscarried."

Susan backed away, wiping her eyes on her sweatshirt—one she had kept from their college days. She didn't seem to know what to do with her arms. Finally, she wrapped them around her torso as if she was chilled or—Steve dared to hope—yearning for another embrace.

Steve's eyes fell on her face, the nose reddened by weeping. It was just about the most delightful thing he had ever seen.

"Where's your shoes?"

Steve shrugged. "At home."

"Is your t-shirt on backwards?"

His smile was somber but loving; his brown eyes gazing unabashedly into her blue. "I haven't seen you without makeup in years."

For a blip in time, her guard went up.

Steve could feel strands of hair floating on top of his head. He never felt more present. "You look beautiful," he gushed, speaking from the heart.

Susan looked up into Steve's eyes. He held her gaze. Her lips parted as if she was about to say something, but her eyes drifted, making their way down to his hand. She grabbed the purse, a look of horror in her eyes.

"Is this blood?"

"Mr. Forrest?"

Steve and Susan spun around to where a woman in a white coat and dark slacks approached. She wore a stethoscope around her neck like a favorite cat.

"I'm Doctor Allen," the woman said, removing her glasses.

"How is she?" Steve demanded.

"Stable."

"I'm her mother," Susan said. "What happened?"

"Clinical spontaneous abortion, commonly known as miscarriage."

Susan's voice was shaky. "Will she be all right?"

"She should be, but we'd like to keep her for a day or two in case the rejection was incomplete."

Steve shivered under the clammy t-shirt. "What do you mean by incomplete?"

"We need to verify no tissue remains in utero."

"Oh God!" Susan cried, masking the outburst with a hand.

"What was she," the doctor pressed, "twelve weeks?"

"Yes," Steve said, "twelve weeks...why?"

"A fetus is not considered fully formed until the thirteenth week," the doctor said. "Theoretically, remnants may still remain inside her."

"Is that dangerous?"

Doctor Allen smiled at Susan. "Not under my supervision."

Susan let out a nervous laugh, but Steve remained unconvinced.

"There was a lot of blood," he blurted out, feeling obligated to share this information with his daughter's physician.

"Bleeding is the most common symptom of miscarriage," Doctor Allen lobbed back, unperturbed by the news. "How old is your daughter?"

"Seventeen...why?"

"Did she go through NVP," the doctor said, "morning sickness?"

"No," Steve said, thinking back. "Wait! Yes, but only once or twice, early on."

The doctor reflected on the information. "I ask because it's been proposed that morning sickness reduces the risk of miscarriage, but that's still under debate."

296

"Doctor," Steve said, lowering his voice, aware of the delicacy of the topic, "um, where…is it possible—"

Doctor Allen smiled reassuringly. She knew what he was trying to ask. "The tissue passed in hospital."

"Oh, thank God!" Steve said, releasing a lungful of air.

Susan stepped up. "Can I see her?"

"Yes, but I recommend one at a time. You don't want to crowd her. Your daughter's been through a traumatic experience, both physically and emotionally. What she needs is rest."

Susan turned to Steve, her eyes beseeching. "I need to see her…she needs her mother."

Steve gracefully consented. "I'll head to the cafeteria for coffee."

Steve escorted Susan to the elevator before stopping by the washroom to rearrange his t-shirt after airing it for a spell under the hand dryer, finally combing water through his hair with his fingers to make it more presentable. When he stepped barefoot outside the door, he did something he had never done before, something explicitly instinctual. Instead of asking directions or following signs, he moved through the halls until he picked up the scent of freshly brewed coffee.

The cafeteria had only just opened. Hardly anyone was there. Steve paid for a coffee and headed for a table. He didn't realize how exhausted he was until he slumped down into a chair. Through the windows, the first hint of daylight reminded him that he needed to call Josh. He would have to call Bill too and ask for the day off, but it was a little too early for that.

While Steve hunched over his coffee, a man strolled into the cafeteria who immediately grabbed his attention. The housecoat was left opened like a cloak, revealing a hospital gown far too short, exposing a copious amount of skin. He regarded the thick brown, hairless legs—legs that required sturdiness to support such a tall stout frame.

"Indian," Steve whispered to himself.

Steve watched as his brethren bought a coffee and drained it where he stood. As the Indian turned to leave, their eyes connected. It may have only lasted for a fraction of a second, but Steve was sure he detected a flash.

The Indian moved toward him. Steve averted his eyes, looking down at his coffee, hoping he didn't just pick a fight.

An enormous hawk nose pointed downward at him. "Badger?"

"Sorry?"

"Your totem spirit?"

Steve stared up at the Indian. "Wolf."

"Wolf?"

"Did someone say wolf," a little nondescript man said two tables away, turning around in his wheelchair. "A fine animal, none better."

"Yes," Steve said, hesitantly, not knowing what to make of the situation he unexpectedly found himself in. He regarded the elderly man, someone who much more closely resembled a badger than he.

"The gray wolf, *Canis lupus*, was the subject of an article I wrote. All dogs owe their existence to them, you know."

"Do they?" Steve said, noting that the man, like the Indian, was wearing a housecoat. "Are you a journalist or something?"

"A wildlife writer—retired, of course," the man said, sipping his coffee with a shaky hand.

Steve and the Indian waited while the elderly man safely set down his cup.

"You know what I find particularly interesting about wolves?"

298

"What?" Steve said, sitting in the shadow of the Indian.

"Mated pairs typically remain together for life. Isn't that inspiring?"

"I guess," Steve said, not too convincingly.

"You know what else?"

"What?"

"Genetic markers reveal its place of origin to be the Himalayas, way up high on the top of the world. Imagine the journey it must have taken over the millennia to reach Washington State."

Steve's mind flashed back to the wolf he had met on his way down the mountain, the morning after his night with the spirit rocks. He still debated whether it was real. "There're wolves here in Washington?"

The Indian's laugh bounced off the cafeteria walls. "You should know better than anyone," he said, heading off toward the doors.

"They're endangered here, you know," the old man said, "protected under state and federal law."

"Wait," Steve called out to the Indian. "What's yours?"

"What's my what?"

"Your totem spirit?"

"Salmon," the Indian called back as stepped out into the hallway. "I always find my way back home."

******

"Can I sit down?"

Since KariLyn came home from the hospital, Steve had kept a close watch on her—carefully gauging her emotions—but he didn't interfere or try to sugar-coat the harsh, life-altering event she had endured. For almost two months now he had remained observant. As a budding

Buddhist he knew that the miscarriage was as vital an experience for KariLyn as falling off Everest was for him.

"Sure," she said, offering a tentative smile.

KariLyn was in emotional paralysis that first week, but it wasn't long before she was back at school, studying harder than ever before. Suddenly top of the class wasn't good enough for the driven teenager who had doubled down with renewed energy, going for gold.

"What's up, dad?"

Steve smiled from across the kitchen table loaded down with textbooks. In many ways, KariLyn was the image of her mother who incidentally had stepped up her game in her daughter's life. Susan had been insistent on coming by once a week to pick her up for a mother-daughter outing.

Steve was curious how his ex-wife reacted to her first trip to a thrift shop, but how could he ask when she had refused any number of invitations to come inside? Susan hadn't once stepped into the house, always ready with an excuse.

"Life is full of *dukkha*," Steve said, looking lovingly at his daughter as he repeated the words once said to him.

"Is that a curse word?"

"No, honey, it's a much more meaningful word than that."

"What does it mean?"

This was the first time Steve attempted to talk to KariLyn since she lost the baby—a real talk, the long-overdue one he put off until now, waiting for the right moment.

"It was a word the Buddha used a long time ago to describe suffering, pain and anxiety—things that make life difficult," he said. "He used the word as the basis of the Four Noble Truths."

KariLyn's interest seemed to spark. "What's that?"

"The Four Noble Truths are the central teachings of Buddhism."

"Which are what?" KariLyn said, clicking her pen tip closed.

Steve combed his fingers through his hair. He doubted whether he was qualified to instruct on Buddhist principles, but he was determined to try. Before attempting, he instinctively swept the room to see if he could spot any shadows lurking, listening in.

"Simply put, the first Noble Truth explains the nature of *dukkha*, the second its origins, the third the truth on how to liberate oneself from it and the fourth explains how that's accomplished."

KariLyn twirled the pen in her fingers, thinking. "That seems pretty straightforward."

Steve couldn't help but laugh. "It's not as simple as that, honey. There're books thicker than these on the subject of the Four Noble Truths," he said, laying his hands on the textbooks spread out over the kitchen table.

"Why are you telling me this?"

It was a hard question to answer. The truth was that Steve wanted his daughter to understand something he was only just beginning to understand himself.

"Partly because you asked me to," Steve said, lovingly, "The Buddha taught that *dukkha* is a part of life since life itself is transitory, ever changing. Happiness one day leads to sadness another, and sadness eventually leads to something else."

If the look on his daughter's face was any indication, Steve was about to lose her. He tried to stick to the point.

"What I mean to say is only in accepting pain and suffering can they be overcome."

Little folds formed between KariLyn's eyes. "That's not a very satisfactory answer, dad."

"Dissatisfaction!" Steve said, striking the table. "That's *dukkha*!"

Along with her siblings, KariLyn had by now gotten somewhat used to her father's theological outbursts of discovery. She was no longer put off by them at any rate. "What's the origin of *dukkha*, the second Noble Truth?"

Steve sat back in the chair. "Desire, both for things we want and to get away from those we don't. They have to do with cravings, sensual pleasures, ignorance…things like that."

KariLyn looked down at her textbooks, her eyes unfocused. "I was a fool."

"No, honey—"

"Yes, dad, I was," KariLyn insisted, looking up to meet his gaze. "I was a fool for love. I know that now. Mom said the same thing about herself."

Steve suddenly found himself sidetracked. He wanted to know more of this unexpected disclosure. He would've probably pursued it if KariLyn hadn't cut him off with a question.

"What's the third Noble Truth again?"

Steve took a moment to gather his thoughts. "The truth in how to liberate oneself from *dukkha*."

"How's that done?"

Again Steve was filled with doubt in his ability to answer such questions, but he didn't have much choice in the matter. He was the one who brought it up.

"It's done by coming to recognize *dukkha*, pain and suffering," he said, adding, "and by understanding its origins—where it comes from inside us."

KariLyn smiled. "Not so simple after all."

"No, not so simple."

Steve didn't recognize the sweater his daughter was wearing, a loose-fitting lavender number, worn at the sleeves. It made her look older than she was, much like a college student or a young woman on her own. He

302

supposed she got it at the thrift shop while shopping with her mother.

"And the Fourth Noble Truth?"

Steve was about to open his mouth and improvise, but he was violently diverted, as if struck on the head by a gong. Suddenly, he felt like he found a missing piece to a puzzle he had been working on for months.

"The path!"

"The path?"

"The Noble Eightfold Path!" Steve said, springing from the chair.

KariLyn's long hair got caught up in a whirlwind once she stepped outside the door, following her father into the backyard. It was a damp, blustery late winter's day, more suited for staying indoors. She stood on the deck watching her father as he headed for the pile of scree stones stored by the house.

"What're you doing?"

"We'll need softball-sized stones and a big one for the middle."

Steve did a quick calculation in his head on how many he would need. They then got to it. Being too heavy to toss, he and KariLyn lugged each cold, clammy stone to the middle of the yard and drop it before going back to retrieve another.

"They're not too heavy, are they, honey?" Steve called over the rush of wind.

"I'm fine, dad."

Steve took on the big one, acutely aware of his old injury. It must have weighed close to a hundred pounds. Slowly he made his way with it between his knees, carefully judging the position—the exact center of the backyard—before letting go with a grunt.

"We need to make eight equidistant lines from the center stone," Steve said, sweat beads evaporating in the turbulent air.

"Like a sunburst?"

"Yes, like a sunburst," Steve said in a rush of excitement. "We'll position the stones so each line is three feet long. I'll do the same, following your line. That way we'll have four six foot lines meeting at the center stone."

At that point the job got a lot dirtier. Fortunately, KariLyn was wearing an old pair of jeans with her sweater and not one of her cherished creations. They worked opposite each other, setting down stones in a straight line until they had one six foot in length. Then they worked on the cross-section. Two more lines were set down diagonally after that until they had an approximate six foot diameter sunburst made of eight lines, each three feet in length and all projecting from the center stone.

"It's beautiful, dad," KariLyn said, stepping back into the wind to admire their work, "but what is it meant to be?"

"We haven't finished." Steve picked up a spare stone and placed it inside the sunburst. He stood up to appraise the positioning. "Good, now we're going to make a circle inside the sunburst, one stone inside its edge, following the one I just laid down."

KariLyn looked at her father, questioningly. "Like a ship's wheel?"

"Exactly!"

In fifteen minutes it was done. Steve made small adjustments while KariLyn stood over him, her hair flying about her head. He looked pleased with himself as he stood up, wiping his hands on his jeans.

"We calculated perfectly," he said, giddily. "Not one stone extra."

"What is it?"

Steve flung his arms out to the wind. "It's the Noble Eightfold Path," he said, "the fourth of the Buddha's Four Noble Truths."

Steve long debated what to do in the center of the Zen garden. Up to that point it had remained a barren patch. He considered a birdbath but rejected the idea. Nothing felt right until now. Standing there, gazing at the garden, he felt it was one step closer to being complete.

"The symbol is called the Dharma Wheel."

"Sorry?"

"The Dharma Wheel," Steve said, practically shouting.

It was almost impossible to hear over the sound of bamboo stalks bending taut, snapping against each other, branches creaking above the houses, and the wind whistling through every hollow in the trees where the birds were hunkered down waiting it out.

"What is it meant to mean?"

"*Dharma* is the teachings of the Buddha, the truth as it's recognized after enlightenment is realized," Steve said. "It's the symbol of Buddhism."

"I thought you said it was the symbol of the Noble Eightfold Path?"

"It is," Steve said, his voice cracking. "The eight spokes of the wheel represent the eight elements of the path: right view, right intention, right speech, right action, right livelihood, right effort, right mindfulness, and right concentration—the path taught by the Buddha himself."

The diverging gusts seemed as confused as the expression on his daughter's face.

"But how can a path be round?" KariLyn shouted. "Wouldn't you eventually end up where you started?"

Steve was overjoyed. It was as if each of his daughter's questions were clarifying his own understanding of that which he had just laid out in stone. "The Noble Eightfold Path is a different type of path, Kari. You can't walk it, arriving at one station at a time. You must live it, all eight dimensions at once, to complete the journey."

KariLyn stood looking down at the Dharma Wheel, lost in thought. Minutes passed in gusty silence.

"Sally called."

"Your grandmother…when?"

"A couple of days after I got back from the hospital," KariLyn said. "We've been speaking ever since."

"Why didn't you tell me?"

"What?"

"Why didn't you tell me?" Steve said, raising his voice.

"She said she wanted to talk to me," KariLyn said, sounding a little guilty. "Dad, she wants me to go live with her for the summer, after graduation."

"In Inchelium?" Steve held the hair on his forehead from blowing into his eyes.

KariLyn let the wind propel hers freely as she spoke. "I think I want to go…mom says I should."

Steve couldn't believe his ears. "You've talked to your mother about this?"

"She thinks it's a good idea for me to get to know my roots," KariLyn said. "Sally said she could put in a good word for me for a summer job at a local restaurant famous for its Indian tacos."

Control seemed to be slipping from Steve's fingers. His family—his loved ones—the people who gave him the courage to come back from death, were making decisions without his knowledge, input or judgment. He felt confused, left out, immaterial; but something inside his gut told him it would be okay, to let go, to offer no resistance.

Steve shouted his response to be heard. "If your mother thinks it's a good idea, then I do to."

******

Susan's opinion was clear and to the point.

306

"KariLyn should've been picked to present the valedictory address," she insisted. "Didn't she have the highest grade point average of her class?"

Despite Susan's indignation, it wasn't to be. The scandal of the pregnancy disqualified KariLyn, even if it wasn't said in so many words. The student with the highest grade point average was replaced by a gangly ball of facial expressions whose high-pitched voice amplified shrilly over the auditorium's speaker system.

The day improved after one of KariLyn's teachers made a point of approaching them after the graduation ceremony to express her opposition to the decision. Susan and she became fast friends. All in all it was a happy day until Steve was informed by his ex-wife that she would be driving their daughter to Inchelium two days hence. It was all prearranged without his knowledge.

******

"What's for supper?" Josh said, slamming the front door, sweaty from a touch football game. He ran up the stairs without waiting for an answer.

"What do you want for supper, Talitha?" Steve said.

The big, garish guacamole couch didn't respond. Talitha had put too much effort to give up now. She had been hiding under the cushions since her father arrived back from the washroom, only occasionally shifting positions, making the cushions burp.

"Well?"

The cushions exploded. Talitha didn't look pleased at being found out.

"How'd you know?"

"I heard you giggling."

Talitha stuck out her tongue.

"You know that's the Tibetan way of saying hello, how are you."

The little girl's temper dissolved. A plan popped into her sly little head. She bounced off the couch, taking the last remaining cushion with her.

"Where're you going?"

"I'm going to stick my tongue out at Josh!"

Talitha didn't wait for her father's opinion on the matter. She sprinted up the stairs and out of sight. Steve got up from the lounger to pick up the cushions, tucking them back into the couch before strolling into the kitchen, wondering what to make for supper.

He laid out a number of items on the countertop for inspiration. There was a box of granola, a large can of black beans and a packet of Chinese noodles that he didn't have a clue how to prepare. He decided to make an improvised stir-fry when he heard his son shout from upstairs.

"Talitha's sticking her tongue out at me, dad!"

"Tell her to stop," Steve shouted back, grabbing the wok from a cupboard.

Steve fished some vegetables from the bottom drawer of the fridge, deciding a pasta bean stir-fry would do, but his heart wasn't in it. His mind was on KariLyn, far away in Inchelium.

"Problems, problems," Steve said to himself.

A car pulled up to the house. Steve didn't think anything of it until the front door opened and he heard a thud. He walked out into the hall and stared at a suitcase.

"Is Josh here?" Susan said, stepping through the door with a box in her arms.

Steve's lips felt like rubber. "Upstairs."

"Josh!"

The teenage boy appeared on top of the landing, hair damp and glistening from showering. "Hi mom," he said. "What're you doing here?"

"Get the other stuff from the car, all right? I need to talk to your father."

"Okay," Josh said, jumping down the last two steps. "Moving in?"

"Yes."

Josh stood looking at his parents before shrugging his shoulders and jogging out to the car in his bare feet.

Steve couldn't think. His whole body felt numb. "You're moving in?"

"Yes," Susan said, looking defiant. "If you have a problem with that you can take it up with your landlord."

Steve didn't think to brush away the hair that slid over his sightline—hair now past shoulder length; long enough to tie into a ponytail. "I don't...what...Ryan?"

"No, me," Susan said. "It's my house now."

"What?"

"I bought it."

Susan moved out of the way as Josh came through the door, carrying two boxes, one on top of the other, showing off his growing muscles. She moved into the living room, looking around.

"Oh my," she said, staring at the purple polka dot curtain panels. She next turned her gaze on the couch. "Guacamole!"

"Overlaid with a sunburst pattern," Steve said, feeling obliged to act in its defense.

"Mom," Josh called, coming through the door with a duffel bag slung over a shoulder. "Where does all this stuff go?"

"Kari's bedroom," she said, moving into the kitchen. "Much better!"

"What do you mean you bought the house," Steve said, trying to process the information as he followed behind.

"I bought the house from Ryan, just as I said."

"You couldn't have," Steve said. His face was all twisted out of shape. "He would've told me. We work together, you know. I see him five days a week."

309

"I asked him not to tell you…I wanted it to be a surprise."

That silenced Steve until something occurred to him, and he blurted it out all at once. "Where'd you get the money?"

"The divorce."

"The divorce!" Steve said, a little too loudly. "The money we settled on wouldn't be enough to buy my mother's trailer."

"Not our divorce," she said, throwing him a backwards glance, "the divorce settlement from Jeremy."

Steve felt woozy. He grabbed onto the kitchen table to settle himself. "You can't be divorced?"

"Why can't I?"

"Jeremy's in India!"

"Don't raise your voice to me," Susan said, throwing him a warning glance before opening the door and stepping out onto the deck. "Oh my!"

Steve found his resolve and pushed himself out the door, hands pressed to his hips. "Jeremy's in India," he said again, trying to stay calm.

"Jeremy's been back for months," Susan said, looking dubiously at the backyard. "Is this some sort of nautical-themed rock garden?"

Steve refused to be sidetracked. He wanted answers. "I would've known if Jeremy were back," he said. "He would've called me. We're friends, you know."

"I asked him not to."

Steve's arms flew up in the air. Susan, however, didn't seem to notice her ex-husband's agitation. She had a finger resting on her lips, looking at all the stone.

"How's Talitha supposed to play here?"

At that moment a window sprang open above them. "Hi mommy!"

"Hi baby," Susan said, shading her eyes from the sun.

Talitha was bending out the window, a big smile on her face. "Like dad's Zen garden?"

"Is that what this is?" Susan said, looking up at her daughter. "Don't you want grass to play on?"

"I didn't like it at first, either," Talitha said. "It takes a little time to get used to."

Susan's expression remained doubtful. "But what's all this supposed to mean?" she said, pivoting around, looking from the big stone monolith to the scraggly fir to the ship's wheel centerpiece and finally to the bamboo gazebo.

"It's dad's life in stone."

Josh popped out of the window beside his sister. "All the stuff's up in Kari's room...what's for supper?"

Susan glanced at Steve. "If you two can be ready and out by the car in five minutes, we'll drive to Northlake Tavern and Pizza."

The two vanished in a flash.

"That's where we used to always eat as a family," Susan said. "Remember?" She walked through the door without waiting for an answer, throwing back an order. "Change your shirt."

******

Steve gave in. There was nothing left to do. It was all out of his hands. For the next several hours he seemed to float, following behind like a cloud. He felt as if he were in two worlds at once, the world he knew—the one he could see—and somewhere else—one he thought he could glimpse when he unfocused his eyes.

He sat dazed under the purple ceiling, sitting limp on a red chair in front of the pizza he had barely touched, eyelids slits. Susan, Josh and Talitha, the other customers in the restaurant and the colorful interior merged into a kind of soup. The hubbub of voices slowly transformed into

311

indistinguishable waves of harmony. He found emptiness in what only moments ago was form.

"Dad!"

Steve refocused his eyes. Susan and his kids were staring at him. It was a bit of a shock to see them in their flesh again.

"Did you blank out, dad?"

"The Two Truths," he said, "one relative and one ultimate."

Steve was introduced to the Two Truths at the last intensive he attended, but he didn't really understand it, not really.

"What's the Two Truths?" Susan said, wiping her fingers on a napkin.

Steve locked eyes with each in turn. "Are we eating pizza or do we only believe we are because we perceive ourselves to be eating pizza?"

"Are you losing it, dad?"

"That's the relative truth," Steve said, ignoring his son, "one of two in Buddhism."

"What's the other?" Susan said, automatically.

Steve wasn't sure how to explain the ultimate. His understanding was too raw. "I wish Jack were here," he finally said. "He'd know."

"Father Jack?" Josh said. "That priest who presided over midnight mass?"

"Yes," Steve said, surprised his son remembered.

"Doesn't that make us Christian?"

"We're Indian," Talitha blurted out, lips painted tomato sauce red.

"And Buddhist, too," Susan said, stopping her eyes from rolling. "Don't forget about Buddhism."

"Dad," Josh said, chewing a mouthful of cheese. "If you ask me, Buddhism's a lot like math."

"How so?"

"Well, there's the Noble Eightfold Path."

Susan snickered, smiling at her son. "Jeremy used to talk about the seven steps Buddha walked at his birth, each step producing a lotus flower. He'd go on about the Six Perfections, purifying karma, and the Five Precepts, the basic code of ethics."

"Don't forget the Four Noble Truths," Talitha added, having heard all about it from KariLyn.

"And the Three Marks of Existence," her mother batted back, playing along.

"And the Two Truths," Josh said, in on the joke.

There was a moment of silence before Susan, Josh and Talitha sang out together in unison. "And a partridge in a pear tree!"

The people sitting at the other tables turned to look at what all the laughter was about.

******

"Let me do that," KariLyn said, brushing her father's hands away, helping him with his tie. "Relax, dad," she whispered in his ear. "It's all going to plan."

Steve's fingers were chopsticks. He couldn't seem to pick up anything without dropping it. As the morning sun moved up in the sky the butterflies in his stomach migrated to his knees. Nothing was going to plan as far as he was concerned. He nicked himself shaving and put his socks on inside out.

Steve even clumsily walked through a party-streamer coming down the stairs, dislodging part of the festive handiwork taped to the walls and ceiling. He didn't have time to reattach the loose end, not with all the guests arriving. The streamer floated in the tide of people flowing through the door, reminding Steve of the tassels tied to the horns of the yak that had long ago carried him to safety like a sack of rice.

313

People had been arriving for a good part of an hour. Like two members of a chorus line Denise walked in arm in arm with Betsy. Steve greeted them both with hugs, noting the respectable length of Denise's skirt—just above the knees—as they dropped envelopes into the basket set out in the hallway and made their way through the kitchen and out the back door. It wasn't long after that that Melody arrived, the physiotherapist who got him through those first months of paralysis.

KariLyn tugged her father's tie straight. "You look great, dad," she said, picking lint from his thrift shop blazer.

Steve knew he was probably worrying for nothing. Despite his reservations, everything indeed seemed to be going to plan, just as KariLyn said. He smiled down at his daughter but froze when he heard Talitha shriek from the backyard.

"Don't lean on the Chomolungma Stone!"

A silent prayer of thanks was offered when Steve heard Lila's voluminous voice intercede, defusing the problem.

"You never mind where people lean and just worry 'bout keeping your pretty little dress clean."

KariLyn patted her father on the shoulder and went to help her grandmother. Sally was making her way down the stairs sideways, hanging onto the railing, not used to high heels. She was wearing a tulip print dress her granddaughter made special for the occasion. Steve never saw his mother look so happy.

Most of the guests arrived by half-past-ten: Randy and his wife, Brian and Ryan and the rest of the socially and environmentally conscious lawyers that made up his law firm, a busload of residents from the Greenlake Retirement and Nursing Home, Deputy Garcia and his very pregnant wife from Kittitas County, even Master Feng and his teenage grandson. But one guest hadn't arrived—the one Steve wanted to see most.

It wasn't as if he didn't try. Steve was on the phone with the parish for weeks, trying to get in touch with Jack, but he couldn't get a straight answer, not even after contacting the diocese. "Yes," they promised, "we'll do our best." Little if anything came of it. He was worried about his friend and frustrated by the bureaucracy.

"It's not as though I'm trying to contact the pope!" Steve said to a particularly apologetic cleric.

Tom Louie arrived late, shuffling through the door with a bundle in his arms. Steve was about to offer assistance when someone beat him to it, striding in behind the old man. The shaman didn't come alone.

"You shouldn't have, Tom," Steve said, looking dubiously at the bundle of fur.

"It ain't for you," Tom said. "Where's your son?"

"My son?"

"I got something for him."

Steve stalled a moment before calling out. "Josh!"

The teenager trotted into the hallway with a lightness of step, looking sportive in his newly repurposed navy blazer.

"This is Tom Louie," Steve said, pulling the boy toward him. "And this is my son, Josh."

Tom shoved the bundle into the boy's arms. "Here," he said, looking relieved to be rid of it.

The pelt gave off an odor of dusty old road kill. Steve was grateful Susan was upstairs getting ready and not down here to witness the defilement of her son's blazer.

"Thank you," Josh said, not knowing what else to say.

"I'm giving all my stuff away, you know."

"Why?"

"Because I'll be dead soon," Tom said, matter-of-factly, "and won't need this stuff no more." The old man poked at the yellowish-gray bundle, looking up at Josh. "Know what it is?"

"Fur?"

"Open it up?"

Josh held it in an arm while pulling away the prickly layers. Inside was a carved, gnarled stick, the color of mahogany. Two eagle feathers were tied to a notch on one end.

"It's a coup stick," Tom said. "Belonged to my grandfather. In his day a young brave proved his courage by riding into battle with just such a stick. He'd strike his enemies with it, bust their heads open 'counting coup.'"

Josh's expression brightened.

"That stick's at least a hundred years old," Tom added, peering up at Josh, his eyes gleaming bright. He cupped a hand to his mouth and leaned into the boy's ear. "Expect dreams if you put it under your bed, powerful warrior dreams." The old man then turned to the man in pigtails and gestured him forward. "This is Michael Moonbear. He's been in training with me to take my place. When you're ready, he'll act as your shaman."

Steve ran his fingers through his hair while Michael Moonbear and Josh shook hands. He debated whether to intervene.

"You go put that under your bed," Tom said, "and wait to see what happens tonight."

Josh tucked it under an arm and sprinted up the stairs.

Tom seemed satisfied, nodding his head. "Alright, that's done…get me to a chair."

A cheer rang out when Steve stepped out onto the deck. He waved, smiling broadly, a little embarrassed by the attention. It was a packed house.

"Looking sharp," Steve said, watching Michael Moonbear help Tom into a chair.

316

"Thanks," Jeremy replied, dapper in his expensive suit, standing by a table where a hi-fi system was set to go. "Who's that blond over there?"

Steve followed Jeremy's gaze. "Melody, a physiotherapist...pretty, isn't she?"

"Mind introducing me at the reception? You owe me one, my friend."

Steve laughed. "You've got a deal."

The priest sent from the local parish in lieu of Jack was in deep discussion with the Buddhist monk who would be offering blessings. They presumably had much to talk about. The Buddhist ceremony was secular while the Christian unapologetically sacred.

Steve patted Jeremy's shoulder and stepped off the deck, bending down to kiss Helen's cheek. The crooked smile that sprang on her face dislodged the cat eye glasses. He righted them for her.

"How's she doing?"

"As well as can be expected," the Professor said, leaning into Helen's wheelchair. "I'll tell you, she wasn't going to miss out on this. Denise spent a good hour with her this morning, doing her hair and makeup."

Steve bent into the old man's ear. "Don't forget there's a Porta-Potty set out in my neighbor's backyard and a Greenlake staffer for any emergency."

"We were briefed on the bus," the Professor said, winking.

Suddenly Steve felt a lot more confident. He sprang back onto the deck and made his way into the house, crossing into the living room, filled with items taken out of storage. The guacamole couch had been replaced with a much more fashionable camel-colored sectional, but the purple polka dot curtain panels had somehow survived, at least for the time being.

Steve stepped into the hallway at the very moment a vision in white was descending the stairs. Both were caught

317

by surprise, but all the superficial conventions and formality washed away in a tide of longing. Words spilled stupidly from his mouth.

"Whoo-wee?" Susan said, smiling brightly. "I guess that means you like my dress."

The dress was kept secret. KariLyn and Sally worked on it for the better part of two months.

"Recognize it?" Susan stepped off the stairs and twirled around to set it off, not at all put off by the infraction to the rules that stated that a groom was not supposed to see the bridal dress until the bride stepped onto the aisle.

The dress didn't have any tangible structure to it. As she twirled it spun in ribbony bands of sheer silk and tulle that spilled gracefully to the floor from two braided shoulder straps. The way it seemed to float it could have been stitched together from strands of cloud.

Steve shook his head, lost for words.

"It's my wedding dress, silly...the one I wore the first time around."

Steve stared in wonder. "It looks nothing like it."

"That's the point," Susan said. "I wanted to take something old and make it new, just like you and me. Has the priest arrived?"

Steve breathed deep to get his head straight. "Sure did, and the Buddhist monk too."

"So we're ready?"

"I think so," he said, starting to feel butterflies again.

Susan kissed a finger and dabbed his nose so not to smudge her makeup. "Say it again."

"What?"

"Whoo-wee!"

Wu-wei was what Steve actually said, but he was never going to tell. It just spilled out of his mouth the moment he came upon Susan in that celestial, repurposed dress. That moment he felt a sense of interconnectedness, an integral part of his surrounding environment. He wanted to breathe it in and touch it, to welcome happiness without interference or doubt, to live this moment of bliss.

"Whoo-wee!" Steve said, embracing his inner cowboy. He stroked her hair, glad she left it loose around her shoulders.

"Come on, you two! Everyone's waiting," Josh said, tap-dancing down the stairs in his dress shoes. "The faster you remarry the sooner we eat."

"What happened to your blazer?" Susan said.

She stepped up to brush away what looked like giant strands of cat hair.

"Don't know," Josh said, smiling innocently.

"You boys never change," Susan said, shaking her head, but at the same time fully aware how much the man she was about to remarry indeed changed. She backed off and gave her son a once over. "All right, tell your sisters to get in here, pronto. Steve, you position yourself in front of the Temple. We'll meet up there."

"Okay."

"Got the ring?"

"Yes," Steve said, slapping a pocket before setting off.

Susan held up a hand. "Wait!"

Steve and Josh put on the brakes.

"Tell Jeremy not to turn on the music until he hears me signal from the kitchen window, and make sure he's standing ready to lead me down the aisle."

Owing to how the chairs were set out in compliance to the awkward layout and restrictions of the Zen garden, the aisle was going to be more like a meandering stream, but Steve knew they would make the best of it and get to where they needed to go.

One chair had been left empty, way back in the shadows under a spray of bamboo, behind the

319

Chomolungma Stone, a "reserved" sign taped to the backrest. When asked whom it was reserved for, Steve would only say he expected a guest—one for whom he would symbolically invite to his wedding as the Buddha had invited it in for tea.

Looking at her, all determined and organized, a mischievous smile curled Steve's lips.

"You know, it's a full moon tonight sweetheart."

Susan's eyes widened. She gave him a look. Some things weren't supposed to be said in front of the kids.

******

Brother Peter said a little prayer as he walked down the line of cars parked on the side of the road. Some were fancy luxury models and others scrapheap jalopies, but he paid no heed. He was taking strength from the day, sunny and mild, and the birds singing in the trees. He couldn't bring himself to eat anything, not since breakfast at least, and then only a slice of bread with cheese to calm his nerves.

He dreaded the task before him, but he had his orders. In retrospect, it was astonishing how a simple request from a dying priest could snowball like it did; but the matter was taken seriously, for anything out of the ordinary could be construed as unorthodox—even heretical—in the estimation of the Church.

Brother Peter resembled more the monks of centuries past, cloistered in monasteries—those who rejected ordination and the right to preside over Mass, dedicating their lives to contemplative prayer—or so they might have thought. That was what he thought when deliberating whether to take the vows and commit to consecrated life, but living in a religious community was a lot like living anywhere else. He was expected to work, to help with the daily operation as it best suited his abilities;

320

and he was more than willing to help, especially with those in need.

The Church was quick to recognize this strength in him. Indeed, since first arriving they watched the young novice, how he gravitated to the elderly, the bedridden and the terminally ill—those whose souls would soon depart on their greatest and final journey. Brother Peter would sit with them when they could no longer get out of bed, feed them when they could no longer feed themselves, schedule their medicines and read them passages from the Bible to calm them.

Brother Peter became a nurse at the Church's expense. Since receiving his license to practice, he had been assigned numerous clergy, some stricken with disease while others laid waste by time. He took to it straight away. It wasn't just a job; he got something out of it in return. When his patients breathed their last it was as if they left something behind for their nurse, something he cherished. Each patient felt like a gift that brought him one step closer to Christ's waiting arms.

His latest assignment was the most difficult in his career. Brother Peter never had such a spirited patient before. He had been briefed, of course, told of the priest's eccentricities, his bilateral leanings. At first he acted as driver, chauffeuring the ailing priest around the city, being directed to drive to places like synagogues, mosques and Buddhist temples. Some days were spent staring out to sea.

All the same, the priest finally succumbed to the will of God, and like all the others, he would leave something behind for his nurse; but it wasn't a gift this time around. It was a request, the cause of the crisis to come. Brother Peter was bending over the bed, listening through a stethoscope when the priest whispered in his ear.

"I want to be cremated."

Brother Peter sat up and smiled. Up to that point, death wasn't discussed between them, and that in itself was unusual. It gave him strength. Finally, the two would have a serious conversation, something the young cleric could relate to.

"Yes, Father."

Cremation was still frowned upon by certain members of the clergy. It was hard for some of the older priests to accept it—those who could remember when Mass was said in Latin—but cremation wasn't unusual these days, nothing out of the ordinary.

"Have me inurned in the cemetery."

"Yes, Father, of course."

"And spread some of my ashes in the sea."

At first Brother Peter wasn't sure he heard right, but looking down into the bright blue eyes he knew that he did. "I'll pass along your request."

"And mail a handful to this address."

Brother Peter watched in horror as the dying priest reached over and grabbed a pad from the bedside table, scribbling down a name and address. He tore off the sheet and then wrote a single word on another.

"Mail this note with my ashes."

Brother Peter's mouth went dry as he read it, knowing it would set off a storm of controversy. "I'll do my best, Father," was all he said.

The priest smiled up at him, and Brother Peter smiled back. It was true the face atrophied, but the smile was genuine and the eyes sincere, radiating a look of perfect peace. It was a shock when he realized that the priest was dead, looking up at him with that saintly smile.

A hasty committee was put together to resolve the problem. An elderly priest known for his pre-Vatican II leanings spoke up first.

"It's blasphemy to deal out remains in this way...isn't it? We're not a deck of cards."

Several of those who sat around the table offered opinions before an administrator by the name of Drake intervened. He was a known clerical climber, someone who wanted to step up the ladder of the Holy See. Grandstanding was his specialty.

"If you ask me," Father Drake said, "it's a plan to try to reincarnate himself under the nose of God, using us to sanction it by carrying out his wishes."

"Really, George," the deacon said. "Let's not add to the problem at hand."

The Reverend George Drake took offense at being spoken to in such a way, and by a deacon at that, a lowly delegate of the bishop. He slammed a fist on the table, making everyone jump. "Has God taken his soul to Heaven or does he now reside in *Nirvana*?"

The deacon decided to dissolve the committee, thinking it best to act alone, but that very day a call came in that was to complicate the matter. Of all people, it was from the man who was bequeathed a portion of the ashes, himself requesting that the now deceased priest preside over his upcoming nuptials if he "felt up to it."

The deacon deliberated on the matter until developing a migraine. If the problem wasn't grave enough, the man was to marry the woman he previously divorced, and the woman in question was only recently divorced from another man herself.

"Lord, give me strength!"

The situation was so unusual that the deacon wondered whether there was even precedence in canon law. Books needed to be consulted before coming to a decision, but the man kept calling back, insistent, making an already sticky situation stickier. The deacon finally decided he had little choice but to call the bishop who, upon hearing the news, called the archbishop for guidance. A plan was finally orchestrated.

As Brother Peter approached the house, nerves got the better of him. Fears muddled the order in his head.

323

"I know a man much like you," the dying priest had said to him, "finding his way by helping others."

Brother Peter wondered if the man that lived in this house was the one the priest referred to. He had seen him once when he went to fetch his charge. He remembered the backyard, full of stone monuments and bamboo, nothing like the garden at the rectory. It seemed reckless somehow, out of order. Something about it made him nervous.

Brother Peter stopped behind a tree in sight of the house. From where he stood he could hear the chatter of people, waiting for the ceremony to start. The priest chosen to preside over the nuptials was handpicked by the archbishop—a cleric who spent his career traveling the world as a missionary and knew nothing of the people involved. He would soon be traveling again, off to Africa for several years—out of earshot in case he talked.

"Life's a journey," the dying priest said that final week, blinking up at his nurse.

Brother Peter was busy checking vitals, having just finished taking the patient's blood pressure. It was a common enough saying he remembered thinking, nothing out of the ordinary, not like the epiphanies that would spill out of the priest's mouth at the drop of a hat—the ones so shocking to the nurse's ears.

"Yes, it is, Father."

"But riding the back of an ox isn't the easiest way to get around!"

The patient was always making jokes, trying to get his nurse to forfeit the self-control he coveted. Brother Peter dealt with the situation by smiling politely and attempting to turn the conversation around, not taking the bait. To him, nursing was God's work. There wasn't time for frivolity.

Brother Peter took a deep breath and set off from behind the tree, marching up to the house and stepping onto the walkway. He was in view of the mailbox—his salvation—but through the door was a woman dressed in gauzy white, looking out at him. She opened it and spoke.

"If you're here for the wedding, you better hurry. It's about to start."

"I have a delivery for Mr. Forrest!"

The words came out pitchy. The only thing Brother Peter could think to do was smile to cover up his embarrassment, and that's what he did. It felt unfamiliar on his face, sinful almost.

The woman smiled back. "Is that a wedding card?"

"Yes," Brother Peter said, improvising like the archbishop said he should if something went wrong.

"Give it to me," the woman said. "There's a basket for that here in the hall."

Brother Peter handed it over, his heart racing, terrified she would glance at the name written on the envelope, and in doing so guess the contents; but at that moment two girls rushed into the hall, giddy and excited, one almost a woman and the other still a child, both dressed in identical plum and periwinkle print dresses. The envelope got dropped in the basket with the others, forgotten for the moment.

He made a hasty retreat, suddenly aware what the priest intended for his ashes. The contents were meant to be spread over that Zen garden in back of the house. As he had lived his life, the priest would commit his ashes between religions in death.

Brother Peter was perspiring by the time he reached the rectory car. It was worse than the archbishop anticipated, he thought, and with the ashes that card with the one word scribbled on it.

"*Inshallah*?" The archbishop read when Brother Peter handed it over weeks earlier.

"It's Arabic for 'God willing,'" Brother Peter said, embarrassed by his outburst of emotion.

The archbishop said nothing, staring at the card until finally sealing it in the envelope with the ashes. He sighed as he handed it back to Brother Peter, who would never forget the words that followed.

"Who are we to criticize," the archbishop said, twisting the ring on his finger—the one given to him by His Holiness himself. "Wasn't Jesus buried a Jew?"

EPILOGUE

If you meet an enlightened man in the street,
Do not greet him with words, nor with silence.

Meeting, they laugh and laugh –
The forest grove, the many falling leaves!

We sleep with both legs outstretched,
Free of the true, free of the false.

For long years a bird in a cage,
Today, flying along with the clouds.

-- The Zenrin

327